Kitchen Afloat

Galley Management and Meal Preparation

Kitchen Afloat

Galley Management and Meal Preparation

Joy Smith

SHERIDAN HOUSE

First published 2002 by
Sheridan House Inc.
145 Palisade Street
Dobbs Ferry, NY 10522

While all reasonable care has been taken in the publication
of this book, the publisher takes no responsibility for the use
of the methods or products described in the book.

Library of Congress Cataloging-in-Publication Data
Smith, Joy
  Kitchen afloat : galley management and meal preparation / Joy Smith.
    p. cm.
Includes bibliographical references and index.
  ISBN 1-57409-131-X
  1. Cookery, Marine. I. Title.

TX840.M7 S65 2002
641.5'753—dc21

                                      2002010777

Production Management: Quantum Publishing Services, Inc., Bellingham, WA
Composition/Design: Jill Mathews

Illustrations by Mary Valencia

Printed in the United States of America

ISBN   1-57409-131-X

*In loving memory of my parents, Marie and Peter Daddona,
who taught me that food is love and family is forever.*

Acknowledgments

I heartily thank the many wonderful people who helped make Kitchen Afloat a reality. Lothar and Janine Simon and everyone at Sheridan House did their usual expert job at bringing this book to print. Mary Valencia, once again, created beautiful hand-drawn illustrations. My husband, Gil, Lisa Musumeci, and Diana Duryea provided critical support and wisdom throughout the writing process. My children—Meara Kirsch, Lisa Poole, and Richard Anderson—and their spouses—Joe, Mike, and Marianne—were always ready with encouragement, as were my many dear friends.

Contents

Kitchen Afloat
Galley Management and Meal Preparation

Introduction

It's that time again. The sun is low on the horizon threatening to drop out of sight and your crew is famished. After an exhilarating day on the water, all that fresh air has evoked visions of thick, grilled steaks and stuffed potatoes. You know you're in trouble when you head to the galley to fix dinner and all you can come up with is a can of peas that smells funny and the remains of a bag of pretzels. You're at the end of the fishing line. You're chum.

Whether you've been dubbed the cook by choice or by default, your job is important. Quelling ravenous appetites and having a cache of appealing and nutritious sustenance on board will keep you and your crew healthy and energetic enough to accomplish the most strenuous boating tasks. A can-do attitude will help you stay afloat as you learn to look ahead, be organized, and think creatively.

This book will coast you through the intricacies of your galley, help you tailor supplies and provisions to your cooking and cruising styles, and teach you to plan and execute workable menus both at the dock and under way. Before long, meal making will be effortless. Your crew will not only pronounce you a magician, they'll even quit with those jokes about throwing you overboard.

Chapter 1
Learn to Love Your Kitchen Afloat

A tight, confined space that does the rumba spells "challenge" loud and clear. While there are times when it might be fun to dance in the galley, the thought of juggling foods while doing so can be daunting. Add a badly designed galley to the music of some boisterous waves and you're more apt to be doing more bumping and bruisin' than cooking and cruisin'. Conditions for on-the-water food preparation are seldom ideal; and having a perfect galley is more a dream than a reality. Learning to set up your galley for safe cooking begins with accepting it, understanding it and making changes that will improve its flaws. Focus on what you have, rather than what is lacking, or amiss.

GETTING ACQUAINTED WITH YOUR GALLEY

I realize that not everyone has a full-scale galley, so let's start by defining "galley" as the area on a boat dedicated to food preparation. In even the simplest setup, understanding how galley components operate and learning to use them efficiently will simplify the cooking process. Other than a willing cook, the essentials to meal making are safe work areas, enough fresh water, a means of keeping foods and beverages cold and fresh, and a source of cooking heat.

We aren't fussy about our first galley. Still in a camping mode, our meals are simple—sandwiches, and plenty of cold soda and beer. We think "disposable" and give more attention to having enough paper towels and trash bags aboard, than to worrying whether there's water to wash dishes or to drink. So, when we acquire a boat with a real galley, we're so happy to no longer stumble over a cooler that we give little thought to where the built-in icebox is located. We chortle over the wee sink and miniature stove, and open all the drawers and cupboards like a child enthralled with a new dollhouse. Convenience? Efficiency? Who cares!

This euphoria lasts about two weeks as we spend more time in what has become our kitchen afloat. Our initial delight is replaced by an insistent yearning for more counter space, a bigger sink, a stove that works and a cooling system that doesn't require bags and blocks of ice to operate. Oh, if we could only find spots for all the pots, dishes and groceries we haul aboard; and when we need them, find them easily. Once you have moved into your boat, you will be disappointed upon realizing that your adorable galley is inconvenient and inefficient. It's only human to want more space and reliable galley systems. However, the sad truth is that you've bought it, you've got it. So let's deal with the here and now and see what we can do to help you fall in love with your galley all over again.

A GALLEY ROLLS WITH THE WAVES

One of the major problems is that a galley moves. When the boat is doing the Texas two-step on the waves, everything within is keeping time as well. Under heel, a sailboat "smiles" from port to starboard. A fast moving powerboat planes and "thumps," in addition to some side-to-side rocking and rolling. Boat motion affects everything in the galley starting with where it is situated within the boat, and extending out to its contents—making it essential to take steps to keep you, the cook, intact, as well as the vittles you are preparing.

Location, Location, Location

Amidships is normally the most level section of a boat, so the closer a galley is to this area the less it will be affected by motion. A galley near the engine room will be spiked with noisy vibrations and unwelcome warmth, and when the captain takes the boat apart to work on the engine, the cook will be leaping over tools or an open bilge to reach the galley. The most convenient galley is situated near the companionway, but out of the way of through traffic.

On many boats, the galley is adjacent to and on the same level as the saloon—a combination dining, lounging and convertible sleeping area. The interior of some powerboats, trawlers, catamarans or sailboats with pilothouses may be divided into upper and lower levels, with the saloon on the higher level and the galley set down in sort of a well. This type of galley is a snug place to prepare food, and because it is a confined area, wet spills can't creep into the upper saloon. However, as steps are involved, shuttling glasses, plates and platters filled with food between the saloon and the galley can be risky.

What Shape Is Your Galley?

Where and how appliances are situated within the galley also impacts its efficiency and your safety. Like

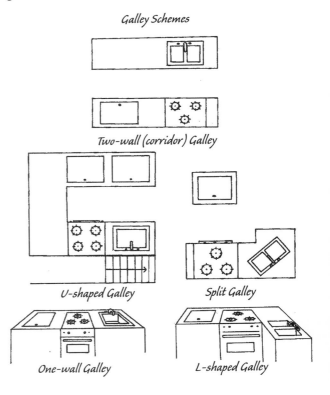

Galley Schemes

Two-wall (corridor) Galley

U-shaped Galley

Split Galley

One-wall Galley

L-shaped Galley

kitchen layouts, most galley configurations are variations of a few basic shapes: U–shaped, L-shaped, one-wall, and two-wall or corridor style. All galleys are small, making them fairly convenient to work in, as there will be so few steps between the sink, stove and icebox.

A galley in which the sink, stove and icebox are enclosed within a tight, continuous "U" is the safest, because it cradles the cook within a three-sided area. A U-shaped galley also makes it very easy to move food between the sink, stove and icebox while remaining, essentially, in one spot. Other galley schemes lose some of these advantages, as they are open on two or more sides or all of the appliances are not situated in the same area of the boat. A corridor or two-wall style, open on two ends, allows side to side sliding; while a strip or one-wall galley, where all three utilities are in a line, offers the unharnessed cook the least protection from being flung across the cabin, unless it is located opposite a bulkhead or some sort of rail.

Prevent Accidents in a Split Galley Scheme

A split galley scheme is also common. In this case, one major appliance, usually the icebox, is situated out of the main galley, often on the opposite side of the boat. With this type of layout, a cook in the throes of meal making needs to be particularly careful to avoid colliding with crew scampering up and down the companionway or through the center of the boat.

To avoid accidents in a split galley:

- Place a nonskid mat on the walkway just under the companionway stairs to slow people down and prevent slipping.
- Make fewer trips between appliances by planning more carefully. Collect and group items you need to remove from or take to the ice chest so trips are productive.
- Place a spare cooler in the cockpit for beverages to eliminate trips below.

APPLIANCE SETUPS

The typical galley includes a sink, stove and icebox. The locations and styles of these appliances affect their on-the-water performance, as well as yours.

Sink Site

The most practical location for a sink is amidships, and if it's near the companionway, you're in luck. A sink provides a safe haven for loose or fragile items that won't need attention until port; such as a thermos of hot coffee, an herb plant, dirty plates, empty Coke cans and small bits of trash. Ideally, a sink should be deep enough to hold sufficient water to allow dishwashing when the boat is heeled. Before you buy a boat, give its sink the eyeball test by envisioning your largest pan in it. Most sinks fail, as they aren't large or deep enough to wash and rinse sizeable items. If you are tussling with this problem right now, here's how you might improve your sink's usability.

- Replacing the faucet with a high-necked style will add more clearance space underneath.

- Installing a simple, 360-degree swivel nozzle to the tap will allow you to hold an oversized pot over the sink at an angle and rinse its sides without creating lakes on the countertop.

Double Sink Dilemma

Double sinks are popular and handy for separating tasks. But I have yet to come across a nautical version large enough to accommodate much more than a small pot or plate. If you've inherited a doll-sized twin set, there isn't much you can do other than accept it or replace it. Given a choice, I would opt for a large single sink anytime. By keeping a small plastic dishpan in a large sink, you can have the benefits of a double sink without losing space.

Sink and Stove Nearby

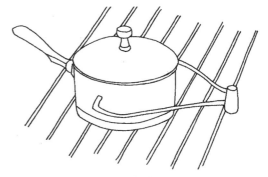

If your sink's next-door neighbor is the stove, passing pots of food between the two will be a snap, and there will be less opportunity to drop or spill hot food. It's also nice if there is enough room to step aside if a pot of boiling stew decides to catapult off the stove, as may occur in heavy seas.

Gimbaled Stoves

Most marine stoves are gimbaled, which means they sway from front to back in harmony with the boat's

Sturdy, well-placed fiddles keep pots intact.

movement. A rail across the front of the cooktop and sturdy, well-placed fiddles (or clamps) to hold pots in place will further protect pans from sliding and tipping over. Likewise, a front lip on oven racks will keep baked goods from falling forward when the oven door is opened.

Placement affects the way a gimbaled stove will move on particular styles of boats.

- On a sailboat, a gimbaled stove situated along the port or starboard side will tip backward or forward, depending on the boat's tack; while a stove located crosswise abeam will be more stationary.
- Most of the motion is up and down on a powerboat, so crosswise placement will be least stable, and a stove situated forward or aft of the center of the boat will tend to swing either toward the cook or slightly away. A stove located port or starboard will be relatively stable on a powerboat.

It's easy to forget that a gimbaled stove will move like a free spirit, until someone accidentally bumps into it and unseats a hot pot. There are occasions when it is safer and more convenient to keep the gimbaled function in the lock position. This also makes the stovetop steady and level enough to use as a work surface. Some boats may have a stove, possibly electric, that lacks the gimbal feature. These stoves either are not meant to be used underway or are situated on a super stable boat.

Iceboxes in Motion

When the door of an upright refrigerator swings open, food is apt to fall forward, so shelves should have bars to restrain the contents. Plastic baskets will help contain small items. When shopping, avoid purchasing foods and beverages in glass jars and bottles, which could tumble out and shatter. Instead, choose plastic bottles, vacuum-sealed cartons and aluminum cans. Some iceboxes have both front and top openings. With a top-opening lid, it's much easier to grab a snack from an icebox or cooler while underway. To avoid having the lid slam shut on a head, hand, arm or fingers, be sure your top-opening icebox has a means of securing the open lid—a hook or support of some sort. See chapter 12 for more on organizing a top-loading icebox.

Look Out Overhead!

A cabinet or microwave oven situated over the stove can become a hazard once the stove is fired up. Overhead doors that swing open can conk the cook in the head; and those over a hot stove may overheat and catch fire. Ensure that latches and locks on cupboards and drawers are functioning properly, so they won't pop open and flood the cabin with their contents while you are underway. Keep cabinet doors shut; tie handles together if necessary.

NONSLIP WALKWAYS

Wet or damp companionway steps or interior walkways can be treacherous. The type of flooring material or covering in place can either alleviate or contribute to this problem. Boats that don't expect to get wet inside, such as powerboats or large sailboats, are often fully carpeted. Carpeting is very safe, but unless it can be easily removed for cleaning, it is almost impossible to dry once it gets wet. It will mildew underneath, stain easily and pick up cooking odors.

I have read that unvarnished teak is truly nonskid, wet or dry, but trying to keep it looking nice could be a disadvantage. Hard-soled floors with any type of finish on them—varnished teak, rubbed tung oil finish, fiberglass or linoleum—are fairly nonslip, until they get wet or splattered with a bit of cooking grease. Then they can become truly dangerous. To prevent slipping on a hard-soled floor, place a few rubber-backed mats in areas likely to catch water, such as under the companionway and in front of the galley sink. Reduce accidents on interior steps that are not ridged for safety by applying stick-on carpet or bathtub strips. Never wax steps!

LIGHTING

Once day has faded into night, most galleys become more difficult to work in due to poor lighting. Ideally, there should be a light over each major appliance and workspace. If you cannot easily wire in additional lights, opt for battery-operated, stick-up versions sold in houseware departments and gadget catalogs. Fluorescent strips provide better lighting than incandescent bulbs. Having dual-colored lights, white and red, is essential for overnight cruising, since switching on a red interior light will not impair night vision.

IS YOUR GALLEY AN OVEN?

Don't be fooled into thinking a galley placed just below the companionway will have plenty of air. It seems so at first glance, but often this isn't the case. Galleys become real hot boxes when warm air collects and gets trapped in recesses. Trying to work in a steamy galley underway, without proper ventilation, can make a cook seasick—not a good thing! Resolve any ventilation problems by having an opening porthole or a dorade vent installed over the stove. A fan is also a good idea. Vents and fans work in harmony to funnel fresh air into a galley and move it around. These can be a godsend in rainstorms or on offshore passages, when all the hatches and portholes must be shut. A fold-up fan installed over our stove keeps me sane while I am boiling up a pot of lobsters on a hot summer evening and provides welcome relief whenever heat builds up in the galley.

BRACE YOURSELF

Hard corners and protrusions make for bruised body parts. While working on a meal underway, take care that handholds and foot braces are in place to keep you from creating a new galley dance. Teak handholds are available from any marine store. A simple strip of wood screwed into the galley floor can help anchor feet and prevent slipping and sliding. When glued or screwed onto countertops, a strip of wood will also keep jars, boxes and other supplies from sliding forward and crashing onto the floor as the boat bumps and lurches. Finally, be sure there are places in the galley where you can clip on a safety harness when you need to—although being strapped into a galley is hardly my idea of boating fun.

Section One:
Water Ways

In the ancient Chinese principle of *feng shui*, water and its movement are essential for bringing harmony and balance, or *chi*, into our lives. As a result, it may comfort you to know that as boaters we've got a leg up on this. Water is all around us. We float on it, swim and dive into it, get doused with it when it rains, bathe in it, and we drink it. Just as three-quarters of the earth's surface is ocean, a similar percentage of our body is composed of water. Water completes the circle of life and is essential to support it.

Water is considered a great purifier and cleanser, salt water even more so. Spiritualists use salt to deflect evil—and some recommend we bathe in salt water, even wash our clothes in it as a means of purification. As boaters, salt water has its use in dishwashing and some forms of cooking, but should never be used as a thirst quencher. Drinking ocean water has been the downfall of many a marooned sailor, as it can cause serious dehydration and eventual death.

As seagoing sailors, it's up to us to assure that we have enough salt water under our keels to keep from going aground and enough fresh water on board to keep us healthy. In this section we will discuss the many means of procuring, storing and purifying water so it will taste delicious and be safe to drink and use in cooking.

Chapter 2
The Fresh Water Challenge

If fresh water is so essential, why does it have to be such a nuisance to get aboard? Weighing in at a little over eight pounds per gallon, water is heavy, and we need a lot of it. A family of four, for example, uses an average of six gallons a day for drinking, cooking and washing. There is always the option of installing a watermaker to convert the staggering amount of salt water around us to fresh water. But what most of us do, in fact, is provide for a source of water to use for bathing and washing, and carry aboard bottled water for drinking or cooking.

BOTTLED WATER

For a weekend aboard, our family of four may cart aboard as much as four gallons of bottled water (34 pounds) to drink and use to make coffee, or anything else that might be tainted by foul-tasting water. In truth water stored on board tends to develop an "off" taste. Shortly, we'll get into suggestions for resolving this problem.

Bottled water has become so popular that you can find it in almost any size or configuration, and you can purchase it at even the smallest market. Today, it's almost a status symbol to tote along a personal water bottle, and considered acceptable to take a slug of it wherever you are and whatever you are doing. By using bottled water, we are guaranteed that it is pure, and that it is imbued with no additives or chemicals. As a convenience factor, boaters who formerly relied on gallon jugs as a sole source of drinking water now supplement their supply by including packs of personal water bottles. From a health standpoint, this is all for the good, since it makes it convenient to substitute plain water for carbonated drinks, and storagewise, water does not need to be kept ice-cold to taste good.

Today, jug water is kept on board as a backup drinking source, but used when measured quantities of water are needed, as in making coffee or reconstituting beverages and dry mixes. Gallon jugs with handles are the easiest to manage, but if you are so inclined, you can opt for larger containers that come with spigots. Purchase only sealed bottles. The style with a screw-on cap is less likely to leak when wedged in a tight spot on the boat; but to be safe, stow any water jug in the head, a locker that drains or in the bilge. Recycle used water bottles and jugs by washing thoroughly and refilling them with water from a taste-tested source.

If you plan to purchase empty jugs for filling, select those rated and built for water storage. Uncap and sniff them. Avoid those reeking with a plastic odor.

Rubbermaid sells a 6-gallon carrier for about $15. Collapsible 5-gallon polyethylene jugs, which cost about $10, are the handiest style, because you can squish them flat and stash them away once they are empty. Polyethylene may deteriorate if left in direct sunlight for long periods, so store water jugs you won't use right away in the shade. To freshen jugs between uses, rinse them out with a mild solution of baking soda and water.

Flexible Water Tanks

Using a flexible water tank or "bladder" is another means of having a quantity of fresh water available. Marine catalogs advertise bladders solely designed to hold fresh water. These are available in larger sizes than water jugs, and although they are more expensive (a 13-gallon bladder starts at $70), they are a bargain when compared to the installation of a plumbing system. There are different grades of bladders. Based on the materials used and construction, one manufacturer attests that its bag will "impart no taste to your water." Another's has an inner bladder that can be removed for inspection and cleaning. The advantages of a water bladder are that it fits where hard tanks can't, collapses as it empties, and can be rolled and stored when no longer needed. When full, bladders are so weighty that they are immovable, so don't plop one down anyplace where it can't stay.

Jugs and Bladders

Collapsible Water Jug   *Flexible Water Tank (Bladder)*

One Gallon Jug

BUILT-IN WATER SYSTEMS

If you find all of the above a hassle and opt to add a built-in water system to your existing boat, speak to your boat manufacturer, your marine services department, or someone who knows plumbing. Do it right to avoid creating a piping nightmare. A permanent storage tank will take up lower locker space, so be sure you can afford to give up space under a berth or a saloon seat.

A permanently installed water system is truly a convenience, providing you with a functioning sink and faucet. All you need is to fill the storage tanks with water and maintain its connected delivery system, and your water problems are over. Well, almost over. You need to get the water traveling through the system, which you can do by manually pumping it via a hand or foot pump, or by a water pressurization system. Manual pumping does not require electrical power to operate, while a pressurized water system uses the boat's DC battery or AC electrical power to control water flow and works in the same manner as the plumbing in your kitchen sink at home.

As a power failure backup measure, it's smart for boaters with pressurized systems to also have hand- or foot-pump access to the water system. Manually pumping also has its place when water consumption is limited, since it's easier to draw small amounts. It's also common to have an additional tap to draw salt water, usually pumped.

Pressurized Water

A pressurized water system takes little effort to operate: simply twist or move the knob of the faucet. You'll hear the grinding sound of the pump each time someone turns on a tap and whenever water is running. We usually turn the pressure system control switch off at the panel when we are sleeping, as ours moans whenever the boat shifts position. The person who will be most disrupted by a noisy water system is the one who sleeps in the berth atop the workings.

Troubleshooting a Water System

A constantly complaining water system is an unhappy one. If your system continues to groan long after you've stopped drawing water, this means there is either air in the system or the tank is getting low on water. You can burp a bubble out of the line by running water from one or more of the faucets until air spurts out and the water runs freely. Otherwise, assume your system has an empty stomach and either get out the hose and feed it some water, or switch the system over to a second, full water tank.

Still having trouble coaxing water from the tap? Try checking the control panel to be certain the water pressure breaker is turned on. If this is okay and no water is flowing from your tap, look for kinks in the plumbing or obstructions in the tank vent. Otherwise, search further for electrical problems, corrosion, or faulty connections.

Water Tanks

Water tanks are the "water jugs" of a boat. Their construction and your management of their condition will affect the quality of the water that comes from the tap. Built-in fresh water tanks are usually constructed of polypropylene, marine-grade stainless steel or aluminum. Polypropylene tanks are lightweight and inexpensive to manufacture, but they will add a plastic taste to the water they contain. Stainless steel tanks are heavy and more expensive to manufacture because they require experts to weld them together, and although they won't impart a metallic taste to water, they will pit over time if chlorine bleach is used regularly to clean and disinfect them (as it should be). Aluminum fresh water tanks suffer from calcium buildup, due to the chemical reaction between this metal and the minerals in the water, which will affect the taste of the water, and may eventually clog up the pipes if the tanks and lines aren't flushed and properly cleaned. Keep in mind that all metal tanks must be bonded to prevent electrolysis. If you notice pitting on the *exterior* of your metal tanks, there may be a defect in your grounding, which may be causing a chemical reaction.

Keep Water Moving

Left standing in your tanks for a few days or more, water will surely begin growing something nasty and may even become contaminated. If you have clean tanks and keep the water in them moving and refreshed, you should feel comfortable drinking the water on your boat. If you have more than one water tank, be sure to switch over to the second tank once the first one is empty, so you use up the water in both tanks. The next chapter discusses ways to ensure that water drawn from your tanks not only tastes delicious, but also remains safe to drink.

WATERMAKING

What better way to have an ongoing supply of fresh water than to make it yourself? To the coastal cruiser, owning a watermaker means not having to tie up to the pier to refill the water tanks as frequently. A good friend we cruise with for a couple of weeks each summer has a hefty watermaker on his boat. While we wash our dishes in salt water and take stingy showers to avoid having to seek dockside water, his wife and daughters use freshly made water as if they were at home. When our friend brags about having to "make water," we know he's not referring to a trip to the head. It's hard not to be just a tad jealous. Most often, however, it is the offshore cruiser who requires this fancy device. In situations where finding clean, fresh water is difficult, having a watermaker ensures a continuous supply of safe drinking water.

Think back to your high school science class and you may recall how the process of reverse-osmosis is used to convert salt water to fresh water, which is exactly what a watermaker does. It's actually very simple. A watermaker is a pump with filters. The more powerful the pump, the more pressure it can exert to push water molecules through its semi-porous membrane, leaving mineral salts behind and allowing only fresh water through the filter.

Choosing a Watermaker

Watermaking systems vary considerably and are expensive, so choose wisely. Begin by defining your needs. How many gallons of water will you realistically require? How will you power the unit? Also compare which watermakers deliver the most water in the least amount of time, consume the lowest amount of power and take the least amount of storage space.

Battery or electrical power drives the watermaker, so you will be limited in your selection by the type and amount of energy available to you. Energy to power electrically operated units, such as watermakers and refrigerators, is created by using a boat's engine to power the batteries while motoring underway or while running at anchor or at the dock. This, of course, translates into increased fuel usage.

Serious boaters often supplement their boat's battery power by using a wind generator or solar panels. Powerboats and large sailboats commonly use a generator, which is the most reliable as a supplementary source of energy, to charge the boat's operating systems. An inverter does not provide energy, but merely converts battery-driven power to electrical power.

Types of Watermakers

Handheld watermaker pumps will be of little concern to the galley cook, as they are emergency devices kept in ditch bags, so most commonly used watermakers are battery-operated. A small 12-volt watermaker will meet the freshwater needs of a 40-foot boat, but depending on the make and model, may draw as much as 38 amps in the course of an average day. Most units require that the engine be run to keep the batteries charged while making the water. An efficient 12-volt pump, for example, may require 8.5 amps to deliver 9.5 gallons of water per hour. A 12-volt maker does not have the capacity to make as much water as quickly as a more powerful 120/240-volt AC unit.

The 120/240-volt AC motor-driven watermaker pump is noisier, but more efficient than a 12-volt style. It requires either shore power or a generator to operate. This unit can make more water in less time because it has the power to create more pressure than the 12-volt watermaker. The kicker is that if you don't have a generator, you will not be able to operate this unit unless you are plugged into shore power. However, if you are on shore, you probably don't need to make your own water. Thus, 120/240-volt AC watermakers are most commonly found on large boats that can sustain power for long periods.

Caring for a Watermaker

A sitting watermaker gathers dried minerals on its filters, so the best way to keep a watermaker running smoothly is to use it regularly. If you will be away for several weeks, flush fresh water through the system before you leave to prevent mineral buildup. Another potential problem with any watermaker is that it is processing salt water, which contains highly corrosive chloride ions. Take care to prevent electrolysis, as the pump and its workings are metal. Read and follow the manufacturer's directions to keep your pump free of problems and operating smoothly.

RAINWATER

The heavens routinely douse us with an ongoing source of water that I don't want to ignore. Rainwater fills our reservoirs and lakes and soaks into the ground to replenish wells; it is delivered to our homes as pure, fresh drinking water. In fact, all of us are so dependent on rain as a water source that when we have a dry spell we suffer water shortages. There's some old-time glamour in capturing rain as it falls from the sky and collecting it in a bucket or whatever is handy. How much more natural can we get? I always picture the person lost at sea in a rubber raft, surrounded with water and dying of thirst. The rain is his savior, rinsing the salt off his sunburned skin and rehydrating him. Somehow I don't see many pleasure boaters regarding rainwater as their salvation. If it rains we are more apt to complain because it has spoiled our sailing plans or our hairdos than we are to glory in its collection.

Yet, when performed properly, amassing rainwater is a bona fide collection method used by many voyaging sailors to great effect. Let's take a moment, however, and consider rainwater as a true source. First, we have water that has come to us through our atmosphere, which in many areas is not too clean to begin with. Then we must consider the sterility of our collection device. Would you drink water that has been sitting on a dirty canvas bimini top or out of a bucket that has been used to hold fish, even if it's been scrubbed out? Using untreated rainwater is a desperation measure that has its place in keeping a lapsing water supply replenished. If you do plan to use rainwater, ensure it is bacteria-free by allowing it to boil it for at least 10 minutes or passing it through your water purifying system before consuming it.

Chapter 3
Savory Sipping

When I was a kid, we gave little thought to how our drinking water tasted. We let the water from the kitchen tap run until it got cold, stuck a glass under it, and then drank it. Today, we are so sensitive to water purity and fearful of chemical additives that many of us have moved away from drinking tap water completely; opting instead for the bottled variety. Thus, it's no small wonder that so many of us shy away from consuming boat-stored water. While it may be clean and potable, its taste can make one doubtful. By the time you complete this chapter, I hope you will be armed with enough information to help resolve this issue. By being selective about your water source, caring properly for your water tanks and taking steps to filter bacteria and chemicals from water drawn from your supply, you may be surprised to find yourself actually drinking your boat's tap water, like we do.

LOOK TO THE SOURCE

Begin your quest for good taste at the source: your water supply. Before you fill up your tank, taste the water in the area. If it is unsavory, your options (other than resorting to bottled water) are to take your boat to a marina serviced from a different water supply, one that passes your taste-test; or to take measures to filter off the chemical-causing problems at your port. Most marinas are located in areas served by city water supplies. Depending on the community, this water may be laced with good-for-you chemicals that will impart a particular flavor to it—chlorine and fluoride are common additives. As a rule, well water is delicious, but your chances of obtaining it for a boat fillup are slim.

Take care when you haul out that hose that you won't be adding to the problem. Use a clean plastic hose, one that has only been used for water—an old-fashioned rubber hose will add to the taste problem. Check that both ends of the hose are clean before connecting them and that the area around the water on your boat's input valve is free of debris that might fall inside.

Hose Intake Option

Some boats may be fitted with a fresh water intake valve—a "hose intake option." This is pretty nifty for accessing water while at the dock. The nozzle of an ordinary water hose screws directly into a hose intake opening on the boat, and water flows directly into all the taps. The intake valve feeds into a "T" in the output pressure line from the pump, fitted with a built-in check valve to control pressure. Water taken in this way uses the "T" connection to bypass the water tanks, leaving them undisturbed. As this method also bypasses the pressure water pump, it is quiet and won't complain each time you turn on a tap. We absolutely love this feature on our boat. It's easy to screw in a spare water hose leaving our water tank supply intact. This works especially well when we are preparing our boat for a trip because we can take long, luxurious showers, yet depart knowing our water tanks are topped full.

FILTER OFF BAD TASTES AND OTHER DELIGHTS

A good water filter can improve the taste and assure the potability of tank water by ridding it of bacteria, impurities and minerals. Water filters vary considerably in the level and type of filtering they do. Some low-level filters are mere sediment strainers. They will protect you from the horror of finding something floating in your water glass, but won't do a thing to improve palatability or kill bacteria.

External Filtering

External water filters have become a household and galley item for many of us because they help rid city water of its chemical taste. They are inexpensive, ranging from $20 to $200, and can be found in most houseware departments. They improve the taste of small amounts of water, purifying it as you need it. However, as they are freestanding, placement and space might be a problem. The Brita pitcher is most common, but needs to be stored upright in a cozy spot to avoid spillage. I've seen the Brita tank used on board in the sink area. The weight of the water inside seems to keep it intact, but on a small boat such a unit will always be in the way. One model, a PUR, attaches at the faucet, but I have not tested it out. Bear in mind that any type of filter placed directly onto a tap is liable to reduce the water flow.

Built-in Water Filters

An in-line water filter installed just upstream from the fresh water pump will remove chemical tastes, as well as any impurities or bacteria. Selecting a filter for your boat can be confusing, because there are literally hundreds of systems on the market, all of which function at varying degrees. Low-level filtering systems are not designed to be purifiers, thus cannot protect against microorganisms, while activated carbon filters improve taste. Odor-specialized, ion-exchange filters can remove hardness and some toxic metals and minerals, while distillers will remove bacteriological contaminants, minerals and salts. More sophisticated processes can remove the most harmful contaminants, without affecting beneficial salts or healthful minerals.

For years we struggled with a variety of filters, yet our water still tasted awful and we were still lugging heavy jugs to the boat, along with every one else at our marina. Then we discovered the Seagull IV[1] at a New Jersey boat show, and just one taste convinced us. If this filter could improve Jersey water, it could certainly solve the problem aboard our boat. The Seagull unit sells for between $300 and $400, depending on the model, and is well worth every dime.

According to Seagull's literature, "Its superior filtering system is the only technology certified to meet the USEPA Standard for Microbiological Purifiers that does not require chemicals, electricity, double processing or hold time." This standard requires protection against all forms of microbiological organisms, parasitic cysts, disease bacteria and viruses throughout the rated life of the product. I am certain that by now there are other equally excellent filtering systems on the market that will purify water in a similar manner. Some filtering systems do, however, require power to operate.

It's easy enough for anyone who needs to enhance or repair a water system to locate instructions from the wealth of technical information available on nautical water systems and plumbing. When we first installed the Seagull filter, we did it on our entire water system and our tap and shower water ebbed to a dribble. As we only needed good-tasting water for drinking and cooking, we solved this problem by installing a Y-valve at our galley sink and attaching the filter onto the portion of new hose connected to a separate, small drinking water tap. I believe the Seagull filter now comes with directions for doing this.

For several years now, we've enjoyed drinking tap water on our boat that tastes as good as bottled. Friends can't tell the difference. In fact, we fill their jugs for them on days they don't want to bother going ashore. Our system came with a 10-year manufacturer's warranty, and other than changing the filter at the start of the boating season, it's been maintenance free.

YUCKY TANKS, YUCKY WATER

For years, my captain and I blithely added fresh water to our tanks without thinking much about it. Before we installed our Seagull filter we only used tank water for washing up and brushing our teeth, so we never even considered the sediment that may have accumulated in the water tanks, or wondered if our tanks were sterile. Had we had opaque stainless steel or aluminum water tanks, our negligence might have been excused. But we didn't. Ours were semitransparent, polypropylene tanks, and it wasn't until our water quality fell from distasteful to putrid that we began to investigate. It was karma that we finally unscrewed the locker cover to peer inside. And spying something greenish and slimy drove us to leaf through old maintenance manuals. It turned out that we were supposed to have been treating our water with chlorine all along! Tell me we weren't the only ones this clueless.

Deep Clean a Dastardly Tank

Regardless of how much water you decide to tote to your boat or to run through a filter for improved taste, it's always reassuring to know that the tank water on your boat is safe to drink. We often assume that by boiling water it will be potable, but while it's true that boiling will kill most germs, especially if you boil the water for at least 10 minutes, chlorine is the best way to kill them all. If you are not certain about the purity of your tank water, use the following procedure to sanitize new water systems, tanks where water has been standing for some time, or water you suspect is contaminated. Make sure you also treat all distribution lines being served from the tank:

- To a full tank of water, add $2/3$ cup (6 ounces) of chlorine for every 10 gallons of water. A commercial brand of chlorine, such as Clorox or Purex, is fine as long as it is unscented and does not contain any other active ingredients or deodorizers.
- Run water from each tap or outlet until you smell a heavy chlorine smell throughout the boat. If you have installed a water filter, remove the cartridge before disinfecting.
- Close off the taps and allow the chlorinated water to sit for two to four hours until the chlorine smell disappears. (This is not a good time to have a party on the boat.)
- Drain tanks and lines completely and refill them with fresh water.

You won't need to repeat this disinfectant process as long as the water system remains intact, isn't contaminated, or isn't interrupted to install new equipment. If your water retains a slight chlorine odor or taste, try flushing water through again and again until it dissipates. As a last resort to remove the chlorine taste, you can either boil the water before using it or try adding a little white vinegar to counteract it. It's a never-ending battle, isn't it?

...And Keep It That Way!
Once you've ensured your tanks are clean and sterile, help them stay that way.

- Always seek the cleanest, most dependable water source available.
- Add a chlorine compound to the water storage tank. Allow 1 teaspoon of chlorine for every 10 gallons of water.
- Install a water filter to remove bad tastes, odors, and disease bacteria that may still be viable.

I've read that you can wash out water tanks with soap and water. This is best done when the boat is in dry dock where you can flush out sudsy water with lots of fresh water. Gravity will help the tanks to drain empty. Even though this method will clean the tanks, you will still need to embark on a chlorine maintenance program to keep standing tank water bacteria free.

Close of Season Care
At the end of each season, follow standard close-up procedures for winter storage. Flush all water systems and pour in non-toxic propylene glycol antifreeze. Pump it through the system until pink water spurts out the through hull opening. In the spring, flush tanks by filling with fresh water and pumping it through, until all the antifreeze has been washed out of the system; and then refill the tanks with fresh water. You may need to repeat this several times until all signs of antifreeze have disappeared. I read somewhere that vodka can be used as antifreeze, as well. We've never tried it, as it seems a waste of a good bottle of Stolie.

Vinegar Cocktail

Once a year, treat your water system to a shot of vinegar to remove mineral buildup in pipes, plumbing and tanks. White vinegar is a nontoxic, inexpensive, and highly effective means of doing this. Buy it by the plastic gallon. Try this method either at the beginning or near the end of the season before adding antifreeze.

- Drain tanks. Mix 1 quart vinegar to 5 gallons of water and pour this mixture into empty tanks.
- Allow vinegar solution to agitate for several days. If the boat is moving, it's even better.
- Flush tanks clean and then refill with fresh water. If you smell vinegar, flush tanks once more.

BE A WATER MISER

Most of us are accustomed to the convenience of using our kitchen sinks at home. We have a large sink or a double sink, counter space for a drain board or for preparation, and unlimited water for cooking and cleanup. Using water as if you were at home only works when your boat is parked where you'll have constant access to a public water supply. (Here's where that hose intake option we talked about earlier comes in handy.) Water is one commodity we don't miss until it's gone. The only thing worse than having a water supply run dry with a sink full of dirty pots and dishes is to be caught mid-shower with a fully lathered head and body.

We are constantly working against a diminishing onboard supply, so unless you have ready access to refills or enjoy the luxury of a watermaker, learn to be a water miser. By paying attention to how often your water tanks need to be refilled, you can predict the lifespan of a supply. On our boat, two full tanks of water last my husband and me for five days, as long as we don't embark on a water fight. There is a tendency to use water more freely on a boat kept in a slip, but if you live on a mooring, taking the boat to the wharf to refill water tanks can be an inconvenience. We used to moor our boat at a marina that was overdue on dredging; if our water run into shore didn't coincide with high tide, we ran aground—and did without a bit longer. Replenishing water tanks is also a nuisance on vacation, when we crave nothing more than to languish at anchor, but must instead locate a dock to pull in and fill up.

Experience will show that there are sneak water wasters aboard. For instance, if your water system is pressurized, the water flows more freely and is certain to disappear more quickly. People are more conscious of water use and tend to use less when they have to work for it by manual pumping. If you want fresh water to last as long as possible, shut the pressure water system off at the control panel to force anyone drawing water to use the manual pump. If someone attempts to use the tap in the head, you'll hear them squawk, "There's no water." But in truth, this method is common to offshore sailing as it keeps the water supply as intact as possible.

Use Salt Water to Conserve Fresh Water

Especially if you plan to cook on board, it makes sense to be conservative about water consumption, and taking advantage of the wealth of seawater in which your boat is floating can dramatically extend your fresh water supply. Salt water, although unsafe to drink, is great for dishwashing, and if it's very clean, it also has limited uses in cooking. Use it for making a batch of spaghetti or rice, or doing any other type of cooking that requires a quantity of water to boil for at least 10 minutes. One cup of seawater contains approximately two teaspoons of salt, which is too salty for most tastes, so dilute it with fresh water.

Also use salt water for some of the nasty cleanup jobs. There's lots of it readily available, so you can freely flush the gook off messy cooking pots and dinnerware. If your boat is not equipped with a salt water tap, it's easy enough to have one installed. Be sure to choose a different tap style than your fresh water tap to avoid making a careless mistake that will ruin a meal. Even though you use salt water for some chores, you will always need a certain amount of fresh water.

Use Less Clean-up Water

As chief water user, the cook can take measures to conserve water and ensure there will be enough left over for a shower and shampoo later. Begin by confining food preparation to a small area. Also try to work on a "disposable cutting board," i.e., instead of using a dish to peel a peach, slice a watermelon or make a sandwich, use a paper towel or paper plate, and when you are through gather the mess and toss it away.

Once food preparation is completed, no matter how we try to avoid it, there will always be items that require washing and can't be thrown away, such as the pan used to heat up the baked beans, the steak platter, or the knife used to spread mayonnaise.

Save cleanup water by mixing in plastic bags instead of bowls. Avoid scrubbing messy pans by choosing cook-in-bag foods. If you are traveling on an offshore passage, rinse and reuse plastic bags, as these cannot be tossed overboard.

Dishwashing Water Diet

Put your dishwashing on a water diet whenever fresh water is sparse. In dire cases, use salt water for steps 1 through 4 listed below. Salt water disinfects, so it will clean dishes and pans sufficiently, although a salt residue will remain unless the items are given a final rinse in fresh water. Also, dishes can be placed in a mesh bag and dunked overboard to soak and pre-clean.

1. Scrape off as much stuck-on food as you can from plates and pans. Use a paper towel to wipe them down, if necessary. If you have a salt water source, you can flush off gooey debris—baked-on egg, spaghetti sauce—from pans, dishes, and utensils.
2. Condense items to be cleaned by stacking and grouping them as you scrape or rinse them. Set plates atop one another. Stand utensils upright in a dirty glass or pan. Place the stacks or piles where they will be accessible to the sink.

3. Make a soap bath in either one side of a double sink, or in a pan or bowl placed in a single sink. If you don't have hot water available on the boat, do your best with cold water. If I have a pot to wash, I often rinse it and use it to hold soapy dishwater.
4. Begin with the cleanest items, such as the drinking glasses. Use a wet soapy sponge or dishrag to clean items, and set them aside without rinsing. Don't go wild on the soap or you'll be rinsing forever and wasting water. One trick to avoid using too much soap is to add some water to the soap container.
5. To rinse, I often use the trickle method. Reduce water flow to a steady dribble, and then rinse each item separately, catching the rinse water in a basin to use for large items. This takes a while, but does a good job. You can also try running fresh water into a clean sink or pan and then dumping in the soaped utensils. Afterward, dip each item into the rinse water, and when the water gets too foamy, dump it and replace it with new water. Otherwise your next meal will taste like soap.

Once you've gotten this method down, train the rest of the crew on it.

Section Two:
Keeping It Cool

It's hard to believe we are dependent on something as elusive as cold air. And, once we manage to get hold of it, it must be contained like a caged animal, lest it escape, leaving warm air and spoiled food in its wake. We've relied on ice and other coolants to provide cold, and insulated boxes and mechanical refrigeration to keep cold in check for as long as I can remember. As boaters, we've many options for both acquiring and maintaining enough cold air to keep our foods safe to eat and our drinks icy cold. We'll explore them all in this section.

Chapter 4
Around the Ice Block

The beer is warm! And what's that horrid smell? Didn't we put ice in here a few days ago? For boaters trying to keep milk and steaks from spoiling and drinks cold, having enough of the right type of ice is as essential as wearing foul-weather gear in a storm. Ice is a slippery quirk of nature produced whenever and wherever water freezes, delivering mounds of lacy snowflakes, pounding us with piercing pellets of sleet, dripping daggers of icicles from our eaves and causing cars to skid around roadways as if they were drunk. Water is a free spirit until it freezes, at 32° F or below, to take on the shape of its container. We can discipline water's amorphous ways by allowing it to freeze into useable shapes—cubes or convenient size blocks. That way it works *for* us, instead of against us.

There are several means of cooling foods and beverages, but ice is the most common. It is readily available, nontoxic and doesn't require power to produce cold. Ice works by absorbing the warmth from the air around it, leaving it cold. The amount and type of ice used and the insulation of its container determine how much cold air is produced and how long a supply of ice will last. Although water-based ice is the most familiar, ice can take on other forms, such as frozen foods or drinks, gel packs or dry ice.

In order to stay cold, ice must be kept cold; well insulated carry bags, coolers, and ice chests will assure this. The farther we travel with ice, the more attention it needs to prevent it from transforming into a dripping mess, so be prepared to pamper it. Until we owned a boat, we took ice for granted and used it primarily in drinks. Now, it seems we're always stalking marinas for it, hunting down ice machines, or hauling gargantuan ice-filled coolers and ice chests.

ICE PICKING

Although most ice sold in the United States comes encased in plastic bags, foreign countries often supply it *au naturel*. Buying ice is like buying air; it will trickle through your fingers like money at a mall. Opt for frosty cubes or blocks "smoking" with cold air. If the ice looks slick and shiny or has a watery surface, it has already begun to melt and won't last as long. In the United States, 5-pound packages of block ice or bagged cubes are the most popular and also are the easiest to handle and place in a cooler or icebox. A 5-pounder costs a dollar or more per bag. Larger

22

quantities of ice are cumbersome, but they will stay frozen longer, due to their greater mass.

Any ice you buy or obtain, like water, will only be as good as its source. Choose ice made for human consumption. Beware of buying ice from a fishing port, where it is used to chill fish, as it may have been delivered through a hose as slush and contain special icing chemicals. When in doubt, ask; or get your ice elsewhere. You can't run ice through a water filter to purify it before whirling it in the blender for piña coladas. Running out of ice on a pleasure boat can become an emergency around cocktail time, so know where to find it. Most often, it's easiest to buy ice at a marina or at a nearby market. Some marinas or launch services will bring ice to your boat for a modest surcharge. I have found the convenience of not having to schlep around in search of ice and then tote it back worth the extra cost of a delivery service.

Cubes on the Loose

Types of Ice

Loose ice cubes are fabulous for quick-cooling cans or bottles of soda, beer or other beverages. When dumped out of their bag, they'll snuggle into crevices around cans and bottles, driving away the warmth. However, unbagged cubes melt more quickly than bagged cubes or ice blocks, as their many small surfaces absorb more heat; before long, your chilled goods will be enjoying a bath. The most practical use for loose cubes is in a portable cooler that can be easily drained. Avoid using loose cubes to chill down a freezer, as they are apt to melt together to form a blanket of ice that will need to be chipped out or defrosted.

Bag Ice

Cubes in a Bag

Ice cubes will last longer and are more controllable if left in their original plastic bags. If perchance you were sold naked cubes, as may occur in a foreign country, protect their modesty by bagging them yourself—in plastic, of course. Place bags of cubes near the top of the cooler, where they will be accessible for drinks. (A jab or two with an ice pick will loosen cubes that have stuck together.) Remember that each time you lift the lid or open the door to the icebox, you invite in warm air to sabotage your cubes. If you are hosting a party and need to frequently retrieve ice, remove the entire bag to another cooler, ice bag, ice bucket or to the galley sink.

Loose Cubes

Block Ice

Block Ice

A chunk of ice is as slippery as a skinned skunk and, if dropped on your foot, will surely dent your sole. Because of their limited surface area, ice blocks will remain solid about four times longer than the same weight in cubes. Leave blocks in their plastic bags so when you lift or touch them with wet hands your fingers won't stick. (To free up stuck fingers without injuring yourself, pour some warm water over them.) Use gloves or ice tongs to safely manage bagless block ice. Place blocks at the bottom of the icebox, preferably on top of wooden, stainless steel or plastic grating to keep them from sitting in water—which absorbs the cold and escalates meltdown. To coax an ice block into place, use an ice pick to chip at its corners until it rests flat. Block ice is a nuisance to use for drink ice, unless you enjoy chopping it into shards a la Sharon Stone in the film *Basic Instinct.*

For a stay aboard, a combination of blocks and cubes works best to maintain cold in an icebox—the blocks for long-lasting cold, and the cubes for dual-purpose chilling and personal use.

HOW MUCH IS ENOUGH?

As a coolant, ice is dependable until it performs its magic act and reverts to water. The capacity of an icebox and its degree of insulation determine the length of time you can rely on a block of ice to hold a desired box temperature. Experiment to determine how best to manage the ice supply for your particular unit by keeping track of the amount needed to attain a consistent 40°F, as well as when and how frequently you need to replenish it during a stay aboard. Blocks of ice are the mainstay of consistent cooling, so it's vital to monitor their progress each day. Your icebox may require more or less ice than ours did. Pay attention, and before long you'll be adept at estimating the life span of a block or bag of ice in your unit and will know how much ice is needed to keep it sufficiently cold.

This is what worked for us, based on a 12-cubic-foot top-loading icebox.

- If we were just down for the day, one bag of cubes got us through, unless we indulged in blender cocktails—true ice cube hogs.
- On short or weekend-length stays, we began with one block and two bags of ice cubes, then added one bag of cubes per day.
- On stays lasting a week or more, we began with two blocks of ice and two bags of cubes, supplementing the supply with a new bag of cubes each day. Typically, we needed to add a fresh block of ice every couple of days.

MAKE ICE

Ice is ice, whether you buy it or decide you'll pack up cubes or blocks made at home. Use zippered plastic bags to carry ice cubes to the boat. Stuff bags as full as possible, squeezing out excess air before sealing. Make your own ice blocks by freezing plastic bottles or jugs of water. Freeze them overnight, or until the bottles are solid. Reuse empty jugs or bottles by first washing them thoroughly, then refilling them with fresh drinking water. Remember that water expands as it freezes, so leave some space at the top of a container before capping it.

Also, zippered plastic freezer bags are sturdy enough to fill with water and freeze. Leave air space at the top, fill and seal bags, and then lay them flat in the freezer to solidify. Frozen jugs and ice bags can ride to the boat in the cooler and be transferred into the icebox aboard your boat. Set frozen jugs of water at the bottom of a cooler or icebox, as you would ice blocks. Tuck in smaller bottles or bags wherever you can, grouping them for more effectiveness. As the water melts, pour it off for drinking or cooking. If you are counting on using frozen water as drinking water, remember to leave some bottles out to defrost.

"Food Ice"

Whenever you chance to tuck a frozen can of orange juice concentrate, bagels or waffles directly from the freezer into the cooler, you are using what I've dubbed, "food ice." Or maybe I should call it "free ice." Using food as ice is a space-saving and inexpensive way to chill your beer, as well as your perishables. Capitalize on the concept and pop food items earmarked for the boat (that can be safely frozen) into your home freezer. Noncarbonated beverages, individual boxes or canned juices, frozen vegetables, dinner meats, and pre-made casseroles and breads are good candidates. Steer away from freezing potentially explosive glass-bottled and fizzy drinks. Carbonation builds up into solid bubbles that need room to expand and often will—all over your freezer.

Put items in the freezer until they solidify, then use them in your cooler as you would ice packs. The hitch is that as these items defrost or are consumed, your cooling agent disappears and you risk spoilage. For this reason, you should only use food ice to supplement or enhance your normal ice supply. By using food ice, you'll require less water-based ice, and will have less melt water. Once the food ice has been consumed, your only residuals will be trash.

GEL PACKS

Ice can be messy, and it certainly isn't reusable once it's disappeared into a puddle at the base of the cooler. This is why encased-gel ice packs are everywhere picnic goods are sold. Gel packs work well for small coolers and as a supplement to ice. For maximum cooling power, stack several gel packs together. Sometimes called "blue ice" or "cool ice," gel packs come in several sizes and shapes to fit into cooler tops or to hold cans. They are relatively inexpensive and will last for a long time. The gel inside should be an FDA-approved nontoxic, biodegradable material that can be refrozen repeatedly. Gel packs work best when used for keeping pre-chilled foods and beverages cold. Those with hard plastic outers won't tuck in or bend around irregular surfaces, but they are almost indestructible. The more flexible, plastic soft-pack style will do the same job. Take care not to puncture the outer coating of a soft gel pack, usually a rather tough vinyl. To make soft gel packs most effective, manufacturers suggest depressing the outer bag to remove dead air space inside before freezing. Defrosted ice packs are useless and can create a storage problem, unless you have a means of refreezing them aboard. Allow packs to dry completely to prevent mold before packing them for home.

Some soft packs can alternate as heat packs with a spin in the microwave oven. One brand sold at boat shows, Techni Ice, comes in a roll of flat sheets, which makes them as easy to store as a box of plastic wrap. These are filled with a dry, nontoxic substance that is initially activated by soaking the sheets in water. Once puffy, the sheets can be frozen and used, and reused, as ice wraps or heat pads. Activated sheets will normally last an entire season or longer without leaking or needing another soaking. I've found them convenient for rolling around beverage bottles or for layering. Nonactivated sheets can be stored indefinitely.

DRY ICE

The term "dry ice" seems an oxymoron because we think of ice as water-based. We hear talk of how wonderful this product is as a coolant, yet it never seems to be around. I was wondering about it, so I did some research and found dry ice has very specific uses. After reading all the warnings, my conclusion is it has no place on a boat. I know you're curious, so here it is.

Dry ice is frozen, or solidified, carbon dioxide (CO_2); the gas we exhale as we breathe. It is one and one-half times heavier than air. Frozen CO_2 is translucent, like snow, and is compressed into pellets or blocks for many uses. Dry ice is much denser than traditional ice and weighs about the same as a standard brick. It is also much colder than ice— around -109°F—which is a definite advantage.

Unlike water-based ice, dry ice doesn't melt, but goes directly from a solid state to a gas and literally disappears. If you will think back to your old science class, solids are supposed to liquefy before they vaporize as a gas. Dry ice got its name because it bypasses a liquid form. Dry ice will disappear, or sublimate, at a rate of 10 pounds every 24 hours in a standard insulated container. The more dry ice you have in the container, the longer it will last.

Uses

Some boaters are turning to dry ice as a supplementary refrigerant, and placed at the bottom of an icebox or boat freezer, it will help to keep the temperature consistent and extend the lives of ice blocks and cubes. My most recent experience with dry ice was when we used it to pack food supplies in a large ice chest destined for the Grenadines for two weeks of chartering. The airline balked. It couldn't store our ice chest in the baggage compartment along with pets because CO_2 emits fumes that can be toxic in an enclosed area. (We'd never thought about this.) You can imagine how embarrassing it was when the airline personnel called in the fire department, whose members arrived wearing boots and fireproof gloves, to take our cooler outdoors and remove the "dangerous" substance. Our food, luckily, made it to the Grenadines without spoiling thanks to the airline's donation of loose cubes from the bar. But that was the last time we used dry ice.

The reason folks turn to dry ice is that it will keep perishable items fresher and frozen longer than traditional ice, without the hassle and mess. It works best for shipping or storing foods that will be left undisturbed for a day or so. It is the only form of ice that will keep ice cream frozen. My studies on dry ice turned up some fascinating uses for it. In food preparation, dry ice snow is added to ground beef and sausage to rapidly lower the temperature of the meat, which retards bacterial growth. Also, it provides carbonation in drinks and at the same time chills them.

The other uses aren't food related. Dry ice is used to make fake fog for special effects—wouldn't that be a hoot at the marina? —and rubbing a little dry ice into a dent in your car will remove the ding. A block of it placed in a picnic area will keep mosquitoes away, and it eradicates gophers, since dry ice fumes are heavier than air so they go to the bottom of gopher nests.

Managing Dry Ice

If you feel dry ice will be beneficial to you in some way, use these precautions recommended by dry ice houses.

- Plan to pick up dry ice as close as possible to the time you will need it.
- Bring an insulated container, like an ice chest or Styrofoam cooler. Plan to use this same type of container for packing, as it will slow the ice's conversion to a gas.
- Always store dry ice in a properly designed container.
- Keep the lid or cover closed when not in use.
- Do not expose dry ice to high temperatures, as this makes it convert faster to a gas and pushes more CO_2 into the atmosphere.
- Ensure adequate low-level ventilation in the area where the ice is stored.
- Fill empty space with wadded newspaper as you remove items from the container. Any dead space will cause the dry ice to disappear faster.
- Don't transport dry ice in the cab of a truck or the passenger compartment of a car.

The Good

- Dry ice is nonflammable.
- It leaves no residue.
- It's pretty—it looks like snow.
- It does not support life, i.e., bacteria.
- Dry ice cools colder and takes less space than traditional ice.
- Dry ice will freeze whatever is directly next to it.
- Its use extends the life of frozen foods in a cooler.

The Bad

- Dry ice is extremely cold. Only experienced people with proper instruction should handle it.
- Wear eye protection and insulated gloves. Dry ice can cause frostbite on bare hands.
- Dispose of dry ice in a well-ventilated area away from the public.

The Ugly

- Dry ice can't be stored in a standard refrigerator or freezer. It is so cold it will cause the thermostat to turn off the freezer.
- CO_2 will cause any airtight container to explode, so be sure to store your dry ice in a vented container.

Dry ice is a chemical that feels cold as it becomes a gas. It is expensive and has a fixed life span. If you plan to use it, take the time to understand the precautions involved. Also, don't allow it to touch food that isn't wrapped well, because it's toxic.

So you see, ice isn't as slippery as you think. Once you get acquainted with all forms of ice and learn to make the most of the special properties of each, you may never again have to say, "Phew! What stinks"? The trick is to always stay one ice block ahead of the game.

Chapter 5
Cart-able Cooling

Cold storage begins and ends with the lowly cooler. We use coolers year-round at home to pack food and drinks for the car, the office and school lunches. I'm old enough to remember the brown paper lunch bag, and I shudder at the thought of all those sandy, warm baloney and mayonnaise sandwiches we wolfed down at the beach. Perhaps the bacteria were lounging, as well, because we never seemed to get sick from tainted sandwiches. Back then, calling lunch meats "cold cuts" was more a prayer than a description. Today, coolers work overtime during the boating season to manage the safe transport of perishables— the chicken for dinner, deli turkey, tuna salad, milk, cheese—to and from our boats.

CHOOSING A COOLER

Choosing the right cooler for the job is determined by the need for either short- or long-term storage, the quantity of perishables that needs storing and the specific uses you will have for it. Are you using your cooler to transport foods, ice down beverages, or preserve caught fish? A cooler that works fine for a day at the beach or an afternoon of sailing may not be powerful enough to maintain food freshness over a weekend stay. Bear in mind that because it is insulated, a cooler can also keep foods warm.

Portable coolers come in various colors, shapes, capacities, insulation levels and price ranges. Manufacturers often indicate cooler capacity by liquid volume, the number of 12-ounce cans or the number of quarts held. A small cooler may hold four quarts (one gallon), while a larger model may contain as many as 320 quarts (you do the math—I think they use large numbers to impress us). Better quality coolers indicate their degree of insulation by relaying the number of hours a particular cooler will hold its temperature.

Managing a Portable

Just because a cooler is called portable does mean it will be easy to move. When packing for the boat, the number and sizes of coolers you will need will increase in proportion to the length of your stay. An unused cooler takes up space so if you don't need it for cold storage and you must keep it aboard, be creative. Can you use the cooler for other types of storage? To keep dinner warm? We've found a clean cooler makes a serviceable punch bowl for an impromptu dock party. To avoid being saddled with a pile of leftover coolers once you have stowed everything aboard, select one practical-size cooler to remain for miscellaneous uses and return the others to your car.

Small coolers with carry straps that sling over the arm work well as long as the cooler is empty or all that's packed in it is your lunch. A cooler chock-full of canned and bottled goods gets to be too heavy. If the handles of your cooler are situated more than an arm's breadth away, this is a clue that it's meant to be either carried by two people or dragged. It will be nearly impossible to single-handedly move one of these monsters into a dinghy and then up onto a moored or anchored boat.

Coolers on Wheels

Large coolers with built-in wheels and retractable handles may seem the ideal solution to moving around a weighty cooler. But it's still necessary to weigh the convenience of being able to easily roll a cooler against the hideous task of maneuvering it up onto and about the boat. The wheel apparatus also makes luggage and coolers that much heavier when empty. After examining a few of these in stores, I've concluded that large, wheeled coolers are best suited to a campground. I saw an advertisement for a collapsible rolling cooler,[2] though, which has possibilities. Should you succeed in hauling one of these aboard, remember to contain the beast where it can't spin free.

Some boats have insert lips or braces specifically designed to hold a rigid portable cooling unit. You can also purchase a set of fasteners designed to clamp down heavy appliances, sold at marine supplies locations.[3] If you can't find a safe spot to stash the cooler, clip or tie it to something immovable where it will be accessible, yet out of the way. Run a piece of line through its handles, or secure it by its strap.

Cooler Bags

Soft-style cooler bags are easier to manage than their rigid relatives, and they are collapsible, which makes them a delight to stow. For our regular winter trek to the islands to charter-sail, we pack clothes, cameras and any other items that need extra padding in our cooler bag for the trip. We then use the bag to keep drinks iced and portable during our cruise, after which we dry it out and repack it for the flight home.

Our first instinct, when we think of a soft cooler, is to reach for the popular drugstore variety intended for short-term use: a picnic at the beach, lunch foods or beverage chillers. These bags work best when used with gel-pack inserts, but most are not insulated enough to keep the pack frozen for more than a few hours. Drugstore cooler bags are inexpensive and sold everywhere; but they can't take much abuse, may leak water when packed with ice and can easily be punctured or torn. Sizes range from lunch for one to lunch for many. Most come with handy Velcro closures, convenient carry straps, and are available in zillions of colors and patterns.

For serious cold storage, invest in marine-grade soft cooler bags. Although more costly, these are constructed of high-grade materials, have superior insulation and are completely waterproof. Marine-grade soft coolers match a good-quality hard cooler in durability and insulation quality. Their webbed carry straps are durable and can withstand excessive weight without snapping. Drain off water from melted ice by dumping the bag over on its side. Marine-grade soft coolers will not deteriorate, even when left in strong sunshine, and if they get dirty, they don't mind a gentle spin in the washing machine. If you do this, pull up the lining before tossing it in the machine, so it too can get clean. Then hang the bag outdoors to air dry.

Years ago, it was difficult to find these fabulous coolers, and many boaters still aren't aware that they work as well as the chest style. Today, however, I am pleased to see them widely advertised in marine catalogs and stocked at marine supply stores. These come sized to hold six, 12, or 24 cans or bottles. Given the nature of a soft cooler, larger capacities would be too heavy to carry. I have found my cooler bag indispensable and have added several sizes to my repertoire. My original bag, purchased many years ago, is still a workaholic.[4] The only problem I have found with soft coolers is that whenever I loan one out, I need to beg to get it back.

Hard Coolers

Hard coolers and ice chests come in grades, as do soft coolers. Their rigid, boxy shape makes it easy to store flat-bottomed items, like juice jugs and milk cartons, as well as items you don't want squished—fruits, vegetables, and breads. The terms "cooler" and "ice chest" are used interchangeably, but ice chest implies a more substantial, better-insulated box. One manufacturer boasts that its ice chest has 25 percent more insulation than traditional ice chests and will keep food preserved for "five days in 90° heat"—a feat that's hard to beat. Some ice chests offer more storage capacity than the average built-in icebox. You can spend $15 for a simple 12-quart ice chest, or buy a 320-quart hippopotamus for $450.

Look for those that best meet your cruising needs, as well as your pocketbook. Ice chests geared for fishermen's catches will have special features, like a built-in fish scale or cutting board. A sturdily built cooler makes a handy seat; some come with removable cushions. There are a ton of options from which to choose:

- long warranties against warping, fading, cracking, denting, peeling, chipping and rusting
- fully insulated body and lid
- lids that are hinged and will stay in place when opened
- child-safe snap-lock latches
- lids with extra built-in functions, such as holding a refreezable gel pack, a divider tray and a cutting board that stores inside the lid
- heavy-duty handles that lie flat and out of the way
- on larger coolers, a threaded drain plug that allows you to hook up a hose for mess-less draining. Leaking water will make your boat floor treacherous, so be sure the fitting is tight.

Pack an Ice chest for the Long Haul

A heavy-duty ice chest is invaluable for keeping a backup supply of meats and dairy products fresh while you enjoy a trip, unencumbered by the need to locate a grocery store. Once you've properly packed the ice chest, the most important rule is to leave it shut. Begin by planning your trip menu (see Section 8). In this "untouchable" chest you will store dinner meats, seafood, deli-meats, cheeses, milk and other perishables that you will not use for the first couple of days. Pack supplies in order of use, according to your menu. For example, if you plan to grill steaks on your last night out, these will vacation at the bottom of the chest.

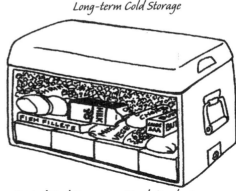

Long-term Cold Storage

Rest of Food, Beverages, Hardy Produce
Loose Cubes
Frozen Foods, Meats, Seafood, Dairy
Block Ice

Layering Technique
Follow these steps for layering foods and ice to maintain safe food storage temperatures.

1. Place a layer of ice blocks to cover the bottom of the ice chest, using an ice pick to shape the blocks so they fit snuggly and lay flat.
2. Add frozen foods, dairy products, meat, and seafood, keeping them as low as possible in the icebox.
3. Add a layer of loose ice cubes.
4. Add the remaining food, beverages, and hardy fruits.
5. Fill the empty space at the top with a final layer of loose ice cubes.
6. Now, shut the lid, hide the chest, and vow to open it no more than once every day or two to retrieve items for transfer into your main icebox or refrigerator.

Beverage Coolers
The beverage cooler is a functional variation of the hard cooler and designed to hold noncarbonated drinks, like lemonade or iced tea. One- to 3-gallon containers come with a carry handle and a spigot to simplify pouring.

PORTABLE REFRIGERATORS AND FREEZERS
Electrically or battery-operated portable coolers work on the same principle as built-in iceboxes and refrigerators, which we'll discuss in the next chapters. These have a place in boating, as long as there is a consistent power source and a means of transporting them when full. Most run on either 12-volt DC battery or 110-volt AC electrical power, but you can also find propane-operated units. Typically, portable refrigerators can be used in either an upright front-opening position or a top-opening position. Set the unit in a secure spot, preferably on the floor, where it is close to a power outlet. A thermostat is essential to any refrigeration system, even a

portable model. Some may contain a small freezer for ice making. A refrigerator, especially one that includes a freezer, will weigh more than the same capacity cooler. Generally 12-volt DC and 110-volt AC powered models start at $500, which I think is costly for such a paltry bit of storage. If you keep the boat in a slip and it is equipped for dockside power, plugging your power cord into a 110-volt AC dock outlet will allow you to effortlessly operate any type of refrigeration without drawing down your boat's batteries.

Thermoelectric Coolers

If you are in the market for a small, inexpensive refrigerator—about $100—and don't mind doing without a freezer section, consider a thermoelectric unit. A high quality thermoelectric cooler can maintain an interior temperature of 46°F. It is reliable, weighs less than a traditional portable refrigerator and can be used either standing upright or on its side. Some thermoelectric coolers can switch over for use as a food warmer, and may get as hot as 150°F. These are also reasonably priced. They operate on 12 volts DC, but you can buy a 110-volt AC converter kit.

A thermoelectric cooler is easy to maintain and uses no environmentally harmful chemicals to operate. The unit cools electronically without using Freon, compressors or evaporators. It works like a standard refrigerator, by absorbing heat from the inside of the unit and transferring it to a heat radiator. A fan blows the heat into the environment. To perform the same cooling job as a normal refrigerator, a thermoelectric cooler requires several times the energy. These units take a long time to cool down warm or room temperature foods and drinks, so their best use is for keeping previously chilled foods and beverages cold. Pre-cool a thermoelectric refrigerator by running it for a while each time you restart it.

Chapter 6
Live-aboard Iceboxes

The nice thing about having a built-in cooling unit aboard is you don't need to haul it anywhere. Like a cooler, an icebox is simply an insulated box that lives on your boat and waits to be filled. The term "icebox" is a remnant from the pre-refrigeration era, when ice was essential to cold storage. In today's world, however, a refrigerator is also considered an icebox, despite the fact that power-driven cooling methods may be in place.

FILL'ER UP

An icebox loaded with cold food won't need to work as hard as an empty or partially full unit, and will hold its temperature longer. As items are removed, dead space fills with warm air, causing the coolant to work overtime to rechill the area. This means that ice will melt more quickly and additional ice or power will be needed. To give your cooling process a break, keep the icebox filled. As the food level lowers, insulate the dead space with some sort of protective material. There are many options on how to do this.

Keep in the cold with a filler material, anything bulky you can spare. Newspaper is one of the oldest, most universal insulators. A few old issues stacked atop your cold provisions will ward off a warm-air attack. Although newspaper disintegrates when wet and can leave black smears, it is usually on hand and easily disposed of. An extra blanket, folded towels or a pillow will also work as long as you can keep the items dry by storing them in a large plastic trash bag or by layering a sheet of plastic between the linens and your groceries.

For small areas, bubble pack can also work quite well. Bubble pack comes in sheets, so it is flexible and can be tucked in and around food items. Several layers can easily fill inches of dead space. When you aren't using it in your icebox, wrap the bubble pack around glass or fragile items for safe storage. I've seen articles that suggest filling zippered plastic food bags or small drawstring trash bags with packing peanuts. These may work well to displace air in large voids, but remember that these bags of fluff will be bulky to store elsewhere and rather messy should the bags split and leak. A neater and more effective way to eliminate the lost energy problem might be to use a sheet of insulated material.

Front-loading iceboxes have a special problem, as cold air falls forward and out each time the door is opened. A reader's solution offered to a sailing magazine[5] suggested mounting strips of soft plastic, available by the roll, to the top inside area of the door opening. This keeps in cold air, while allowing a hand to rummage through the goods.

Keep Out!

We get so accustomed to opening and closing our refrigerator doors at home that we are apt to carry these habits over to the icebox on the boat. One of the most common deterrents to keeping food cold is people. Each time someone lifts the lid or opens the icebox door, warm air rushes in and gets trapped, leaving the coolant to fight it off. Here are some things you can do to help your ice supply last longer and minimize unnecessary invasions.

- Put drinks in a portable ice chest and keep it handy to the cockpit.
- Don't hold open the lid and peer inside deciding what you feel like making for lunch. Think about it beforehand, then quickly retrieve everything you will need.
- Organize your icebox so like items are consistently stowed in the same place (dairy items on the bottom left, deli meats at the top rear, etc.) so you won't waste time hunting. If you think anyone will take the time to consult it, you might even diagram your use of space and mount it nearby.
- When a crewmember needs something, either get it for them rather than allow them to rummage around and abuse your domain, or train them on the proper retrieval method.

GENERAL MAINTENANCE

All that ice you have loaded into the cooler will become water that will soak off labels and eventually saturate milk and juice cartons. Small items will sink lower by the hour, as blocks and cubes liquefy and threaten to drown them in the pool at the bottom. Although a little water—an inch or so—is desirable for maintaining icebox temperatures, be sure to watch the water level and routinely drain off or pump out excessive water. When you do this, make certain the seacock is open so the water will drain and that the drain hole is not clogged with paper, food bits or other obstructions. If you have placed a grate at the bottom, keep the water level no higher than the grate.

Routine Cleaning

Clean out and reorganize your icebox or refrigerator regularly. It's not an especially distasteful job so long as you don't put it off forever. I like to tackle this project just after breakfast or before grocery shopping. Whenever you deem it is time to do it, you'll find it takes no more than five or 10 minutes to sort through its contents, wipe up spills, pump out extra water, discard past-their-prime foods, restock beverages and add fresh ice. Tuck a box of baking soda on a shelf inside to keep your icebox smelling fresh. If there is no dry place to put it, use a refrigerator deodorizer encased in plastic and poked with a few holes.

End of Stay Close-out

If you have no means of keeping a refrigerator or icebox cold while you are away from the boat for an extended period, clean out the box and leave it to air-dry by propping the lid or door open before you depart. The first time you forget to do this is usually the last, because you'll be welcomed aboard with a snootful of putrid smelling, mold-blackened foods on your return.

Warm, moist areas are playgrounds for the terrible two: mold and mildew. To avoid fighting with this pair, make it a priority to attend to the icebox *before* closing up the boat. Begin by completely emptying the icebox. This is especially important if you have been using ice, since everything will be slicked and soggy with moisture. Set unopened or nonperishable beverages in the sink or on the countertop to drain off and dry while you are away. Wet metal cans leave rusty rings, so place a paper towel or dishtowel underneath them to avoid staining. Remove remaining ice and either dump it overboard (minus its plastic bag), give it to a neighbor or put it in your cooler to take home. Pump out or drain all the water from the icebox. Wipe down the interior with dish detergent, baking soda and water, or a mild solution of chlorine and water to prevent or kill mildew and remove stains. To allow the interior to dry completely, remember to leave the icebox lid or door ajar. Pack homebound perishables into a cooler, along with any leftover ice.

IS IT WORKING RIGHT?

An icebox of any type is only good if it's efficient. If it seems that you are always low on ice and you haven't been using it for making blender drinks, be ruthless in tracking down the culprit. It's possible there is a physical problem with the seals, insulation material, or drainage. It's also possible that you are not using your icebox correctly.

A good ice chest or refrigerator will have high-grade insulation to maintain cold for long periods. To keep heat from seeping in, the lid needs to fit snuggly and be lined with at least one row of rubber gaskets. Replace worn, dried-out gaskets. Check the seal for leakage by closing it on a piece of paper and then trying to pull the paper out. If it comes out easily, replace the seal. Keep the seals in fighting form by cleaning them regularly with a solution of baking soda and water. Once they are dry, apply a thin layer of petroleum jelly to prevent the seals from sticking, bending out of shape or drying out.

The most commonly used insulation material is polyurethane foam. Foam is bulky, so sometimes boat manufacturers skimp on it to make the icebox appear larger. When foam gets old, it becomes porous and absorbs moisture, which causes ice to melt quicker, food to take longer to chill and, in the case of a refrigerator, causes the compressor to work overtime to bring down the temperature. If you think your icebox should keep things colder than it does, it may be time to add to or replace the insulation material. You can buy blocks or sheets of foam at a building supply store and glue it around the icebox, as long as there is adequate space. Instead of foam, some experts recommend using high-vacuum insulation panels. A 1- to 1$\frac{1}{2}$-inch-wide panel is equivalent to four to six inches of polyurethane foam.

For supplementary installation, you might try tucking in a sheet or two of Super "Q" Ice Saver.[6] This is a slim, $1\frac{1}{2}$-inch-thick, specially constructed insulating sheet designed to lay on top of loaded ice chests to divert heat up while keeping cold down. According to the manufacturer, testing proved that this product maintains the ice in the chest "2.37 times longer than normal." Super Q can be ordered cut to size. A $\frac{1}{2}$-inch-thick blanket is equivalent to about $4\frac{1}{2}$ inches of conventional fiberglass or foam insulation, and costs about 6 cents per square inch. Another such item, recommended by author Dave Schaefer, is Reflectix insulation. This flexible foil sheet, available by the roll from home supply stores, can be cut to fit any space. Use it to line a poorly insulated box or to tuck over and around foods.[7]

Allowing ice to take a bath at the bottom of your box will cause it to melt faster. Experts say it is unhealthy to allow an icebox to drain directly into the bilge, even in a fiberglass boat, because this water is contaminated with bacteria from rotting food particles. Instead, icebox water should drain directly overboard or into a separate sump box equipped with an automatic bilge pump. Not all boat designers are paying attention, however; one of our earlier boats had the icebox drain switch toggle with the salt water tap. The only way to drain the icebox was to switch it over and let it drain out the tap into the galley sink.

I expected our new boat to have a proper drain, but I looked and discovered the refrigerator and freezer drain hoses sitting not so prettily, immersed in the slime of our bilge water. I had to go in with rubber gloves to switch the drains on or off. In giving this matter some serious thought, I've decided that the drain-off water from an icebox can't be any more contaminated than the bilge water. So, unless you plan to wash dishes in, bathe in or drink the water from the bilge, I can't see this as a major problem.

CHILL-LESS BOATING

Not everyone has the space or inclination to deal with much more than a simple cooler, and there will always be situations when cold storage is a problem. Your ice supply may be nonexistent or dwindling fast, or the refrigeration system on strike. Keep wine, sodas and beers cold the old fashioned way by dangling them overboard in a retrievable net. Use lines long enough to prevent the bag from clanking against and damaging the hull. Of course, you can always pretend you're in Europe and drink warm brews.

It's possible to get by without any form of refrigeration by wisely choosing your food supplies. Most fresh vegetables, fruits, and breads will remain fresh for a short period without refrigeration. Look to nonperishable staples for meal making and snacks by maintaining a supply of canned and dry nutritional foods—beans, tuna and peanut butter—for example. I recently picked up a wonderful cookbook touting the benefits of a meatless galley. The recipes were enticing, and none of the ingredients required refrigeration.[8]

Chapter 7
The Gift of Refrigeration

Ice is nice, but ah, luxury of luxuries—refrigeration! Do we need it? Of course not. Nevertheless, many boats are equipped with this wonderful indulgence despite the hefty amount of power that refrigeration requires. Refrigeration systems frequently live on large sailing yachts, powerboats with generators, or boats that spend a good deal of time dockside. On brand-new, sleep-aboard boats, refrigeration is a dealer option. Although this power-driven convenience is more expensive than its manual cousin, the icebox, it takes a bit more discipline to operate. However, I can attest that its benefits far outweigh any problems.

Having refrigeration instantly expands an icebox. No longer do multiple blocks and bags of ice usurp valuable space. Food remains dry, labels won't soak off, and less moisture means less mold. And, if you are able to keep your boat refrigeration system running continuously, you won't need to shuttle that same tub of butter back and forth, because you can confidently leave it aboard. Your end-of-stay cleanup becomes a distant memory, and cold beer and enough milk and juice for breakfast greet you on your return. Having refrigeration is most often a cook's goal. I've had a refrigeration system for a several years, and although we've dealt with an occasional problem, I don't miss messing with all that ice one bit!

CONVERT YOUR ICEBOX

If you want a refrigerator, and this just *isn't* a good time to be buying a new boat to get one, it's possible to convert your icebox over, like we did on a former sailboat. New alternatives for accomplishing this are being offered every day, so scan through the latest catalogs and talk to manufacturers to determine what style will work best for your boat. Other than the standard fare, consider an inexpensive ($200-600) 12-volt DC electric unit that, as one manufacturer claims, will "quickly and easily convert your icebox into a reliable energy efficient refrigerator."[9] Even though some manufacturers claim their refrigeration systems can be owner installed, most require professional installation.

UNDERSTANDING REFRIGERATION

Like the portables we discussed earlier, there are different styles of refrigerators— top loading, front loading, or a combination of both. The typical box is cavern deep. An upright-style refrigerator contains rows of easily accessible shelves, which make the unit much easier to organize than the chest style. On these, the coils and mechanics are hidden.

Recreational vehicles typically use the less efficient, absorption-type refrigerators, which operate on liquid propane gas. But most marine refrigerators are electrically operated. Both types have a closed system in which the refrigerant circulates. The fundamental principle of refrigeration is that when a high pressure liquid or gas expands, temperature reduces. Refrigeration systems rely on a thermostat to regulate the temperature of the box.

Marine refrigeration systems are designed to survive exposure to salt water and plenty of boat motion. They use a nontoxic and nonflammable refrigerant, a nonsparking motor, and have safety valves in high-pressure portions of the system. There are two styles of electrically operated marine refrigeration systems: the evaporator system, which operates on the same premise as our home refrigerator; and the holding plate system. Good compressor ventilation, good batteries, tight couplings and good icebox insulation are essential to the performance of both types of systems.

Evaporator Systems

Low-power, evaporator systems are inexpensive to purchase and fairly easy to install. They operate on 12- or 24-volt DC. Smaller boats use a 12-volt/110-volt system. Some styles have a small freezer compartment that *might* get cold enough to make ice cubes, but they generally aren't as reliable as a stand-alone freezer for maintaining below-freezing temperatures. An evaporator system consists of a thin aluminum sheet with internal refrigeration coils, which look like running rows of linear metal tubing. These may be hidden or exposed, depending on the style of refrigerator. A coolant, usually Freon, circulates through the coils to cool the box. The powerhouse of the system is the compressor, an engine that cools by transferring heat from one place to another. A compressor doesn't create cold. The unwanted heat exits to a radiator, where a small fan spins it out into the air.

When installing a refrigeration system, it's best to locate its external workings in a roomy compartment, such as an outdoor lazarette, where the warm air it creates can easily escape. If the refrigeration workings are installed in a poorly vented locker, trapped warm air will keep recirculating, forcing the system to run continuously to get rid of it. Thus, the refrigeration system will consume more power than normal and won't cool effectively.

Holding Plate Systems

Higher-power holding plate systems are used on larger boats. The cooling element is a holding plate filed with a salt solution that maintains the same temperature while changing from a frozen solid to a liquid. The holding plate becomes a frozen block at 18°F. With this type system, it takes a little longer for the icebox to cool down than it does with an evaporator system, but the temperature will hold longer, making it very reliable and consistent. The holding plates are flat, rectangular stainless steel plates about two inches thick that are installed onto at least one side of the icebox. One plate per refrigerator and two per freezer unit is standard. Additional plates increase the speed of cooling, holding power, and reliability of the system.

A holding plate system uses a .75- to 1.7-horsepower DC motor, or a compressor driven directly from the main engine. These systems sometimes use sea water to cool the compressor, rather than a radiator and fan system, eliminating the heat emission problem. Seawater enters the boat via a through-hull water line, sometimes via a separate seawater pump. A holding plate system costs more than an evaporator system and requires occasional professional maintenance to keep it up and running, especially when it must be restarted after the boat has been on the hard.

ENJOYING REFRIGERATION

Refrigeration is very common to powerboats, as these tend to have more powerful engines than most sailboats. However, sailboats and other craft can reap the benefits as well. The first hurdle is learning to manage the power issue. Boats on a slip at dock and wired for AC power can easily operate all electrical systems without draining batteries or need of a generator or inverter.

Off the Dock?

The joy of boating, however, is travel. Suppose your boat is sitting at dock happily chugging along on 110-volt AC power and you decide to go for a ride. The first step is to disconnect the power cord—otherwise, you won't get very far—but then what? The answer depends on how long you expect to be without power. A well-insulated refrigerator will be fine for a few hours without battery or electrical power, so long as the kids don't spend time hanging over it with the lid open deciding what to drink. If you plan to disconnect your refrigeration system for a longer period, however, you can expect it to gradually warm up. What can you do about this situation? That also depends.

A refrigeration system cannot endure long without an energy boost, so you will need to periodically charge it whenever you are moored, anchored or under sail. Are you strictly sailing? If so, fortify your refrigerator with extra ice to help it stay cold longer. If you are motoring or motorsailing, charge your refrigeration as you go using engine power.

How to Charge a Refrigeration System

To charge a refrigeration system, periodically run the engine or, if you have one, the generator. Running the engine charges your boat's batteries and, in turn, delivers DC power to all connected boat systems. Allow the refrigeration system to charge until, according to its thermostat, the ideal temperature of 40°F is attained. We have found that refrigerator temperatures below 38°F cause milk and vegetables to freeze and sodas to explode, so don't go overboard here. Note the start and finish time of this process, then use that number to calculate the time it takes for your unit's temperature to be restored, usually an hour or more.

The size of the box, amount of insulation and the burden of any warm or room-temperature foods and drinks put inside during charging will affect the amount of time needed to complete the charging process. A well-insulated box will hold its temperature throughout the day, even in blistering hot weather. To maintain the cold, charge your refrigeration system twice a day. Most folks do it in the morning and then again at dinnertime. Generators and engines are noisy, so if you are in a crowded marina or anchorage, don't run your engine or generator at times when people want to sleep or relax.

Restarting a Refrigeration System

Has your refrigeration been turned off or inoperative for many hours or many days? You'll need to restart it from scratch. Be certain the lid is shut, and then start up the engine or generator to charge it. Escalate the cooling process by adding lots of ice along with pre-chilled cold drinks and foods. Hold off adding room-temperature foods and drinks until the thermostat reads 40°. Some boats have a timer and a refrigerator charge switch, both of which must be turned on before charging the unit. Turn these off once the box has reached the proper temperature.

KEEPING YOUR REFRIGERATOR HEALTHY

As long as you have consistent dock power, your boat refrigerator will operate as smoothly as the one you enjoy at home, because it is simply designed and there is little to go wrong. All parts are sealed and operation is straightforward. In fact, under normal conditions, a refrigerator will last for years with no more mainte-nance than a periodic washing and seasonal vacuuming of the condenser. The problem is that a boating environment can hardly be considered normal or consis-tent.

Lack of Reliability

Despite all this reliability talk, boaters are often gnashing their teeth trying to figure out what's wrong with their marine refrigeration. Yours may be running all the time attempting to reach a prescribed temperature, or simply refusing to do anything at all—at the least opportune time. The two most common problems with misbehav-ing refrigeration systems are inconsistent power and blocked vents. The blocked vents, we can handle; the inconsistent power, we just need to understand.

Stress, Stress, Stress

If you have a steady source of dockside power, switching off the refrigeration at the electrical panel at the end of a stay is inefficient, unnecessary and puts undue stress on the system. Also, when you return, you won't be able to unload your cooler or put away anything that has not been pre-chilled until later. As we discussed earlier, a refrigerator is happiest when it is running continuously—a nearly impossible feat on a boat lacking a steady power source.

Refrigerators are energy eaters and may consume between 60 and 300 amp hours every 24 hours, the equivalent of running an engine or generator for one to two or more hours a day. To top it off, each time we power down the refrigeration, it takes two to three times as much current to restart it. When power to the refrig-eration is cut off or reduced, condensation forms and the icebox gets warmer. More energy is then needed to get the temperature back down to where it belongs. This creates a secondary problem as the condensation refreezes on the surfaces of the coils or the metal holding plate, leaving it coated with ice. I have enjoyed refrigeration for several years now and wouldn't trade it for anything; but it's important not to underestimate the effect of inconsistent power on anything mechanical on a boat.

Fend Off Ice Build-up

Proper air circulation is key in the operation of a refrigerator or a freezer. One of the most common causes of blocked circulation is built-up ice on the coils or holding plates. When the frost forming on the coils or cold plates is over one quarter inch thick, it's time to defrost the unit. To defrost a refrigerator or freezer naturally, turn the thermostatic control to off, and then leave the lid or door open until the ice is melted. To speed up the process, pour warm (not boiling) water into the box to raise the temperature. As the frost loosens, carefully scrape it off with a plastic or wooden scraper. Never use an ice pick or other metal object. Make sure the drain is open and clear to remove excess water, and scoop ice chips up and out. Wipe moisture from box before closing the door and restarting it. Allow it to reach a proper temperature before restocking it with perishables.

In addition, if your system radiator vent is clogged or blocked, or in the case of seawater, if the raw water filter is choked shut with sea grass or debris, heat cannot vent efficiently and the system will slow or shut down completely. If you know a particular harbor is notorious for sea grass, stay ahead of the problem by checking and cleaning out the seawater and other vents and filters on a daily basis.

Leaky Seals

If you find your unit is accumulating an undue amount of frost, it could mean outside air is coming into the system through a poorly sealed lid, door or liner joints. We touched on this subject in the last chapter. The owner's manual for my refrigeration system says, "90 percent of all refrigeration problems come from leaks and moisture."

Another culprit is leaking coolant. A determined amount of it is needed to properly operate the system. If there is seepage, efficiency goes out the porthole. Check for a coolant leak by looking at the moisture sight glass. If you don't see bubbles or some sign that there is fluid present, you likely have a leak. Repair gauges are more accurate, but usually only professionals use them.

What If?

Our refrigerator conked out the weekend I expected a boatload of company, sending us on a frenzied search for ice to keep our party food from spoiling. If you find you are dealing with a malfunctioning refrigerator, begin by offloading extra beverages into a spare cooler to make room for the ice. Rearrange the contents of the refrigerator so you can place a block or two of ice at the bottom and some bags of cubes on top. If you are plugged into dockside power and accustomed to leaving your refrigeration on, follow the routine cleanup procedure, as you would for an icebox: i.e., remove everything, leave the box open to dry out, and take all the perishable foods home with you. When our refrigeration system was out of coolant one season, I used it as an icebox while we waited several weeks for it to be repaired. My vittles took a deepwater bath before I realized the drain switch wasn't open; it's normally kept shut to prevent warm air from leaking into the box.

If you are putting the boat to bed for the season or won't be using it for a while, wash out the refrigerator and freezer and allow them to defrost. Leave the door or lid propped open to allow air circulation and prevent mildew. It's a good idea to spray the condensing unit with light oil to prevent rust. To prevent frozen piping on holding plate systems, it's necessary to circulate antifreeze through the seawater circuit until the antifreeze discharges.

FREEZERS ARE NICE, TOO

When we bought a boat and found it had a separate freezer, one larger than the refrigerator, I thought, "What a waste!" I would have preferred a larger refrigerator. We actually considered raising the thermostat setting to just above freezing in order to store beer, several bottles of my favorite wine, and all the sodas. But a technician said our freezer wouldn't work efficiently if kept above 18°F. (The moral of this story is that before changing the primary function of any operating system, it's important to check first with experts.)

By the end of the first summer, however, I was enjoying having a freezer, especially since our boat had access to a continuous electrical power source, which helped immensely. In our freezer, bags of ice cubes and blocks stay frozen, so we always have a ready supply. I am also able to keep frozen meats, vegetables and desserts on hand. And I learned that if I stuff leftovers into the freezer at the end of a stay, I can defrost and use them when I return. Sliced bread, packages of bagels and English muffins, and rolls are still delicious once defrosted. Even roast beef, turkey and ham from the deli freeze acceptably, although these are a bit watery when defrosted. It is so handy to reach in and pull out a couple of steaks to grill if we can't get dinner reservations, or to produce a cake for a special celebration.

We are fortunate that our freezer, a holding plate style equipped with two plates, is extremely reliable. Many of the charter boats we've sailed were equipped with a one-plate freezer and failed to keep the food frozen as long or as well as mine. A freezer compartment within a refrigerator will be even less reliable, as it will be less insulated.

If you have a freezer and plan to leave food in it while you are away from the boat, it is critical that its temperature holds to at least 32°F, the freezing point for water. Food that freezes, defrosts and then refreezes may not be safe to eat. To determine if your freezer has behaved erratically, do the following test:

The Ice Cube Test

Place a cup of ice in freezer for a few days. If the cubes remain solid, temperatures have remained at freezing. A cup of frozen water means your goodies have been compromised. If food is slightly mushy, even though cubes are solid, treat it as thawed food and use as soon as possible. Partially thawed food can be refrozen if it still has ice crystals on it.

When you are away from the dock, follow the same procedure to maintain temperature as you would for the refrigerator. We usually spend several weeks harbor-hopping in the summer. I've found that as long as we charge our refrigerator and freezer twice a day, all the food will stay fresh.

By the way, I found out why the freezer on my boat is bigger than the refrigerator. When we provisioned to take the boat offshore to the Caribbean, I was able to stuff enough home-cooked frozen meals and breads in it to sustain a crew of four for several weeks on the water. I still wish my refrigerator were bigger, though. Fresh produce takes space, and being crammed atop everything else needed for our trip caused much of it to become bruised and soggy.

Section Three:
Warming Trends

While we can certainly manage on cold sandwiches and salads in the summertime, these don't provide the comfort offered by hot food. Mornings, we're looking for hot coffee or tea to help us greet the day. In the evenings, a hot meal provides closure after a great day on the water. Like any boating task that begins simply, it isn't long before our needs escalate from burgers and dogs done on a barbecue grill or portable stove to oven roasts and casseroles baked in a marine oven. For indoor food preparation, we'll rely on some sort of portable or built-in stove, maybe even a microwave oven. This section includes a wide range of cooking options available, as well as how to safely operate them.

Kitchen Afloat proverb
Nothin' says lovin' like somethin' in the oven.

Chapter 8
Stove Sense

There are as many ways to heat foods as there are to chill them. Whether you rely on a small portable stove or enjoy the luxury of a full-blown unit with a baking oven and a broiler, you've got the means to put a hot meal on the saloon table. Just as a car needs gas to run, your stove needs fuel; almost anything flammable seems to have been used at one time or another. The most common cooking fuels used by boaters are alcohol; propane gas, also known as liquefied petroleum gas, or LPG; and natural gas, also called compressed natural gas, or CNG.

STOWAWAY STOVES

Boaters requiring mobility and flexibility in their cooking usually own a portable stove. These stowaways have progressed miles beyond the old-fashioned camp stove many of us anguished over as kids. The newest stoves are compact, reliable, easy and safe to use, and operate using replaceable fuel canisters. When choosing any portable cooking unit, look for an auto shut-off valve to prevent overheating when pressure increases, a safe canister loading function and a secure means of keeping both the stove and food on it intact while it's in use.

Stationary Portables

If you are looking for a versatile portable cooker that can be used almost anywhere, you will likely opt for the familiar one-burner butane stove, a boxy unit that weighs about 4 pounds. Coleman makes a two-burner folding stove that will expand your cooking options. With both models, everything is contained within the stove, so there are no gas lines or hookups trailing when you move it. Replaceable, sealed canisters of propane or butane cooking fuel lock into both units. (Because the amount of fuel used is limited to eight ounces, a canister-driven butane stove is considered safe for marine use.) One canister will provide two to four hours of heat. I bought a single-burner unit at a boat show, but these are also sold in marine catalogs and in camping supply stores.

After one season on board, I concluded such a stove's best use is on the wharf, where it can't skid about like a fireball. It now lives at home in my basement and is called into action when a winter storm cuts off our electrical power. If you have or are considering using this flat-bottomed baby aboard, avoid the temptation to plop it atop a nonskid hot pad on the cockpit seat or on a galley countertop. Even if you guard it like a pit bull, a sudden lurch could send it flying. To keep such a stove in place, some manufacturers offer models with suction cups on the underside, called "sea feet." These don't meet the American Boat and Yacht Council's standards of retention. But my feeling is that any feature that helps the stove to get a grip on a flat surface is better than nothing at all.

If you find this portable stove convenient as a permanent galley fixture, devise a means of screwing it in place. Perhaps you can place the portable cooktop in the same well that once held a poorly operating built-in stove, or even secure it atop the original stove, so long as it's free of fuel and truly non-operative.

Gimbaled Portable

The safest, most practical stove for onboard use is the portable gimbaled stove. Like the single-burner unit, it is self-contained and can be stored out of the way until dinnertime. Now, for the perks. You can use it on a moving boat! The stove is circular, has a supportive rim around the burner that is high enough to keep a pot intact, and it's gimbaled to stay level with the boat. There's no longer any need to be concerned about a hot stove running amok, because it is mounted securely to the bulkhead. The larger units operate on propane fuel, using 16 1/4-ounce canisters, which will provide more than three hours of cooking time on a high setting.[10] Are space and money scarce? I saw advertised a mini stove small enough to fit in the palm of a hand that claims to deliver up to 8,000 BTUs and sustain continuous heat for at least one hour using butane or propane canistered gas.[11]

BUILT-IN STOVES

Hooray! You have a real stove, built into the galley. With luck, you've got one with lots of safety features and made of sturdy, noncorrosive stainless steel. It is likely to be gimbaled and has a cooktop with two, three, or four burners equipped with sea clamps, also known as fiddles. You'll enjoy using your stove, or maybe not. Stoves can be moody about getting and staying lit and keeping consistent temperatures; meaning your meats, casseroles, cakes and pies may not emerge looking as appealing as they do at home. Still, you can take comfort from the fact that no one will care except you. Everything always tastes better on the boat.

Fear of Frying

Bona fide cooks have confided to me that they've never lit the oven on their boat, much less cooked anything in it. Some even shy away from igniting the top burners, preferring to use the area as additional counter space. I guess it's easier to pretend there is no stove at all than it is to do battle with one. Fear of fuel is a common affliction affecting new boat owners—and those of us who've risked our lives trying to get a stove going.

Being able to flip a dial or press a touch pad to turn on our ovens at home spoils us, and fussing with a match to light an alcohol or gas stove seems like traveling back in time. Help is coming in the guise of improved stoves and features

such as easy-starting ignitions, slide-under oven doors, standard thermostat controls and split-style part electric, part fuel stoves. Read on and perhaps you'll gain
the courage to light up and enjoy cooking afloat.

Alcohol Anyone?

Do you own an alcohol stove? I wouldn't be surprised if you do, especially if yours
is an older boat. Alcohol stoves are widely used because they are inexpensive and
simply constructed. An alcohol stove has all its parts contained within: a hose
connects the fuel to the stove and an interior tank holds the alcohol. To move the
fuel from the tank up and out through the burner, it's necessary to build up pressure
by pumping a small knob at the front of the oven. Experts claim pressurized alcohol
stoves work well as long as clean, low-carbon content fuel is used—and there must
be well-behaved alcohol stoves out there somewhere or they wouldn't be still viable marine options. But when we had ours the words "work well" are not what I
would have used. It took a man's worth of effort to get going and I can't tell you
how many times we singed eyebrows and arm hairs and scorched the deckhead in
our attempts to warm a simple can of soup.

   I didn't realize it at the time, but many alcohol stoves are also designed to be
used with kerosene. Kerosene is readily available, cheaper and more efficient than
alcohol. Okay, so it smells up the boat and a fire extinguisher is needed to douse its
fires. But I would have happily clipped a clothespin to my nose and given it a try to
see if our stove liked it better; especially since I discovered that alcohol costs twice
as much, takes twice as long to boil the same amount of water and is four times
more flammable than kerosene. It's true that an alcohol fire is one of the few that
can be doused with water—but as fire can be spread by water, this needs to be
done carefully. Another potential hazard with an alcohol fire is that the flame is
nearly invisible, so it's hard to tell if a burner is on.

How to Use a Pressurized Alcohol Stove

Here's what manufacturers suggest doing to get an alcohol stove working. Maybe it
will help you simplify the task and feel more comfortable using your stove.

- Make certain the fuel tank is full each time you use the stove, since a
  full tank requires less pumping to build up pressure. It takes about 30
  pumps to pressurize a full tank, more for a partially full tank. Use a
  funnel to pour the alcohol directly into the tank and wipe up spills to
  avoid starting a fire while igniting the burners.
- Light the burners by turning the main control knob to on and pushing in
  the preheater knob and then igniting the flame. The flame will be
  yellow at first, then turn blue. If the flame remains yellow, it will fizzle
  out, so go back and preheat the burner for another 10 seconds. Use the
  main control knob to regulate the flame. (The directions don't tell you
  that you need to be a three-handed wonder to accomplish this.)
- When you are ready to start the oven, make sure the main burner knobs
  and preheating knobs are closed. Hold a lighted match or igniter at the
  side of the preheater outlet, then pull the preheater knob out and light

the alcohol or kerosene vapors. Hold the knob down and allow the fire to burn for 30 to 45 seconds.

• To keep your coveted blue flame cooking, maintain the pressure with occasional pumping. If a burner smokes or burns unevenly, quickly turn the main control knob counterclockwise as far as possible, then back again. Keep a lighted match handy in case the flame blows out.

If you've done all this and have emerged victorious and unharmed, go pour yourself a cold drink—preferably something strong. You've earned it. Dinner is imminent!

The Blessings of a Non-pressurized Alcohol Stove

The new alcohol stoves from Sweden have restored my faith. Origo makes a stainless steel, nonpressurized stove that doesn't require pumping and is safer to operate and much more reliable than the traditional alcohol stove. The beauty of this stove is that it has a sealed canister system, which means there will be no liquid alcohol sloshing about inside. Simply pour denatured alcohol into the burner canisters, and it will be absorbed and bound into a nonflammable wool material. Capillary action, not pressure, draws the alcohol from the storage canister to the burner where it can be ignited. A steady flame will boil a quart of water in six to eight minutes, and a full canister will last for six to eight hours. All this and the price is still reasonable. Nonpressurized stoves sell for between $150 and $350. Origo also makes a combination alcohol-electric stove for about $500 that allows you to use shore power when available and safe alcohol underway.

Gas Stoves

If you have a gas stove, you're in luck. This is one of the easiest stoves to manage. After years of tangling with my uncooperative alcohol stove, we bought a boat equipped with a CNG-fueled stove. With three children under 12 aboard, I was giddy with delight that I could comfortably prepare full meals aboard. Natural gas comes in skinny lead canisters, about half the capacity of propane canisters, which sent us searching for a place to buy refills once or twice during the season. Our present boat uses propane. I see little difference in both for cooking.

Propane fuel, the same used in outdoor barbecue grills, is more popular than natural gas because it is more readily available. A full tank of propane should last all season, unless you spend an inordinate amount of time in the galley. Both propane and natural gases are instant lighting, although natural gas doesn't burn as hot as propane. Natural gas is lighter than air, so leaks tend to drift out of the boat, but propane gas will sink, so leaks may accumulate in the bilge, creating a fire hazard. All gas is explosive, but by taking sensible precautions like installing the gas tank in a cool, well-ventilated area—preferably in an outdoor locker—and avoiding leaks, you can enjoy the ease of gas cooking with little concern.

Safe Installation

Store the gas cylinder away from potential fire hazards, such as a gasoline-fueled engine or hot exhaust pipes. The fuel supply should have shut-off valves both at the tank itself and at an electrical panel. On gimbaled stoves, the gas supply line needs to be flexible, as well as fire resistant, and must be approved for the particular type of gas (propane or natural) that you are using. Use one continuous length of hose between the supply and the stove, and keep the number of fittings to a minimum, as every connection is a potential leak.

Avoid Leaks

Do you smell gas? First, make sure that all the burners on the range are shut off. Test your fuel system whenever you open the supply valve on the gas cylinder. Open the manual and solenoid valves, note the reading on the pressure gauge, then close them. The pressure should remain constant for at least 10 minutes. If it doesn't, it indicates there's a gas leak in the system.

The Bubble Test

To sniff out a leak, mix some detergent in water and then apply this mixture to all connections and other suspect points. Check for bubbles. Whatever you do, don't be foolish enough to test for a leak using a lit match. Once you isolate the problem spot, make repairs and retest using the bubble test before igniting the stove.

How To Use a Gas Stove

Using a gas stove is familiar, as many of us have them at home. Like today's home stoves, newer-model marine gas stoves use an electronic ignition starter to spark a flame, making it unnecessary to fiddle with a lit match.

Begin by making certain the gas system on the boat has been turned on, both at the canister and on your boat's control panel. Many stove models are tamper-resistant. A simple twisting of knobs will not light any burners or allow gas to enter your boat. On the stovefront, push in the selected control knob as far in as it will go and turn it clockwise to high. At the same time push the spark ignition button or hold a match to the area until the burner is lit. Continue holding the burner knob all the way in for about 20 seconds to heat the thermocoupler and allow the gas valve to stay open. This should deliver a steady blue flame that you can then lower and adjust using the associated knob. If the electronic ignition fails, turn the burner off and apply a lit match to it before returning the knob to the high position. If a burner sputters before igniting, it may need a few seconds to purge the air out of the gas line.

Light the oven burner using the same procedures as for the stovetop burners. Close the oven door carefully to ensure the flame won't be extinguished. Before lighting a broiler, adjust the oven rack to the position needed. Broil with the door ajar and check the food often. Manufacturers recommend that you not run the broiler for more than 20 minutes at a time and suggest that the oven and broiler can be run simultaneously for 10 or 15 minutes to preheat the oven faster. If you do this, don't forget to turn the broiler off before baking, or you'll be serving an extra-crispy casserole.

If there doesn't seem to be much heat coming from a burner and the flame is burning low or sputtering, you might be low on fuel. Check the gas gauge and make certain the valve on the gas cylinder is fully open. If this doesn't solve the problem, maybe the burner orifices are clogged. Remove the burner caps and clean them (once the burners have cooled down, of course). Also, if you are a die-hard boater who is attempting to cook despite below-freezing temperatures outdoors, expect that your stove will balk. In frigid weather, propane gas will not flow as freely.

If you leave your boat unattended for a long period of time, particularly in hot, humid weather, the high-temperature lubricant in the gas control may settle, making it difficult to turn the control knobs. Just clean the valve and relubricate it with a little high temperature grease.

Oven Thermostats

With marine stoves, especially the less sophisticated ones, it's often difficult to determine the exact temperature of the oven at any given time. Food may take longer to cook or may burn at the edges, leaving the middle raw. This is because, in addition to the standard oven thermostat we use at home, some marine oven manufacturers have complicated the process by devising an "infinite heat valve thermostat," which is said to "alleviate the erratic temperature swings common to a thermostat-controlled oven." My oven has such a thermostat, and for the life of me, I still can't figure out how to obtain an accurate oven temperature. Several burnt batches of brownies later, I partially solved this problem by hanging an oven thermometer on the middle rack and fiddling with the heat control.

The manufacturer suggests setting the oven by keeping the oven burner on high until the temperature begins to reach the desired setting, then turning the flame down and adjusting the setting until it holds at the desired level. "Thereafter, check occasionally to see that it remains level." Good luck. I understand newer stoves now have the option of a traditional oven thermostat. Given the choice, I would opt for that.

Diesel and Sterno

In addition to alcohol and gas stoves, you may be interested in a diesel or Sterno stove. Diesel stoves are heavy-duty units that put out a great deal of heat, so much so in fact that radiant heat will warm the cabin—a delight in cold weather, but a nightmare during the dog days of summer. As a fuel, diesel is clean burning and easy to light.

Sterno, on the other hand, isn't too popular, because it doesn't generate enough heat to do any serious cooking; although, it is fine for small, quick heating jobs. One of the oldest, simplest fuels, Sterno comes as a gel, packed in a can and is available in most supermarkets or hardware stores. As it burns, Sterno turns to a gas and disappears. Smother the flame by putting the lid on the can. If you plan to cook with canned Sterno on the boat, you can drag out an old fondue pot, or just its stand, and use it in the sink. Otherwise, you'll need to devise another way to raise a pot a few inches away from the flame.

Non-options
Gasoline is unsafe as a stove fuel and should never be used for cooking on a boat. I'm also going to totally ignore wood-burning or coal stoves, as these are normally used for heating our bodies, not our food. Campfires on the beach and large-wheeled portable stoves are certainly means of heating food, but these are strictly shore items.

Electricity as "Fuel"
Electricity is probably the safest source of cooking heat because there is no open flame. The concept of using electricity as fuel almost seems too civilized for boating, yet electrically operated stoves are an easy solution for those who have ready access to 110-volt AC power. Powerboats especially come equipped with electric stoves. Some model stoves combine electricity with propane or with alcohol, making it convenient to cook using either method. There are also some plug-in, mini electric stoves on the market.[12] In the next chapter we'll discuss in detail one of the most popular "electric ovens," the microwave.

HOT TIPS

- No matter how damp and cold it may be, avoid the temptation to use your range as a cabin heater, even if it has an automatic shut-off safety feature.
- The whole range becomes hot when the oven is on, especially the top portion of the back of the range, so don't try to swing it up or lift it without using potholders. A hot unit is also dangerous to children and pets.
- As a safety precaution, I recommend keeping the oven's gimbal function in the locked position when the boat is at dock and you have foot traffic in the galley area.
- Whenever you are baking, check frequently to make sure the oven burner has remained on, especially when you lower the oven temperature. A low setting or low fuel conditions may cause the flame to sputter out and die. With a gas stove, escaping fumes are hazardous.
- As with any hot food or hot cooking device, keep potholders handy and prepare a heatproof spot to receive a hot cake pan or casserole after you remove it from the oven.
- Make it a habit to keep the stove in sight when you are cooking on it or in it so you will be handy to avert a problem. Pots may boil over; greasy spills can catch fire.
- Don't store flammable materials, such as plastic containers, wooden spoons, and dishtowels where they can melt or ignite.
- Extinguish grease fires by smothering them with baking soda or by using a fire extinguisher mounted near your galley.

Oven Cleaning

For years I dodged cleaning my oven at home, until finally I acquired a self-cleaning oven. Well, you won't find a marine self-cleaning oven, so the best way to avoid a major cleanup project is to wipe up food spills or burnt food before they cook on. Routinely use a sponge soaped with liquid household cleaner to clean the inside and outside of the stove. Remove crusty or stubborn stains with a nonscratching cleanser or scouring pad. Stay away from steel wool or other metallic pads. Using these will embed fine steel particles into the surface of stainless steel, causing it to rust in a marine environment.

Self-fueled Meals

I'll bet you didn't know you could enjoy a hot meal without using any kind of stove or warming device. I recently read about a product called HeaterMeals, available at truck stops and camping supply stores, which is self-heating. I have no idea how these meals taste, but, according to the article, they were originally developed for the U.S. Army and come packed as individual meals. To activate the heat, add water to a specially provided bag of reactive metals that comes packaged with the food product. In about 15 minutes, the meal will be hot. These meals sell for about $4 apiece, don't require refrigeration and have a shelf life of several years.[13] Wouldn't these be handy to have aboard for emergencies? How about slipping a couple into the ditch bag for the survival raft?

Kitchen Afloat proverb
Why ride the ferry, when it's faster by speedboat?

Chapter 9
Nuke It!

It's true. No purist boater would be caught with a microwave oven, much less anything electrical. However, many folks with 110-volt AC access are finding that a microwave oven is a reliable and practical way to cook. Microwave ovens have been on boats since the mid-1900s, when a chocolate bar in a Raytheon employee's pocket melted near a running magnetron machine. After changing his pants, the intrigued fellow hovered near the magnetron with corn kernels, and they popped. A raw egg cooked so quickly it exploded. Two years later, the first commercial microwave oven hit the streets, a big boy about the size of a refrigerator that sold for about $3,000. Traveling ocean liners and trains bought them to defrost and heat meals in their kitchens. It wasn't until 20 years later that less costly countertop microwaves began appearing in households and, today, on our cruising boats.

HOW IT WORKS

When microwave ovens first became available for consumer use, it was like the coming of the television set, a marvel. We've come to take the miracle of cooking without heat for granted, and many of us vaguely remember how the microwave process works. The answer is sex. Only, the sex in this instance isn't between people, it's between the water molecules in food. When an oven is turned on, a small antenna near the magnetron sends microwaves through a metal pipe, called a "wave guide." The walls of the oven then reflect the microwaves, which causes them to bounce back and forth between any water-containing items in the oven. Soon, all the water molecules are jumping about, rubbing up against each other and having a hot old time. This orgy that takes place within a particular food or beverage creates heat, which cooks by driving the exuberant water molecules from the middle of the item to its outer layers, essentially steaming the food.

WHY BOTHER WITH A MICROWAVE?

Microwave cooking is fast, safe and efficient. What more could a cook ask for? Use it to heat up leftovers, defrost frozen foods and cook raw foods.

Put your hand inside of a microwave oven after you've just heated something in it. Because the oven itself doesn't heat up, it will feel cool, except for a bit of lingering heat from the item you've just removed. This makes cooking in a microwave safer than using a conventional stove. With no open flame or hot parts to be

54

concerned about, even kids can safely use it. There has been concern expressed about harmful microwave rays escaping from the oven. But today's microwaves will not operate unless the door is closed. Repair bent or damaged doors and be certain the seal is tight, and all those little waves will remain in the oven where they belong.

It's fast. You can literally serve a meal in minutes when you nuke it. And when you've finished dining, you save water by washing fewer dishes and pans, since most foods can be cooked in their storage containers, on a serving plate or directly on the oven floor. Unlike a conventional electric oven, a microwave oven heats only the food, so it will consume less of your hard-earned power.

Food isn't apt to bake onto the interior of an oven, even if it spills. Slopovers or spatters will clean up with a few swipes of a sponge or paper towel moistened with a little dish detergent and water. Most ovens have a glass spill catcher tray, which can be removed for washing. For the most part, a microwave oven will run without a complaint for many years and requires little more than electrical power to keep going.

CHOOSING A MICROWAVE OVEN

So many boats now come with built-in microwave ovens that it's possible you already have one of these miracle workers aboard. If you plan to buy one, there are a few things to keep in mind.

Where to Put One

The time to determine that you've no space for a microwave is *before* you buy one. Begin by perusing catalogs and the like to check the measurements of ovens at the small end of the spectrum. Then take a hard look at your galley. Where will you locate one? A microwave will be happy anywhere that's stable and allows for ventilation. Usually, the vent is at the top of the oven. Can you remove the door to a locker so the oven will be boxed in? Or, mount it under a cabinet? A 110-volt AC outlet should be nearby. Make sure that the spot you've selected affords enough clearance for opening the oven door, and avoid situating it above the stove. Once you've determined a convenient and safe spot for a microwave, take depth, height and width measurements of the area to ensure your final choice will fit.

What Kind to Buy

The average pleasure boater can get by with a standard household microwave. Touch-pad selectors are moisture-resistant and cause fewer problems than control knobs or push buttons. If you plan to be on the water more than a few months out of the year, I suggest you go whole hog with a marine-grade unit, which is constructed of corrosion resistant materials and built to resist vibration damage and avoid interference with onboard electronics. The bad news is these are twice as costly as household microwaves.

Combo Microwave/Convection

If you are looking at household microwaves, you may come across a combination microwave-convection oven that will fit on your boat. When in the convection mode, the oven will cook by distributing heat, like a traditional stove; however, convection cooking is faster because warm air circulates around food, instead of collecting at the top of the oven. The entire oven can be used for cooking, and since a convection oven does not require preheating, you save time and thus use less power.

Cooking Power

Choose the oven with the highest wattage that meets your dimension requirements. As a rule, a larger oven delivers more power than a smaller one, so you'll have to be particularly vigilant. I discovered the importance of wattage years ago when we inherited a no-name brand microwave that took longer to heat a cup of water than did my stove. I used it as a storage locker. I presently own a 1994 GE Spacemaker II, which is small, yet delivers a very adequate 600 watts. In a catalog, I noticed a 500-watt mini-microwave by Samsung that will fit in a 13- x 11- x 12-inch space. Most microwave ovens have a power control setting, allowing full power cooking or a portion thereof—a must for delicate foods.

MICROWAVE COOKING

If you've owned a microwave oven for years and are comfortable using it aboard, you may choose to skip this section. The most common uses for a microwave are defrosting and reheating, but it is also a quick means of cooking raw meats, seafood, eggs (without the shell, please), vegetables, puddings, and much more. Microwave cooking is no more difficult than traditional cooking—it's just different.

Away From Dock

When you wish to use a microwave oven away from the dock, as with any electrically operated device, turn on a generator or an inverter to convert battery power to 110-volt AC. I have found that running the engine keeps the battery charged while using our inverter, and gives it the extra boost needed to operate without drawing down the batteries.

   If you plan to do some nuking while on the move, keep in mind that a microwave oven isn't gimbaled. Cups and plates filled with beverages and food will slip and slide as the boat moves, and their contents are apt to say, "hello!" when you open the door to retrieve them. I solved this problem by setting the bottom half of a sturdy rectangular, plastic container in the oven as a secondary drip tray. Mine has 2-inch-tall sides, fits comfortably within the oven walls and doesn't seem to add cooking time to foods.

Fear of Searing

Even though microwaves have been around for a long time, there are still a few souls who are uncomfortable using one and defer to the stove. Read on if this applies to you. Less is more when microwaving, so be conservative about cooking time. It's easier to zap an item a few seconds longer than to try to revive it once it's been burnt at the stake. In addition to using and losing by experimental cookery, review the manual that came with your oven for the particulars on times and cooking methods. These samples are taken from the manual for my 600-watt oven:

1 cup of water, coffee or other beverage	$1\frac{1}{2}$–4 min.
1 roll or muffin (low to medium power)	20–60 sec.
1 hotdog or sausage	1–$1\frac{1}{2}$ min.
Bacon (per slice)	40–60 sec.
1 plate leftovers	3–4 min.
6 ounces soup	2–7 min.

Most foods that come with cooking instructions also provide microwave directions. Some microwaves take charge of the guesswork by providing programmable settings for cooking or defrosting specific foods like hotdogs, baked potatoes, and pizza; or they have a separate, sensitized reheat button.

Always take a second glance at the cooking time you've programmed to be sure it is what you intended. Our boat was filled with smoke by the time we realized my captain had depressed 40 *minutes*, instead of 40 seconds to reheat a frozen muffin. Should anything inside an operating oven ignite, keep the door closed, turn the oven off and then unplug it or shut it off at the electrical panel.

Enjoy Uniform Results

Because the energy in a microwave oven is not equally distributed, some portions of a food may heat or defrost faster than others. Microwaves penetrate foods from the outside to a depth of about an inch, so small amounts of food will quickly cook through. Larger quantities of food will cook more unevenly, as the microwaves are absorbed before they reach the center of the food, thus cooking the middle more slowly than the outer areas. Dense foods, like hams or roasts, will take longer to cook than porous foods, such as ground beef. The moister the food, the more quickly it will cook, since it's our friends the water molecules inside doing the rocking and rolling. Use a microwave-safe thermometer to check the internal temperature of large portions of protein foods such as chicken, pork loin and lasagna to be certain they are cooked to a safe temperature.

Compensate for Unequal Heating

Distribute food evenly, centering it on the dish or microwave floor. Arrange individual items like baking potatoes in a ring, leaving enough space between foods to allow energy to penetrate from all sides. Place tougher, thicker portions on the outside and thin, delicate ends toward the inside of the platter. Periodically and throughout the cooking cycle, stir or rearrange and turn over pieces of food.

Ring shapes are the best, because microwave energy penetrates from the top, bottom, sides and center. Try to use round platters, casserole dishes and containers rather than oval, square or rectangular ones. Food in a shallow casserole will cook faster and more evenly than the same amount of food placed in a deeper dish. Choose straight-sided casserole dishes, since sloping sides permit outer top edges to receive more energy and overcook. Clear glass allows microwaves the readiest access to the food within.

Place items like breads or crumb-coated chicken, whose exteriors you wish to remain crisp and dry, on a piece of paper toweling to absorb moisture created from steam buildup between the food and the plate or oven floor.

Use Microwave-safe Materials

Paper plates, Styrofoam cups, glass, china or pottery, plastic containers and plastic bags are all microwave-friendly. Turn casserole dishes and dinnerware upside down and check the label. If the item doesn't say it's microwaveable, it probably isn't.

Plastics

Avoid using anything as a cooking container that may melt. Most brands of marine dinnerware, a form of plastic, are tolerant of only short stints in the nuker. I ruined a good plate trying to fry an egg on it in the microwave; the egg became a permanent part of the dish. Some of the newer marine dishes are microwave safe, so opt for these if you are in the market for a new set. Choose high quality plastic containers—Rubbermaid or Tupperware make some—that are meant to go in the microwave. Some have vented covers. Supermarkets sell plastic wraps designed not to disintegrate in a microwave oven. If you don't care to bother with storing an extra box, select a brand that won't shrivel and melt, or you'll be dining on it along with your meal.

Metal, or Not?

Exercise caution when using any form of metal in the microwave. My sources say it's okay to cover areas of food with small amounts of aluminum foil to protect them from overcooking, and even to use metal pans. You will find very specific directions in your owner's manual. Metal slows cooking because it keeps the microwave energy from reaching the food. On the other hand, metal can drive the microwaves into a heat-producing frenzy, possibly enough to cause arcing of sparks and a fire. If you aren't comfortable with taking the precautions needed, err on the side of safety and avoid using metal pans, foil or any item containing metal as a cooking container. This includes dishes with metallic trim or a glaze with a metallic sheen, as well as recycled paper products since some brands can contain metal flecks. Remove wire twists from paper or plastic bags.

Test an Item for Microwave Use:

> If you're not sure about whether it's safe to use a certain item, place the questionable plate, cup or bowl into the oven along with a glass measuring cup filled with water. Set the cup of water in, on it, or next to the item to be tested. Microwave one minute on high. If the tested item remains cool and only the water heats, it is safe for use in the microwave.

Prevent Splattering and Explosions

Don't forget the story of Raytheon and the exploding egg. To prevent bursting from built-up steam pressure, remove the shell before attempting to nuke an egg and pierce foods that are encased in any kind of skin or membrane, like potatoes or sausages. Open sealed jars and plastic containers, or vent them. Some can build up enough pressure to burst, even with the lids removed. Avoid heating baby food in glass jars and beverages in narrow necked bottles, especially carbonated ones.

Retain moisture and prevent food or drinks from splattering by covering them with sheets of paper toweling, waxed paper, plastic wrap or a paper plate or napkin. Venting is important to releasing built-up steam. Fold back a corner of plastic wrap covers and slit or pierce microwaveable cooking pouches and frozen dinners. Lightly cover sugary liquids or sauces to prevent them from boiling over; they get very hot very fast.

Oil temperature can't be controlled, so relegate frying to a stovetop skillet. Cover or contain items that are greasy or fatty. Use only popcorn designed for the microwave to avoid a gunfight between the corn kernels and your oven walls. Follow the directions for heating and stand by until the popping slows, otherwise the next thing you will smell is burning popcorn.

Foods and liquids continue to cook after being taken out of the microwave, so stir them briefly to distribute the heat and calm down crackling. Heat transferred from food will make some plates and dishes hot to handle, so treat microwaved items as if they were being removed from a conventional oven. Use potholders, remove the cover carefully, and direct steam away from hands and face. Manufacturers caution against placing wet newspapers that need drying in the microwave, and generally nix the idea of using the microwave cavity for storage. But I'll never tell, if you don't.

IS YOUR OVEN OFF A BEAT?

I've read that a microwave oven may cook slower as it ages, but my oven is pretty old, and it still works just fine. If your oven is lacking oomph, it may be experiencing minor fluctuations in voltage or reacting to the mechanical stress of operating on power from a variety of sources. Listen as it runs on a medium setting. It should cycle on and off every five or 10 seconds. You should hear it hum softly when it's on and then stop humming during the off part of the cycle. Different power levels will vary the fractions of "on" time and "off" time. If your oven is humming off-key, then it's singing the "Fix Me" song. Unplug the oven and haul it to the nearest microwave service location for repair. Never attempt to fix it yourself.

Chapter 10
Fire Up the "Barbie"

Someone is grilling! Don't just wish it was your steak or lobster sizzling on the grill, *do* something about it—and I don't mean follow the luscious aroma and beg for a bite. Clean out the basement and unearth your old hibachi or stowaway barbecue grill and bring it to the boat. If you don't have one and aren't quite ready to invest in a marine grill, you can find one almost anywhere picnic goods are sold. Remember that standard grills are intended for shore use, and our kitchen afloat is meant to travel, which means that wherever you go you'll need to be able to tote your grill along with you. Opt for one that is lightweight and easy to stow. You can easily find one-time-use charcoal grills, complete with ready-to-light coals.

MARINE GRILLS

When you are ready to move the grilling process aboard in earnest, check out what's available in catalogs and marine stores. Of course, you'll want a stainless steel, mountable style. Most mariners use the kettle grill, which looks like a Weber with its rounded spherical shape. But there are other styles. Think about your needs before you lay down cash for an appliance that will adorn your boat for a long time. Do you prefer charcoal to propane cooking? What size cooking surface will you need to serve your normal crew? How and where will you mount a grill? Will you also use it on shore? What features are essential to your cooking style?

Kettle Grill

Kettle-shaped grills are known for their even and consistent heating, and you can find a small, charcoal model for as low as $80. Larger sizes and feature-laden kettle grills cost more. Buy the stand available with this type grill, so you can use it on shore. Barrel-type grills range from $100 to over $1,000, and their cylindrical shape gives them a slimmer profile. In addition to stern-mounted models, there are pedestal-mounted grills that swivel and can be removed for shore cooking, as well as substantial, built-in grills that feed directly from an existing onboard propane delivery system.

With a lidded style you'll be able to roast or bake. You can use the grate of any barbecue grill as a cooking surface, as long as you don't mind scorching the underside of your pans. I have a friend, for instance, who cooks eggs and bacon for breakfast on a standard grill. (You can preserve pan bottoms by buying a portable cooktop supporter for pans.) Some kettle grills also function as stoves because they have a built-in burner plate and dome system that will accommodate normal pots and pans.

Charcoal or Propane?
As a fuel, charcoal is messy, but the least expensive means of fueling a barbecue fire. Still, ease of use and reliability have brought the propane gas grill to the forefront. Propane storage is easy and neat; and it's certainly more convenient to carry a sealed replacement canister or two than to tote a bag of charcoal. If you intend to use a grill as a primary onboard cooking device, you'll find the most flexibility with a propane style with on and off functions and temperature controls.

Barbecue Accessories
Hardware, camping and marine stores are bursting with grilling accessories. Before loading up on these, ask yourself if you will use the item enough to warrant adding it to your galley supplies.

Grilltop Protectors
Using a hole-punched metal plate made to fit over either kettle or barrel grills will keep vegetables, soft fish and small pieces of food from committing hara-kiri in the flames. You'll find aluminum foil protectors in the wrap section of the supermarket—Reynolds' brand is called "Grill Buddies"—that will do the same job, or you can make your own grill buddies by cutting slits in a sheet of heavy-duty foil.

Baking Containers
For slowly cooking ribs or for cooking a one-pot meal on the grill, try foil cooking bags. They will hold enough to feed four adults and eliminate the need for a pan. A friend uses these bags to keep food warm once it is cooked. You can also make your own enclosures from aluminum foil.

Grill Utensils
Standard, long-handled barbecue tools—spatula, tongs, fork—are the safest to use, as long as you have a convenient spot to store them aboard—perhaps in an outdoor locker with other grill supplies. We don't, and after struggling with indoor storage I've finally given up. If I hang them on a hook, for instance, they clank about like wind chimes and drive me nuts. I have found, however, that for all but a roaring fire, normal-sized kitchen spatulas, tongs and carving forks both meet my needs and fit easily into a utensil drawer. If you go this route, use them with care. Choose utensils with nonmetal handles that won't conduct heat.

Grill Mitts
Weber sells long-armed barbecue mitts that are fire-retardant and provide protection from active flames. Don these when using short barbecue utensils, like I do, or when handling large, hot pots.

Conveying Pans

Use a pan, platter or tray with a rim that will contain juices to cart food to and from the grill. To prevent raw juices from contaminating freshly cooked foods, always place cooked items on a clean serving tray.

Fire Igniters

To get a fire going, many have turned from the traditional match to the convenience of long-handled butane lighters. These are also handy to keep aboard for safely fusing deck lines and for lighting alcohol and gas stoves. (I've taken to using one to light candles.) Butane lighters are inexpensive, and you can either replace the lighter when it runs out of fuel or buy a refillable model. Some fancy styles run on battery power. All igniters do the same thing, so it's a matter of choice and expense. Should you need to fly to reach your boat, as you might when chartering, be aware that these items are all on the airlines' list of no-no's.

Matches

Kingsford sells long, wooden matches for barbecuing, which look exactly like fireplace matches. It's all in the name, I guess. These, of course, would work as well as a butane lighter, but will take as much storage space, or more, and could fail should they get damp or wet. Waterproof stick matches, sold for boating, are short, like book matches, and despite their claims, I've had trouble getting them to light, even when they haven't been wet. I have found that common wooden kitchen matches, which are about three inches long, make the best backup to a butane igniter.

Charcoal Briquettes

Charcoal imparts a woody, smoked flavor to foods that we have all come to associate with outdoor grilling. So many of us have adapted to the taste of propane-grilled food, however, that we forget how wonderful charcoal-grilled foods really are, until we take our first bite out of a perfectly seared steak. To savor the flavor, you'll need a supply of briquettes on hand. For a consistent, long-lasting fire, opt for quality charcoal. Self-starting coals with built-in lighter fluid may seem convenient—one less thing to stow or spill—but defeat their purpose if a lighter fluid boost is needed to elevate a fire.

To avoid having to stow a bag of leftover charcoal, buy small bags of five pounds or less. We have not dared store charcoal aboard in anything but a waterproof bag, since water once got into our outdoor lazarette, soaked open the paper charcoal bag and made a syrupy black mess of every other item in the locker. If you frequently barbecue and like to keep charcoal aboard, by all means invest in an official charcoal storage bag.

THE HEAT IS ON

Wait! Before you light that grill, note the weather conditions and the wind direction relative to the position of your boat. In a light rain it's often possible to keep a fire going by closing the lid or erecting a protective tarp. Squalls, erratic winds and heavier rains can flick flames into the cockpit and steal the burgers from your grill before you know it, sending your beautifully working fire to never-never land.

If you are in a mooring field or anchorage, the bow will naturally point into the wind, which will route flames and fumes away from your boat—although beware of tides or currents that can sometimes push you around the other way. But when my captain and I decided to relocate from a mooring to a dockside slip, we quickly learned the importance of wind direction. Winds gusting straight into a cockpit can whip a calm fire into a panic of sparks and flames that can be treacherous to the safety of the boat and to the people on it. The first night we tried to barbecue, our stern was facing directly into the wind. Being tied to a wharf, there wasn't much we could do to remedy the situation, except to sentence our steaks to pan-frying belowdecks. We owned a kettle grill at the time, which tumbled over like Humpty Dumpty when we tried to use it on the wharf. Finding a suitable stand solved that problem.

Other than finding another means of cooking dinner, the obvious solution is to relocate the grill to leeward. Although it's not customary to mount a grill elsewhere from the stern, it's possible there is a protected spot near the bow or on a side rail of your boat that will enable you to grill aboard without engulfing your neighbors or your boat with smoke. Most commonly, though, if conditions are contrary to back-of-the boat grilling, most folks on slips move their grills to the dock or to the marina parking lot. It's a bit awkward and inconvenient, but you can still enjoy dining aboard.

Cooking Tips

Whether you are cooking with propane or charcoal, make certain the grill is properly heated before tossing on the lamb chops or chicken pieces. Hold your hand about two inches above the grate; if you can keep it there for two or three seconds, the grill is ready. Once you put items on the grate, avoid the temptation to move them about and flip them from side to side until they have had time to sear. Searing foods helps create that yummy crust typical of grilled foods and will prevent them from sticking to the grate. Piercing foods with a testing knife or a fork will drain the juices into the fire.

Different kinds of foods require different levels of heat. With direct heat, foods are placed directly over the coals and will cook quickly. This method works best for thin or delicate meats, seafood or vegetables. Thicker foods, like filet mignon, chicken breasts or roasts do better when first seared in direct heat to seal in the juices and then cooked at lower temperatures. On a propane grill, this is achieved by simply turning down the temperature control. But with a charcoal fire it may mean allowing the fire to die down some before attempting to cook the food, or first searing the food under direct heat and then moving it to a cooler section of the grill where it will absorb less heat.

Read the Ashes

With charcoal cooking, the process is more intuitive. Anyone can cook a burger or a hot dog, but it takes special care to roast chicken halves for a crowd as flawlessly as my Dad did. Using a handmade cinder block grill, he dumped two 20-pound bags of coals on the bottom grate and set the top grate almost two feet up from the coals. Once he deemed the coals were ready, the chickens were laid out bony side down and left to roast for almost an hour. A quick flip to the topside for browning, and Dad's famous chickens were roasted to juicy perfection. Knowing how to "read the ashes" is important in charcoal cooking. A fire that is too hot, for example, will scorch foods, leaving them uncooked inside. White-tipped ashes make an ideal fire for small pieces of food, but seasoned charcoal cooks, like my Dad, know to use lots of charcoal and to wait until the ashes turn almost white before beginning to cook larger food pieces.

Stand By Your Fire

Leave neither food nor fire unattended. Stand by to supervise progress and to be in readiness to extinguish small flareups. Use a doneness sensor to ensure meat is cooked to safe temperatures. Move cooked food to a cool spot on the grill to keep warm or place it on a serving platter and cover it with foil. If you scrape food remnants off the grill while it's still hot, you won't need to fuss much with it on its next use.

To snuff a grill fire that's gone haywire, first close the lid to cut off its oxygen supply. If it's still sputtering angry flames, you'll need to douse it. Water works for a charcoal fire, but will spread a propane fire. Baking soda is a good all-purpose fire-smotherer, but the safest way to handle a fire of any type is with an official Coast Guard approved extinguisher. You do have several aboard, don't you?

Going it Alone

Has the crew abandoned you? It's tough to try to run a barbecue grill and manage side dishes and meal setup and preparation, as well. Organization is key. Choose side dishes that can be prepared in advance and left to chill or simmer gently on the stovetop. Assemble plates, napkins, forks, spoons, knives and condiments on a tray, or set the saloon or cockpit table in advance. If you've enough grill space, cook potatoes and other vegetables alongside the meat. While the grill is preheating, gather the necessary grill utensils, the food to be cooked, your intended serving platter and your favorite drink, and bring them to the grill site and relax. Your work is almost done and everything will taste wonderful. Cleanup? One of the diners can do it!

PRE-SEASON GRILL CHECKOUT

Nothing works forever without an occasional overhaul, and the onset of boating season is a good time to give your grill a facelift. Last year's grease can collude with winter-rotted food to create smelly flareups, smoking and choking. Clean the upper grate by first scraping off the hardened gunk using a grill brush with a scraper. If necessary, spray particularly nasty grates with oven cleaner to soften the goop, then scrub with a steel wool pad and elbow grease. If you dare, take the grates home and cycle them through the dishwasher. (I've even heard people take them into a car wash.) You'll have to settle for presentable, since no matter how hard you work, the grill will never shine like new. If the lower grate that holds the charcoal or pseudo briquettes is wearing thin or rusting, replace it with a new one.

A couple of years ago, we thought our grill was a goner when the fire would hesitantly start, only to sputter out. As always, timing is of the essence. Our grill performed its sulking act with a cockpit bulging with family and friends invited for hamburgers, which we ultimately fried in several skillets in the galley. As the grill wasn't very old, and was a particularly nice one, we put in a call to the manufacturer. The first question the rep asked was: when was the last time you cleaned the orifices? The orifices? Yes, you need to take it apart and run a thin wire through all the little burner holes, because they are probably plugged. Problem solved! Think of it as cleaning the winch; it's just one of those tedious job that occasionally needs to be done.

Check the condition of the lava rock or ceramic briquettes. Replace lava rocks if they are beginning to crumble. I haven't checked the cost of ceramic rocks, but a bag full of lava rocks goes for $2.99 at the supermarket. In fact, you can get a Gas Grill Clean-up Kit for under $10 that includes briquettes. I've read that lava or ceramic briquettes can be cleaned by placing them in a net bag and running them through a dishwasher. After their bath, allow them to cook at high heat for about 15 minutes to burn off the remaining gunk.

Is the gas tank up to date? Each tank has an expiration date stamped on it, so check every so often to determine if it's time to replace it. Propane tanks need to be disposed of by a reputable dealer, who will also be pleased to sell you a new tank.

With a barbecue, much of the cooking mess has departed the galley, leaving it fairly easy to clean up afterward. Also, without the heat of the stove, the boat remains comfortably cool. Make your barbecue an event and involve the crew in helping out. If you plan it right, firing up the "barbie" might mean cook's night off. Can you think of a better way to enjoy dinner out?

Section Four:
Attack Storage Issues ∼∼∼∼∼

Now that you understand how all the components of a galley function and interrelate, it's time to address some of the finer points. We arrive on the boat with mountains of gear, and it all needs to be stashed securely away. But where? How? There are times when this task is so overwhelming all you'll want to do is stand amid the mess and yell "Help!" I can't promise that if you read this section you'll never again complain about storage, but maybe next time you'll at least be able to find a place to sit. Mount your attack on storage by taking advantage of every available inch of space on your boat, using it wisely and completely. Organize supplies inside, as well as out, and before long, everything aboard will have its place.

Kitchen Afloat proverb
    Organization is the key to managing a mess.

Chapter 11
Space-making

Can we *ever* have enough galley storage on a boat? I doubt it. The ultimate convenience is to have everything needed to prepare a meal within arm's reach. Before
you buy a boat, explore all the lockers and drawers in the galley area to be certain
they are the correct shape and size to accommodate frequently used pans, dinnerware and food supplies. A friend once complained to me that the pan locker in her
new 41-foot sailboat was too narrow to hold anything larger than a small saucepot.
Be sure to settle these types of issues before you sign on the dotted line for that
expensive yacht.

One of our earlier galleys had so few lockers I was forced to stash pans and
bowls in a locker under the V-berth; it was such a nuisance to unearth the bedding
that most of the time these sat stacked atop the berth. On that same boat, the only
place that would accommodate canned, boxed and bagged foods was under a
saloon seat. This made it embarrassing to ask a guest to move when I needed to dig
out the salsa and chips for hors d'oeuvres. If you have such a situation, the only
way to combat it is to plan ahead and remove the items you might need in advance, or to create convenient storage space by bargaining with the captain for use
of the lockers closest to the galley workspace.

Technology Has Its Price
Keep in mind that on a boat there will always be a trade-off. Amenities eat up space
you might otherwise have enjoyed for handy storage. I gave up having a dinnerware cupboard in my galley to install a microwave oven. To accommodate the
workings of a refrigeration-freezer system, I surrendered a great towel cabinet in
the head. Now we're talking about putting in a watermaker. I wonder what I'll need
to give up for that nicety?

HUNT FOR SPACE
If a sardine can makes your galley look like a mansion, take a look around you.
Every open and closed area on the boat has potential for increased space. It's there.
Look behind and underneath cabinets and lockers. Can you make an area larger by
removing an interior board? Open lockers that are screwed shut and maybe you'll
be surprised. After owning her boat for many years, a friend squealed in delight
when she found a locker meant to hold a water tank totally empty and available.

Steal Ideas

When you go to boat shows, snoop about for storage ideas. Where is there shelving? What types of doors are on the cabinets? How is space divided within the dry locker, icebox, wine cupboard and other galley cabinets? Talk to other boaters, particularly those who own your same make and model boat, to find out how they solved issues you are struggling with. You can offer them ideas, as well. Years ago we met live-aboard cruisers who owned our exact style boat. I was amazed at the ingenuity they used in redesigning their cabinets, adding custom lockers and external shelving. We copied many of their innovations and, as a result, have greatly increased the amount of useable storage on our boat.

Create Workspace

Scan your galley countertop—the ends, front and sides—for a spot to accommodate a counter extension. On a former boat, we installed a hinged, fold-down counter that added an extra foot to the galley. By boating standards, being able to summon up this much uncluttered space at will is found gold.

Commonly, many of us resort to the tops of the stove, icebox, cooler, sink or any open surface for food preparation. The problem is that our workspace disappears as soon as we open a lid, light a burner or try to run the water. Thus, preparation in progress is constantly disrupted unless it can be easily picked up and relocated elsewhere. The solution is to create a mobile workstation. You can do this in a couple of ways. Have a set of wooden boards made to set snuggly over the wells of the sink or stove. Be certain these can stow away easily and that you don't make the mistake of attaching them with hinges. A less expensive way to accomplish the same goal is to place a simple tray or cookie sheet over the open areas. If necessary, glue rubberized matting to the underside to keep your surface from sliding about.

Think beyond the galley. The saloon table, the captain's chart table, the top of the cooler and a cockpit seat are all dandy spots to spread out and make sandwiches or do some mixing. Or, simply set a basket, baking pan or platter on your lap and use that.

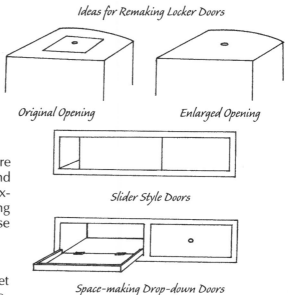

Ideas for Remaking Locker Doors

Original Opening   *Enlarged Opening*

Slider Style Doors

Space-making Drop-down Doors

Maximize Interior Space

Analyze each locker and cabinet within galley jurisdiction and decide on its best use. After owning the same boat for several years, I decided to relocate my dishes from the dinnerware cabinet situated underneath our saloon table up into a small, square locker in the galley. I no longer have to stoop, dig and groan to obtain a plate or two, and the freed cabinet has created a long-sought spot for less needed items.

If a drawer is too short, you may lack a place to store serving utensils. You can't make a locker bigger or change its shape without serious reconstruction, but often you can make it more useable by expanding access to it or reworking the interior. Our liquor cabinet was large but sorely inefficient. It was double the height of the tallest bottle and the openings in the plastic insert, which held the bottles intact, were the wrong shapes and sizes. Our giant bottle of Mount Gay rum was homeless until the local boatyard carpenter came to its rescue by recutting and enlarging the holes in the insert. While we were at it, we realized there was dead space at the top of the locker and added a shelf with dividers and a lip to retain stemware and drink glasses. This was inexpensive to do and has more than paid for itself in convenience.

Examine cabinet doors to see if there is space to add a row of skinny storage shelves inside the door, perhaps to hold spices. Often, changing the way a door or locker opens or enlarging the access to a locker can turn the useless into the useable. Sliding doors require less swing room, but also limit access to items within. Our present boat, a Freedom Yacht, has nifty hinged doors on the cabinets above the icebox and stove that drop down individually to form 8-inch lipped work shelves above the appliances. Perhaps you have doors that can be reshaped in a similar manner.

One of our underberth lockers had a very small opening to it. By redoing the cover, we gained access to the entire locker and can now store bulky items in it that previously wouldn't fit, like the extra sail.

What About the Bilge?

There is no way I would use the bilge on our boat for storage as long as there is enough murky water sitting in it to show my reflection. Yet, I am told that some boats have a dry bilge and that this is an excellent spot to house ponderous items like canned foods, beer and soda. If your bilge has possibilities as a storage area, monitor its wetness by checking it repeatedly to determine if it *ever* gets an accumulation of water, since even a small amount will create enough for a bath when the boat heels. If your bilge gets only slightly damp, encase goods that can't tolerate moisture in plastic for their incarceration there. Set items up and off the bottom by lining the area with Dri Dek or a similar non-rusting grate. Ensure that all items are bilge-ready. A chunk of soggy paper can result in a genuine emergency should it clog up the bilge pump's intake and burn out its impeller. Never stow cardboard boxes where bilge water could possibly wet them. Over time, moisture can cause paper labels to loosen and peel, or become moldy, so remove labels from cans and mark their contents clearly with permanent black marker.

SPACE ORGANIZERS

Ordinary kitchen and bath organizers can help divide and conquer exterior cabin space by maximizing efficiency in drawers, lockers and cabinets. Keep your "space-saver" eyeglasses on wherever you shop. You'll find plenty of items in bed-and-bath stores or in the houseware aisles of your local hardware or grocery store. Seek ideas from catalogs for camping and recreational vehicles and from storage and gadget houses, like Hold Everything, Get Organized and others.

Divide and Conquer

Make your own mobile shelf dividers by using square plastic or wicker baskets to store small items like spices, tea bags and sugar packets. Folding-style plastic milk crates work well in lower or underberth lockers to square curved spaces and keep canned and boxed foods up off the sole. Avoid using cardboard boxes for storage, particularly in southern climates, as cardboard attracts insects. Thanks to a friend who provided us block Styrofoam with cutouts for bottles, we can now safely store two cases of wine in a lower locker. Vinyl coated metal can stackers and stand-alone shelving help organize tall spaces inside lockers without the need to wield a screwdriver or saw. These are inexpensive and, unless they nick, will hold up in a salty, moist environment.

Mount It to Surmount It

String up mesh hammocks to hold snack bags, breads, paper goods and other light-weight supplies. A set of nesting baskets hung overhead holds fruits, vegetables or small items; and the gimbaling effect will keep them safe underway. Hanging shoe organizers with ventilated web pockets will hold dozens of small items and can be mounted on a cabinet door. A fabric or plastic organizer can be cut down to fit any upright locker or wall area. If you use screw-in cup hooks or glue-on, marine-grade Velcro to affix the holder, you'll be able to remove it whenever you wish. Plastic hooks that slip over a door rim also make potential holders for organizers or shelving.

Why dig around for supplies like disposable cups, paper towel holders and wraps when you can mount holders for them right where you'll use them. For cups or mugs, install cup hooks or look for an under-shelf mug holder. I've seen advertised a plastic holder that accommodates several mugs and clips over the shelf and requires no tools to install. Stemmed glasses and cups with handles often cannot be stacked, and by keeping these up and away from the base of the cabinet, you will gain useable space. If you have an overhead area ripe for mounting, install a slotted wineglass holder. Most will store close to a dozen glasses out of the way and in a convenient drying rack.

Suction cup-backed holders are particularly effective and can help corral small items inside a cabinet or out. These are intended to adhere to odd spots like the inside of a sink and to hold lightweight supplies—sponges, sink brushes, steel wool pads—although I have found some are strong enough to hold some weight. Oddly enough, the cheap ones seem to work as well as or even better than more costly, substantial holders. I keep that bottle of dish detergent from dancing behind the sink by popping it into a suction holder. I also use several in the head to hold toothpaste, toothbrushes and soap.

Plastic Bag Holders

Recycled Soda Bottle

Cloth Style

Use screw-in or suction-backed hooks to convert open wall space near the galley into open storage. Hang up a favorite saucepot, strainer or even a small basket to hold matches, keys and other elusive items. Install a spice rack or a utensil holder.

Tame the cluttered piles of paper plates with a plastic holder. The version I saw will hold about 125 paper plates.[14] It is meant to go under a counter, but you might mount one almost anywhere there is space; inside a cabinet, overhead or even in a vertical position over the sink. Looking for a place to stuff all those annoying, but reusable, plastic supermarket bags? Purchase or make a cloth tube with an elasticized stuffer hole on one side and a loop for hanging at the top. These will neatly hold quite a few bags, while allowing easy one-at-a-time removal. I've also seen large plastic soda bottles converted to plastic bag holders, a bulky but easy solution. Use a length of cord to make a loop around the cap of the bottle for hanging, then with a sharp utility knife, cut a hole at the base of the bottle large enough to allow easy insertion and removal of the bags.

Take a few minutes and cruise through the catalogs that I'm sure flood your home daily. You may find just the thing to solve a storage problem in your galley. There is always something new or handy being devised. Remember, if it's easier to reach it will be a joy to cook with.

Chapter 12
Tame Your Top-loader

Cruisers who are blessed with an upright icebox or refrigerator with shelves, like at home, may choose to skip this chapter, as these styles are straightforward to arrange. Without thoughtful organization and planning, however, their top-loading sisters can be black holes of insulted groceries, defying even the cook to locate them.

Putting a dig-in-style icebox in order can be frustrating, unless you've had previous experience with an old-fashioned chest freezer at home or are accustomed to camping with a large cooler. We've all had our share of battles with a cooler to fit and arrange beverages and foods, only to find our brief moment of success dashed once we realize we've forgotten to include the ice. After a summer or two of this nonsense, we eventually learn how and where to arrange items so that everything fits and the lid stays shut.

Managing a top-loading icebox is similar, except most units are deeper than a cooler, making it a stretch to get to the bottom without bending over on tiptoes in an undignified position. This is complicated by the fact that the opening to an icebox is often smaller than the dark cavern it's hiding. Unless you've got good lighting, finding items tucked in dark corners is a challenge worthy of a flashlight. Here, an option to open the unit from the front is a benefit. Iceboxes that aren't especially deep may sprawl horizontally, and several styles have front-access openings. Dual-opening styles present the problems of positioning commonly retrieved items so that you can get at them. There's also the matter of remembering which door is hiding the beer.

The presence of interior shelves can help or hinder the act of loading up large quantities of groceries, depending on where and how the shelves are located. Fortunately, most shelves are removable, which offers the greatest flexibility. Among the four sailboats we've owned equipped with top-loading iceboxes, I can't think of a single occasion where I've found it more effective to leave the shelving in place. In fact, my current shelves are squirreled away—somewhere—on our boat.

Another problem with top-loading units is that the lids are heavy with insulation. On one of our boats the chart table was also the lid to the icebox, adding extra weight. We found it saved injuries to always double check that its spring-loaded hinges were fully up. If you have such a monster, keep children from dipping into it, as they may not take the time to secure the lid open. If your icebox lid has no means of being held erect, install a simple gilguy—an elasticized line with hooks on both ends—inside the lid and secure one end to a nearby wall to hold the lid in place.

ORGANIZE THE ABYSS

Shelves are restrictive because they limit how and where you can place various sizes and types of groceries. To prevent your icebox from becoming a jungle of groceries, make your own visual compartments by deciding where you will group specific food types; then train yourself to habitually place cartons, cans and other items in the same general location each time you are aboard.

How to Stack a Top Loading Icebox

Delicate Foods and Produce
Bag Ice
Meats, Other foods, Dairy
Ice Blocks, Cartons, Cans, Bottles

This is how my top-loader is set up. It is about three feet deep, four feet wide, and has a one-foot-square opening.

- Large cans, bottles and cartons of soda, milk and juice are arranged upright in the bottom of the chest. Juices and milks are on the right, water in the center, and soda, beer and wine are on the left.

- Items that can be jostled, like plastic containers, are placed in the middle.

- The top layer is reserved for the most delicate items—eggs, breads, leafy vegetables and easily bruised fruits.

- Dinner meats and fish—tightly and protectively wrapped—are placed directly under an ice block or bag or in the coldest part of the box.

If you recall from earlier chapters, solid ice is placed at the bottom of an icebox and bags of cubes near the top. In a top-loading box, place bags of cubes on top of beverages and nonfragile items. Remember to use a simple grate to keep foods from tumbling into the drink. Obviously, if your icebox is refrigerated, you'll have fewer problems with moisture and the melt water from ice will be delightfully minimal or nonexistent.

Can Control

Soda and beer are the most frequently sought after, and the most wayward to manage. If you can't relegate canned beverages to a separate cooler, do a few things to control them. One option is to store a whole 6- or 12-pack as one unit. Leave cans in cartons or linked by their plastic rings. Place the first 6-pack at the very bottom of the ice chest. Stack others on top. Place cardboard cartons on end and rip off the top of the box for access. To prevent the cardboard from becoming wet and soggy in an ice-cooled box, set the base of the box in a small plastic bag or container.

I have found an open-topped can dispenser works best for keeping 12-ounce soda and beer cans together and accessible. Move the dispenser around a bit until you find a place where it is balanced. My icebox will accommodate a dispenser horizontally, so I position it across the two sides of my icebox and wedge it between the two lips intended for a shelf. Horizontal rather than vertical placement of the dispenser allows me to easily reach an assortment of beverages, as well as to pile additional cans on top. The dead spot beneath the dispenser works wonderfully for stashing extra sodas or infrequently needed jars of condiments and jams.

I'd gotten so accustomed to relying on a can dispenser that when our plastic model cracked after years of hard labor, I found it devastating to deal once again with an unruly gang of loose cans. You may have to search for an open-topped style, because most can dispensers come close-topped for stacking. I bought a chrome model[15] that I am sure will last almost forever, although I have since seen a simple plastic version for under $3.

Box It or Bag It?

Once the larger items are arranged, it's time to deal with the smaller, more fragile items that tend to get lost. There are two schools of thought on this: some folks swear by using a set of non-nesting but stackable plastic baskets to organize and store like items; others like me enjoy the flexibility of using a combination of covered plastic containers and inexpensive plastic bags with handles, i.e., supermarket bags. Perhaps this is because I've always had narrow, deep, top-opening iceboxes. A sprawling icebox with shelves is more receptive to rigid, boxy shapes.

Regardless of whether you prefer bags or boxes, it makes sense to group like items. Divide items into two or three different groups including, for example, dairy products, vegetables and meats.

Bag large items like heads of cabbage or lettuce since the containers needed are bulky. Lunchmeats and cheeses are easier to grab if stored in a flat rectangular plastic container, although if they are well wrapped I may relegate them to a zippered bag. Round or square containers do a good job of protecting fruits that bruise easily, like plums, peaches, berries, and grapes. I also use plastic containers for foods that may be served, re-stored and then reheated. Whichever style you choose will undoubtedly be sitting atop larger items and need to be removed or shuttled about to get at the goodies below.

CREW PATROL

Unless you set some ground rules, your neatly arranged icebox will soon become a pigsty once the crew dips into it. It's nearly impossible to replace an item without rearranging the box, and most folks won't take the time to do that. For the most part the mess can't be helped. Gravity takes over and any empty spot is immediately filled by whatever else is in the vicinity. Aluminum beer cans will kiss delicate peaches, and a loose jar lid will allow pickle juice to seep over everything. It's not a pretty sight, and before long it won't smell very good either. A frustrating few weeks of dealing with bruised fruit, soggy bread and runaway pickles might make each crewmember unhappy. So what's the solution?

Here are a few ideas that may keep your blood pressure down and keep this problem under control:

- Package food items in leakproof containers.
- Organize supplies in the icebox so you or your crew can quickly find what is needed—draw a map, if necessary.
- Keep loose foods together.
- Limit the number of times crewmembers dip into the box for cold drinks by offloading popular beverages into a separate cooler.
- Guard entry to the icebox like a pit bull—or clue in the crew on your retrieval methods.

CHOOSING AND PREPARING SUPPLIES

It's time to prepare groceries for their deep dive in the icebox. Be selective about packaging. Buy foods in space-saving containers—unbreakable if possible—that can be resealed. Many frequently used items like mustard, catsup, mayonnaise, salad dressings and margarine now come packaged in plastic squeeze bottles that are unbreakable and virtually leakproof. To avoid the boat-home-boat shuttle, bring only the perishable grocery items that you will consume during a stay, unless you have refrigeration that will operate continuously.

As small-size condiments are often either unavailable or costly, transfer quantities of your favorites into travel containers—a half-cup size is just the right size for this. The new disposable plastic containers are suitable for this task. In a wet environment, it's important to protect food from spilling, absorbing moisture and odors, or acquiring leak-over from neighboring foods. To avoid having to deal with a soggy, smelly mess, use plastic bag overcoats to protect paper packaging and vegetables.

Some storage jobs are best accomplished by calling in the "heavies"—high-quality plastic containers such as Rubbermaid or Tupperware brands. Tupperware products are guaranteed leakproof and come in sizes and shapes to suit any task. Leakproof plastic containers are relatively easy to move about since they can sit vertically, obliquely, horizontally or upside down, while keeping the items inside moisture-free. I find a flat, rectangular style works well for deli meats and cheeses, especially those that haven't been packaged in the factory, because it preserves them from external damage and makes them easy to locate and move around.

Use pint-, quart-, and half-gallon-size plastic beverage containers to manage leftover liquids, like milk, juice and soup. These are more durable than cardboard milk and juice cartons, so I often transfer the remains of an opened carton into the correct size plastic container. If you wish to stay with an original cardboard container, be sure to reinforce the opening with some waterproof tape to avoid spilling. If you don't care to maintain a supply of standard plastic jugs aboard, reuse bottles from store-bought water or juice. To avoid contamination, wash them out thoroughly with anti-bacterial detergent. Although these are not as durable as Tupperware-type jugs, they do the job well. Drink bottles with pullout tips are especially good; they won't leak as long as they are stored shut. As you may have already discovered, any container holding liquid, unless it is factory-sealed or specifies that it is leakproof, is liable to ooze when squeezed or under pressure. Camp stores sell bottles made of Nalgene, which will not leak or transmit food odors to drinks.

Bag It or Wrap It

While a sturdy plastic container with a tight-fitting lid offers the best protection, plastic bags and aluminum foil are better for saving space. A good zippered bag is sturdy enough to hold wet foods and liquids; but if you do this, handle filled bags carefully, as they are not squish-proof, puncture-proof or people-proof. Make certain the bag is completely closed. Double-check the seal by flipping the bag upside down and shaking it. If you aren't rewarded with a deluge of its contents, it is safe to stow it away in the icebox or cooler. Place bags on top of other items, laying them flat or standing them seal up, so they won't be pressured to split and spew. Wrapping an item in aluminum foil is another means of achieving an airtight seal; yet, it's hard to be certain the seal is tight enough to withstand a dousing. Thus, I find myself enclosing even foil-wrapped items in—you guessed it—a zippered plastic bag.

Kitchen Afloat proverb
Bad trash makes sick fish.

Chapter 13
Trash Control

There's one thing left to organize, but it's not something we hope to keep around lest the flies and seagulls begin to circle. Trash takes up space, oozes and leaks if crowded, and doesn't contribute one iota to the operation of the boat. Accumulations of meal scraps and empty cans, bottles and boxes grow more aggressive as a trip progresses, and unless disciplined, they will overrun your boat like a band of pirates and leave it reeking like the town dump. All in all, dealing with garbage stinks. Keep the mess to a minimum, corner it in bags and pre-sort it for shore disposal. And whatever you do, don't let it loose to spoil the ocean around you.

CARRY LESS TRASH

Trash control begins at home—or at dock, where dumpsters wait to be filled. If you have ready access to shore disposal (and couldn't care less about the number of bags you need to haul to shore) these-trash saving tips may not be of interest. However, if you will be traveling for several days without touching land, the remains of whatever you take or make aboard are bound to become the most despicable of freeloaders.

- Remove bulky plastic overwraps, outer cartons and other nonessential packaging from supplies before bringing them aboard.
- Repackage bulk foods, like flour, sugar and biscuit or cake mixes into reusable containers and either label them with permanent marker or tape on the name of the item along with mixing instructions.
- Reduce the piles of 12-ounce cans and bottles by purchasing sodas, juices and bottled water in large jugs. Wash out and reuse empty bottles, rather than tossing them out, to keep the number of containers

on board constant. Consider keeping packets of drink concentrates aboard for making up refills.

- Eliminate the need for storing food scraps by controlling the amount of food prepared and dished out to the crew. While it's nice to be certain that everyone is fully sated, it's better to have folks ask for seconds rather than have to scrape uneaten food into the mouth of the garbage can.

- Excessive use of paper products can create useless trash. When mounds need to be kept minimal, forget the paper plates and cups and use standard dishes. Wash them using the water miser method described in Chapter 3. However, it doesn't always make sense to substitute cloth napkins, dishtowels and rags for paper towels, unless you love to do laundry. Cloth items used for mopping food messes can become riddled with bacteria if not kept clean.

MANAGE THE MOUNDS

Control your trash by compacting and separating it. Crush boxes and cans before disposing of or recycling them. Open ends of cardboard boxes and flatten them. Remove the ends of cans, so they can be easily crushed. Some boaters install trash compactors, but these are costly, usurp convenient galley space and constitute a sizeable power drain on small boats. According to the electrician who works on our boat, trash compactors are such a maintenance headache that many folks become discouraged and remove them.

Soupy and gooey food bits can deteriorate quickly and crawl all over the contents of an otherwise dry trash bag. Separate and confine messy scraps to a small plastic bag kept in the galley. If you are offshore, you need to be concerned about plastic disposal. Simply wash out and reuse the same plastic bag until it dies.

Don't we all wish getting rid of our trash was as simple as tossing a bag in a marina dumpster. If you have failed to separate the trash according to the laws of the land, you may find yourself standing amid the flies, dipping your hands into an icky bag to retrieve bottles and cans. Most mainland marinas will accept trash separated into two forms: garbage and recyclable. The disposal problems of small islands will be passed on to visiting mariners. Cuttyhunk, Massachusetts, for example, has six different shore receptacles: green glass, brown glass, clear glass, cans, cardboard and food garbage. At popular stops that are overrun with visitors, there is sometimes a fee for trash handoff. To save your pride, and the need to wash your hands after using the disposal station, keep two separate trash receptacles aboard: one for garbage and one for bottles and cans. Be certain all beverage cans are drained. Wash residue from cans by using leftover dishwater or salt water to avoid smelliness. To avoid tripping over two trash bags belowdecks, keep the can bag outdoors, where it will be convenient for disposal.

STASH THE TRASH

A trash receptacle needs to be handy to the galley and near the food-preparation area, yet few boat designs include a closet or locker to accommodate it. If you are fortunate to have one, you have probably discovered a more efficient use for this space. A fellow boater added shelves to an upright trash cabinet, thereby turning it into a dinnerware cabinet. Another converted the pullout trash bin to a paper goods holder.

On our first boat, we found a spot for a small trash can in the cabinet under the sink, but as the area was open to plumbing, it sat askew and dribbled food bits into the bilge. We settled on installing a small plastic bag holder inside the cabinet door. This worked fine, except the frame of the bag protruded, and with five of us manufacturing trash, it needed constant replacement. In the end, we settled on using a full-size trash bag and securing it to the nearest doorknob, its drawstring handles twisted in a triumphant grin and its bottom lolling on the floor, like a vagrant. In perusing the web, I came across a reusable nylon mesh trash bag that I understand is becoming very popular for boaters. It is flat when empty and can be adhered to or hung against any flat or vertical surface, where it will hold nearly five pounds of garbage. The bag has an elasticized opening on the top and a zippered bottom for easy removal. For messy garbage, this item needs a plastic liner bag. Place several of these strategically about; try the cockpit and the head, and perhaps you can divide and conquer your trash.[16]

One of the most sensible methods I've seen for stashing trash was one in which a trap door installed within the galley opened into an outdoor lazarette. Take a look at the layout of your boat to determine if such an arrangement might work for you. As with any shove and disappear method of disposal, make certain the bag in the locker is firmly in place around the can or the opening to the trash receptacle to avoid fallout. Avoid messy leaks by selecting strong trash bags that won't be easily punctured by a pointed corner or bottom out with weight.

DEVELOP AN EXIT PLAN

Although outdoor storage is the obvious solution to the odor and growth problems common to trash containers, not all boats have space to spare. Develop an exit plan for trash on your boat. Check each bag as it departs the galley, double enclose those that have developed holes or are fully loaded, and then either take them to shore or store them outdoors. On one boat we had a lazarette large enough to fit a family, standing up, where we could put a few pudgy bags that didn't mind rooming with the charcoal grill, extra dock lines and a few tool boxes. We sorely miss that locker on our present boat and sometimes bed down an odiferous bag in the anchor locker. Full bags with no home can hang off the stern of the boat or be trailed behind in the dinghy until they can be taken into shore. It's understandable that some might pray for a strong wind that will blow them away, but be a good environmentalist and secure all bags in place.

CAN YOU THROW IT OVERBOARD?

It's often tempting to "feed the fish" with leftovers or preparation scraps, and it's a reasonable assumption that it's going to good use. In fact, when in the open ocean, it's perfectly fine to toss all food garbage overboard. However, when you are cruising along in coastal areas, use your best judgment. Food particles that disintegrate quickly in warm weather will hang around longer in cold climates. Some tough foods, like orange peels, can take years to break down.

There are a few problems with dumping food scraps when at dock or on anchor. First, many foods float, and it will be embarrassing to watch your dinner leftovers drift off to visit the neighbors. If you've ever thrown a steak bone overboard and heard of flurry of splashing and a big "chomp" you've learned that food scraps attract big fish, making surrounding waters dangerous for swimmers. On some Caribbean islands, it's common for restaurateurs to dump leftovers off the side of a pier into the water. After one such event, we were about to get in our dinghy, when we found it surrounded by several munching sharks, upwards of 6 feet long. In another instance, at dock in Noank, Connecticut, we dumped the leavings of steamed clams we'd enjoyed, and it wasn't long before a trio of fat, striped bass joined our party—and not one of us had a hook!

Nonfood Trash

The majority of mariners are environmentally conscious and know that tossing non-food rubbish overboard while coastal cruising is taboo. Shore currents and tides, along with the circular gyre of the Gulf Stream and other similar ocean phenomena, create a boomerang effect by sending a portion of all dumped trash back to

---

DUMPING LAWS

Coast Guard regulations require you to visibly mount a plaque that cites dumping rules. Read it and bawl.

It is illegal for any vessel to dump plastic trash anywhere in the ocean and navigable waters of the United States. Annex V of the Marpol Treaty is an International Law for a cleaner, safer marine environment. Violations of these requirements may result in civil penalty up to $25,000, fine and imprisonment.

U.S. Lakes, Rivers, Bays, Sounds and 3 miles from Shore.
ILLEGAL TO DUMP
Plastic and paper garbage
Metal
Rags   Crockery
Glass   Dunnage
Food

---

3 – 12 miles
ILLEGAL TO DUMP
Plastic
Dunnage, lining and packing materials that float, also if not ground to less than one inch:
Paper   Crockery
Rags   Metal
Glass   Food

---

12 – 25 miles
ILLEGAL TO DUMP
Plastic
Dunnage, lining and packing materials that float

Outside 25 miles
ILLEGAL TO DUMP
Plastic

State and Local regulations may further restrict the disposal of garbage

local waters. Thus, instead of disposed trash heading out to and remaining in deep waters where it can disintegrate, it returns to litter our shorelines. The Center for Marine Conservation, recently renamed The Ocean Conservatory, performs annual cleanups; someone actually catalogs the amount and type of debris found. Don't let your Coke can become a statistic.

Deep-water Trashing

When we took our boat on an ocean voyage to the Caribbean, I must say it was delightful to be able to rid ourselves of all but the plastic trash. Coast Guard regulations for international waters permitted us to fling paper plates, napkins, soda cans and all food garbage overboard. We were rather shy about doing this at first, but once we got the hang of it, we performed the task like kids on a forbidden escapade. Paper, of course, will dissolve; glass bottles and jars will be eventually be hammered into sand; and cans will rust and erode. Punching additional holes in metal cans assures they won't float in your wake. One of the most stunning sights on this trip was that of a Styrofoam coffee cup bobbing along over 200 miles off the coast of Florida. Styrofoam is a form of plastic, and according to research, plastic can float on the surface of the ocean for 400 years.[17]

NO PLASTIC, PLEASE!

Plastic has been proven to be so lethal to the marine environment that the United States government has put special laws and regulations in place to prohibit all plastic dumping at sea by U.S. vessels. The plastics industry is working on making plastics degradable. But so far researchers have only come up with ways to break it into smaller pieces, not eliminate it.

Because plastic floats, sea mammals, birds and fish who forage for food on the surface of the ocean either eat it and die, become ensnared in it and die or use it for nesting in which case their young die. In the late 1970s a study performed by the National Marine Mammal Laboratory showed that plastic entanglement was killing over 40,000 seals a year.[18] And it's not only sea life that suffers. It was a truly heart-stopping moment when, 400 miles out at sea, we heard the loud thunk of a jammed prop. A peek overboard revealed a long curl of blue plastic rope streaming behind us. We had no choice but to risk sending a man overboard to cut the mess loose.

I can assure you that as much as I tout the use of plastic bags, no plastic ever leaves my boat, except in a proper receptacle. If you are in a legal dumping area, make certain to remove and stash plastic seals to bottles, wrappers for snack cakes and other small shreds of plastic that are easily overlooked. One of the positive things about plastic is that most of it can be crunched compactly. After eight days of sailing offshore, we arrived in Bermuda with one small sack of trash, mostly plastic!

Section Five:
Outfitting Your Galley ~~~~~

The most difficult part of "dressing" a galley is learning that very few supplies are actually needed to cook a meal. In this section, I've covered a wide gamut of cooking and preparation ideas. This is not to presume that all these items are essential—if you opted for one of each, there'd be no room in the galley to cook—but to help you think through your personal needs, evaluate what you already have aboard and determine what stays, changes or goes. It's very possible your present supply is just right, especially if you've already spent many seasons aboard fastidiously fine-tuning your supplies. However, too many of us waste time moving about seldom-used items that would be better off elsewhere.

Take a hard look at what is currently in your galley. If you have a favorite pan you always grab for, it's an obvious keeper. If a particular utensil or serving bowl is gathering dust, take it home and replace it with a more productive shape or size. Follow my rule of two: if an item doesn't have more than two uses and you won't use it more than twice during the season, leave it home.

Once you have established a basic supply it will need little upkeep, other than an occasional weeding out. Pots, pans, cooking utensils and dinnerware can remain on the boat, even during winter storage.

Galleyware Checklist

You won't need all of the items listed below; however, scanning through this idea guide and reading the chapters in this section will help you figure out what items are most important to your cooking style.

Cookware

Pots and Pans

- ❏ 1^1/$_2$-quart saucepan with cover
- ❏ 2^1/$_2$-quart saucepan with cover
- ❏ 8-inch skillet (shares cover with saucepan)
- ❏ 10-inch skillet with cover
- ❏ 4-quart Dutch oven (shares cover with 10-inch skillet)

Ovenware

- ❏ 8- x 8- x 2-inch metal pan
- ❏ 9- x 13- x 2- inch metal pan
- ❏ Foil pans: one pkg. 8- x 8- x 2-inch, one pkg. 9- x 13- x 2-inch
- ❏ Disposable oven-ready casserole and serving dish
- ❏ Box cooking bags

Specialty cookware

- ❏ 8- to 12-quart stock pot with cover and, if possible, drain basket
- ❏ Toaster
- ❏ Teapot
- ❏ Coffee pot
- ❏ Pressure cooker
- ❏ Electric fry pan
- ❏ Breadmaker
- ❏ Microwave turntable
- ❏ Microwave liner

Cooking Accessories

- ❏ Meat thermometer or doneness sensor
- ❏ Matches or fire igniter
- ❏ Barbecue tongs, spatula and fork
- ❏ Grill brush
- ❏ Potholders, oven mitts, heatproof gloves
- ❏ Heavy bib apron

Food Preparation

- ❏ Nesting bowls with cover
- ❏ Colander/strainer
- ❏ Metal and/or plastic spatula
- ❏ Large stirring or serving spoon
- ❏ Large slotted spoon
- ❏ Rubber scraper
- ❏ Paring knife
- ❏ Potato peeler
- ❏ Measuring cups and spoons
- ❏ Rolling pin
- ❏ Blender
- ❏ Can opener
- ❏ Cutting board
- ❏ Vegetable brush
- ❏ Scissors

Serving

- ❑ Soup ladle
- ❑ Steak knife set
- ❑ Bread knife
- ❑ Meat fork
- ❑ Metal tongs
- ❑ Large salad bowl (with or without cover)
- ❑ Salad tongs
- ❑ Vegetable or side dish bowls, or large soup bowls
- ❑ Thermos bottle or coffee serving carafe
- ❑ Covered plastic serving pitcher
- ❑ Baskets
- ❑ Large oval platter
- ❑ Bottle opener/corkscrew
- ❑ Ice pick
- ❑ Place mats, tablecloths
- ❑ Candle
- ❑ Napkin holder
- ❑ Sugar holder
- ❑ Creamer
- ❑ Salt and pepper shakers

Dinnerware

- ❑ Glasses
- ❑ Dinner plates
- ❑ Luncheon plates
- ❑ Soup bowls
- ❑ Cups or mugs
- ❑ Stainless steel flatware set including forks, spoons and knives
- ❑ Steak knives
- ❑ Lobster crackers
- ❑ Pet water and food bowls

Disposables

- ❑ Paper plates and bowls
- ❑ Paper or plastic cups
- ❑ Insulated cups
- ❑ Plastic forks, knives, and spoons
- ❑ Napkins, cocktail napkins

Clean Up

- ❑ Dishpan
- ❑ Dish drainer
- ❑ Dish detergent
- ❑ Kitchen sponge
- ❑ Nonscratch scouring pads
- ❑ Hand soap
- ❑ Paper towels
- ❑ Dishtowels
- ❑ Sanitizing wet wipes
- ❑ Trash bags

Food Storage

- ❑ Plastic storage containers
- ❑ Assorted plastic food bags
- ❑ Aluminum foil
- ❑ Plastic wrap

Chapter 14
Cookware

The more you use the galley stove, the more pots you'll want. On our first boat, my alcohol stove dared me to cook, and I got by with feeding a family of five using one covered, medium saucepot and an electric fry pan—operated dockside. Otherwise, we grilled. Once we upgraded to a boat with a fully operating stove, my cookware needs expanded. I left the electric fry pan at home and opted for more pans and baking supplies.

Most cooks find that one or two saucepans, one large pot and one large skillet will handle the majority of cooking tasks. A medium saucepan with a cover heats up anything from soup and spaghetti sauce to tea water. With a 10-inch skillet you will be able to turn out a variety of breakfast foods—pancakes, French toast, eggs— or to quickly sauté a meal on the night your barbecue gets rained out. Add an 8-inch skillet to your list if you are cooking for two. Many sets come with a Dutch oven, whose cover typically fits the 10-inch skillet as well. The Dutch oven holds about four quarts of water and is good for large quantities of soups, stew and for cooking pasta. Opt for larger rather than smaller pans if spillage is a concern, as it is when cooking on the move.

CHOOSING A PAN

The better the quality of the pan, the easier it will be to cook with and to clean. Thin, poorly made pans heat unevenly, and you've got enough trouble with that already, as you will be using an erratic heat source. When perusing your excess pan collection at home or while shopping for something new, opt for a shape, style and material that won't rust or pit in a marine environment. Pick up the pan and see if you like the feel of it. Is it too heavy to tip upside down using one hand? Remember, you'll not only need the other hand for scraping out food and serving from it, but for supporting yourself in a seaway as well. How is it constructed? Is the handle heatproof? Secure? I once had a large pan with a screw-on handle that always loosened. For years I screwed in the handle each time I used it so I wouldn't dump a pan full of hot food while serving from it. To prevent having this problem, look for pans with forged handles. Will it clean easily? High-quality pans, even those lacking nonstick properties, will come clean without you scrubbing your arm off. Does the pan need special care? How compactly will it sit in a stack? Can it easily be stored aboard?

What's It Made Of?

Stainless steel pans are in many ways the obvious choice, yet stainless steel is a poor conductor of heat. To compensate, quality stainless steel cookware, such as Farberware or Revereware, will have its base bonded to a metal that conducts heat, such as aluminum or copper. Stainless steel cookware is more costly than aluminum, but easier to clean and slower to dent or scratch. I've used my Farberware set for years, and with the exception of some baked on grease that I've failed to remove, it still looks and cooks the same.

Traditional aluminum cookware is fine for short stints on the boat, but a poor option for the long term. Aluminum will pit with salt air or exposure to alkaline or mineral-rich foods, although it is inexpensive, a quick and even conductor of heat, and sturdy enough to take abuse. Aluminum darkens as it pits, but can be brightened by boiling for five or 10 minutes with an acid solution such as vinegar and water or an acidic food like tomato sauce.

Black cast aluminum, such as that made by Nordicware, is a totally different material. It is nonstick and of molded, one-piece construction, yet it retains the even-cooking properties of aluminum. I once saw a large selection at a marine store that included a griddle and waffle iron made to work on a stovetop. It's heavy, like its cast-iron cousin, and doesn't need seasoning to prevent rust. The advantage of using a substantial pan is that it is more apt to remain clamped on the cooktop under rolling seas; the disadvantage is that if it doesn't, you'll know it. Although it is cumbersome to stow and handle, many cooks will use nothing else.

The New Stuff

In your pan-hunting escapades, I'm sure you've either used or thought about some of the higher-grade brands, like Calphalon or T-Fal. My family insisted I needed the best and replaced my most frequently used pan, the 12-inch skillet with the twisting handle, with a very costly "professional" nonstick variety. These pans, however, cannot take the high heat commonly used for pan searing, and as a result I now have a dark red circle at the center of my once beautiful pan that attracts goop like a magnet. A pan this delicate would never make it being banged about my boat. My advice is to look for sales at kitchen stores and houseware departments, as well as go to discount stores like Marshalls or T.J. Maxx. You can also check out cost-saving professional chefs' catalogs[19] in search of quality pans for cheap that you can beat up without guilt.

Nonstick Joys and Woes

Ah, the joys of using a nonstick pan. Food slides out without a whimper, and cleanup is a non-event. However, as I discovered, some nonstick finishes wither with constant use of intensive heat. Scratches caused by metal spatulas, spoons or other stirring utensils also trap food gunk, further defeating the nonstick quality. To delay its demise, avoid dinging the interior surfaces with metal utensils by using those constructed of black nylon or other nonstick-approved materials. When you stack nonstick pans for storage, prevent the bottoms from scratching each other by separating the pans with something soft like a potholder, dishtowel, a piece of bubble wrap or length of paper toweling.

Space-saving Sets

Look for space-saving features like interchangeable lids and nesting sizes. I have never found the need to invest in a stacking pan set, although these are especially space kind. Handles are removable, so the pans nest snugly and will store in less than one cubic foot. An eight-piece set of high-quality stainless steel costs about $350 (no more expensive than a quality traditional pan set), but I've seen lesser-quality nesting sets advertised for much less.

OVENWARE

The cavity of a marine oven is small, daring large pans and casserole dishes to fit inside. Here again, be selective. To save unnecessary toting and disappointment, measure the width, depth, and height of your oven cavity and take this information home with you. Take to the boat only practical pans that will fit comfortably in the oven cavity. I find a 9- x 13- x 2-inch pan fits in most marine ovens and is large enough to warm bread or rolls, or to bake a lasagna casserole. The smaller 8- x 8- x 2-inch size is just right for half-batches of cake or brownie mix. I used to leave hard metal pans aboard, but I've found disposable aluminum foil pans work almost as well. They are inexpensive, can be trashed when you don't feel like washing and reusing them, and stack compactly.

Disposable Pans

Foil pans are available to meet almost any cooking need. Extra-large pans have lifting handles, and some have sealable covers. These come three to a package, and two packages will nest, taking the space of the largest. They are lightweight and won't damage anything if they fly about, and the best part is they are expendable. If you love muffins, instead of bothering with metal cupcake tins, substitute foil cups or foil cupcake liners. These are sold in a tight stack and take almost no storage space. You'll find they work almost as well as the real thing when lined up in a large foil pan.

The newest disposables on shelves are casserole dishes, such as Pot Lux by Reynolds. These can be used either in a microwave or a traditional oven, tolerate a freezer, are sturdy enough to be washed and reused, and make nice-looking serving dishes. Do read the directions included. Oven temperatures shouldn't exceed 400°F, and the dish needs to be placed on a cookie sheet. I imagine a foil pan or a sheet of foil would do as well.

Cooking Bags

Cooking bags, like those manufactured by Reynolds, and vacuum-sealed bags reduce cooking mess and food handling. Reynolds now offers both plastic and foil cooking bags. The plastic style can be used in the oven or microwave. Vacuum-seal bags are similar in function, except they can also be boiled. If you do quite a bit of cooking from scratch and like to prepare meals ahead, even freeze them, it might be worth spending $100 or more on a vacuum sealer. You will also need to purchase the special bags used with the sealing unit. Boaters who use vacuum sealers rave about their versatility. Food keeps longer and stays freezer-burn free because all the air is removed during the sealing process. I think I'll order one!

Cooking bags of any type work especially well for cruising. They are inexpensive and available in sizes large enough to contain a meal for any size family. Seal stews, casserole meals and vegetables in the cooking bags, then lay them flat on the freezer shelf to harden, so they will eventually be stackable. Bring bagged foods to your boat for refreezing, defrosting and heating, and you'll find your meal is "cooked" with nary a dirty pot to wash. The foil bags work well for first-time cooking on the grill or in an oven, but I haven't used them for freezing precooked meals. Also, they are not microwaveable.

SPECIALTY ITEMS

We're always looking for ways to simplify our lives and sometimes a special cooking tool will do that for us.

Large Stockpot

If you like lobster, steamers and other shellfish, or simply enjoy cooking pasta for a crowd, find a spot to store a large, covered stockpot on your boat. Don't skimp on size. The larger the pot, the more lobsters it will hold. (A Dutch oven will hold one lobster—maybe.) Stockpots are deeper and have double the capacity of a Dutch oven, and some come with a drain basket. Your pot can go on the charcoal grill or the stovetop. The pan you choose should be a bang-around type. Here, you might try an aluminum pan, which will heat a mountain of water quickly and be lighter than a pan of another metal. If you choose to store your pan in an outdoor locker, protect it from the captain's gooey stuff by encasing it in a large plastic bag. Utilize the cavity of a large pan for storage by filling it with supplies—extra paper plates, cups and dishtowels—when it's not stovetop.

Toasters

My favorite way to make toast aboard is with my trusty marine toaster. Both the rectangular and pyramid styles are intended to sit, like pans, on a stovetop burner. Neither style requires washing; just a crumb shake-out will do. I much prefer the toasting quality and flexibility of the rectangular model, which is harder to find than the pyramid shape. Because it lies flat, the rectangular model accommodates only two pieces of bread, but these can be almost any kind—bagels, English muffins or rolls.

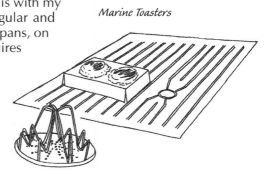

Marine Toasters

How to Make Toast

To use a marine toaster, place it over the burner to preheat, then keep the fire low to prevent the bread from scorching. Use a fork or tongs to both turn the bread to its second side and remove slices as they are cooked. The process goes fast so keep a close watch. If you don't happen to have any of these models and want toast, it can be still be yours. Simply haul out the 10-inch fry pan, heat a pat of butter or margarine to sizzling, and then lay bread slices flat, placing a plate or weight atop bagels and muffins to keep them flat against the hot cooking surface. If your stove has a broiler, it too can be used to make large quantities of toast. Don't forget the barbecue grill is also a toast-making option. If you fire it up for any other part of the meal, slip the bread on as well.

The four-sided pyramid style will toast four slices of bread at one time, but in my experience, it cooks unevenly. Bread slices stand slanted against each side, and the sides fold down flat to store.

Electric Toasters

An electric toaster can be a wonderful convenience, but unless there is a way to secure it each time you set sail, it will be a stowing pest. My two-slicer is presently partying in our basement at home, along with other obsolete boating supplies. If a pop-up toaster is essential to you, opt for a wide-mouth style that will accommodate large breads like bagels without getting them stuck and burning. While you're at it, go for a four-slicer to speed up the toasting process. You many also want to consider a toaster oven instead of a pop-up, as it will take on many more cooking tasks. A compact one will take up just a bit more counter space than a pop-up style, and some models can be installed under a cabinet.

Tea or Coffee, Anyone?

If you frequently boil water to make tea, hot chocolate and instant coffee, or to reconstitute instant soup or oatmeal, you need a tea kettle. A kettle is safer than a cooking pan for boiling small amounts of water, as its wide bottom and narrow neck make it less apt to tip over and spill. It also allows you to fill a cup without splattering.

Coffeepots

In addition to the de facto boating standard—the stainless steel percolator—manual-drip coffee pots, such as Melitta, or French press pots used by coffee gourmets do not require electricity.

"Old Fashioned" Percolator

I've tried most manual coffeepots and have found that the old fashioned percolator still best meets my needs when traveling. It's simple to operate and can be prepared in advance for early morning watches or those of us who can't see straight without that first cup. All it needs is a consistent flame for about 15 minutes, and the aroma of coffee will waft through the air. Nothing boiling needs to be poured until the coffee is properly brewed. Should you scour department and discount stores in vain in search of a non-electric percolator, rest assured you can find a serviceable pot in marine stores and catalogs. You'll also get a wide selection at a gourmet kitchen shop. A stainless steel pot may last forever, but so will an attractive speckled blue or green enameled metal pot.

Manual Drip

A manual-drip pot requires that boiling water be poured over ground coffee through a filtered receptacle perched atop a receiving container. Although the carafe is typically made of glass, thermal plastic is also available and a safer option for the boat. The biggest problems with using the manual-drip method are having a steady enough hand to pour the boiling water without spilling and having the patience to do so slowly enough that the filter doesn't brim over with floating brown coffee granules. I can attest that this makes a real mess. The smart cook will place the receiving carafe and filter arrangement in the galley sink before pouring and pray that the boat doesn't lurch. Making manual drip coffee underway is not for the faint of heart.

French Press

A French press works in a similar manner. Although the carafe is traditionally glass, there are marine versions that are microwaveable or come with an insulated serving carafe. In the French press process, ground coffee is measured directly into the pot, a fairly easy task. Boiling water is then poured into the pot and a stainless steel strainer is "pressed" to the bottom of the pot to remove the grounds from the coffee. This is safer and neater than making manual drip coffee.

Electric Drip

There's nothing like the combination of a good-quality electric drip maker and fine coffee to delight a coffee lover. For this reason, I keep both a manual percolator and an electric drip pot aboard, saving the electric pot for those times when we have dockside power. When choosing an electric pot, or any small countertop appliance, look for one with a small base that won't commandeer a lot of counter space. Many manufacturers make boat-friendly electric drip pots with thermal carafes instead of glass. Although this is a workable solution to the breakage problem, these tend to be larger overall than a glass-based drip system.

To Make Perked Coffee

Fill pot with water to the base of the spout. Then use either one premeasured coffee packet or scoop out eight tablespoons of coffee grounds for a percolator-style pot. Generally allow two tablespoons of coffee per cup. It will be easier to dispose of the grounds and to clean the pot if you use a filter; use the cloverleaf-shaped style that fits into the base of the coffee basket. It has holes in each corner, which slide over the stem of the percolator to enclose the grounds. Put the cover on the pot, light a burner and bring the coffee to a boil. Once it starts to perk or bubble up through the glass bulb at the top of the pot, time it for exactly eight minutes. If you remove the coffee from the fire too soon it will taste like dishwater; too late, it will be bitter.

I once owned a four-cup thermal pot, which I purchased largely because it would fit on the countertop. What I loved best about this pot was that it could be unplugged as soon as the coffee was made, and its protected base remained cool, making it easy to safely serve coffee in the cockpit. What I hated was making several pots each day to keep up with the coffee demand on our boat. Regretfully, I replaced it with a 12-cup standard drip system with a glass carafe—my only glass item aboard except for liquor bottles. There are electric drip systems made to mount under a cabinet, and I've seen slide-out shelves for such pots built into some very luxurious boats.

12-volt Drip Coffee

Marine catalogs and stores have joined the electric drip parade with 12-volt drip coffee pots that plug into a cigarette lighter-style socket. These draw between 12 and 14 amps, and operate on battery power. Although I have not used this type of pot, if it works anything like a 12-volt hairdryer, I suspect it will be slow to heat. I am encouraged that many of the features of the newer 12-volt pots emulate those of electric pots, and that there is a choice of glass or an insulated carafe. If you've no electrical source, take the 12-volt challenge. It might be the right answer to your coffee cravings.

Pressure Cookers

Cooking under pressure has long been a means of saving time and energy. A pressure cooker is a large covered pot that is used on the stovetop like a pan and is designed to build up and then trap steam at temperatures above boiling, thus cooking foods in one-third the time without constant monitoring. Because there is no evaporation when cooking, you also save on water.

In the modern kitchen these cookers have been largely phased out thanks to air conditioning and fast-cooking electrical devices like microwaves and convection ovens.

Offshore, however, the scarcity of electricity, water and space has made these a boon for passagemakers and live-aboard sailors. The units store like an ordinary pan and can be used as serving dishes. You may have heard horror stories about the old cookers or even have had some to tell of your own. But there is no reason to be concerned, so long as you're careful. Temper tantrums are only a problem if the steam is not released properly at the finish of a cooking job. Following the directions is the key to preventing an indignant pressure cooker from "talking back." If you have an old pressure cooker kicking around your basement and are comfortable using one, your boat may be a practical place to make good use of it. I am told that the new pressure cookers are safe, marine approved and guaranteed not to blow a hole through the deck of your boat. Pressure cookers represent an investment of at least $100, so unless you plan to do a good bit of cooking afloat, your money would probably be better spent elsewhere.

Electric Fry Pan

The electric fry pan is the surrogate pressure cooker for boaters with access to 110-volt AC power. This pan makes a great steamer for clams and is large enough to hold enough cutlets, stew or pasta sauce for four to eight people. It can be used not only to fry, but to bake anything from casseroles to birthday cakes. The temperature gauge on the pan allows the same heat control as an oven. Whenever you use the electric fry pan, remember to secure it in a safe, nonslip area.

Breadmaker

I'm going to perform another purist boater no-no and broach the subject of electric breadmakers. Actually, I wasn't

> ### To Bake in an Electric Fry Pan
> To bake in an electric fry pan, place a wire rack in the bottom of the pan, preheat to the desired baking temperature and then place the casserole or cake pan on the rack. Cover the pan and time the bake cycle as if you were cooking in an oven.

even certain the concept was a viable one until I saw a brand-new breadmaker being carted down the dock by a traveling live-aboard couple. Coastal cruising cooks will, I'm sure, have no use for this item as stops are frequent, stays are short and bread is available everywhere. Likewise, most seagoing cookbooks include breadmaking recipes, and many offshore cooks have perfected the art of manual breadmaking in large part because there is plenty of time, the kneading is a stress-relieving comfort to many, the ingredients are simple and the smiles on the crew's faces are rewarding.

If, however, you are like me and your best efforts invariably bake up to the size and density of a brick, and the need for fresh bread is essential to your cruising style, welcome aboard a breadmaker. A boat with a generator can easily sustain the power draw needed for this device, which will mix and bake the bread to fluffy crustiness in a couple of hours. The only mess is in the measuring out of ingredients, which can be done ahead of time in single-loaf batches and then stored in moisture-proof containers or plastic bags. Boxed and bagged mixes will solve that problem. Cleanup is easy. All you need to do is let the dough remains dry, and they will flake right off. A quick wipe with a wet washrag, and the breadmaker is ready for another round. Choose a model with a timer and you will be able to awaken for an early watch to the perfume of homemade bread.

Be aware, however that a breadmaker agitates as it kneads, like a washing machine during the spin cycle. To avoid having it dance off the countertop, sit it down in a spare corner of the floor and place a rubber-backed mat underneath to help keep the noise down. And remember that this breadmaking dervish will take up a good portion of a locker when stowed.

Caution: Too Many Electrical Appliances

The power of a plug-in can easily carry us away into the vast world of small cooking appliances. The choices are endless. With access to 110 -volt AC, you can haul anything to the boat, from a toaster oven to a hot dog cooker. Should you invest in a number of small electrically-operated cooking toys, exercise caution and remember that simple is better. Make sure your boat's electrical system is up to what you plan to do. Heat-producing appliances like toasters and electric fry pans are power eaters. To keep from overloading the circuits, stick to using one appliance at a time. And be sure to run the engine while using an inverter to boost DC power, or use a generator.

Chapter 15
Galley Tools

Bowls, mixers, can openers, garlic presses—there's no limit to the variety of "toys" available to simplify the food preparation and serving processes. Ponder and then pick and choose those that will help you most.

BOWLS AND CONTAINERS

Having a matching set of mixing bowls isn't exactly necessary, but it looks nice and takes no more space than a single bowl. Pick a color that matches your boat's decor and your bowls can sit attractively on a dinner table and even attend parties. If you also need serve, store and heat-up capabilities, choose a set with covers that can go from the freezer to the microwave. The more transparent the bowl, the easier it will be to remember what's stored in it. Since mixing bowls are not straight sided, they will be bulkier to store in a crowded icebox. Spend a few minutes in the houseware aisle and pick round plastic containers that will nest.

No to Stainless

I now have acquired two sets—one came with my boat—and I seldom use either. They are totally opaque so I can't see what's inside, useless for microwaving, their covers never seem to fit right (metal is inflexible) and they make more noise than a tin can band. I *can* verify they are indestructible and will last forever, because they still live in my lost-pan closet. The last time I cooked with one was when I made a doll cake for my daughter's fifth birthday. Her own daughter is nearing that age; perhaps she'd like to borrow the bowl.

Think Disposables

Some of the new disposable containers are very practical, lightweight and surprisingly durable. I've used the same container repeatedly to freeze and store leftovers, and even to reheat them in the microwave. Disposable plastic containers clean so easily—even tomato sauce doesn't stain—that I can't bring myself to throw them away.

Storage bags bear mentioning again because you need to decide what type and how much to stock. Foremost, we have the zippered-style plastic bag, which comes in regular or extra duty styles—the newest even prevent freezer burn. The bags with actual zippers are less apt to open and spill than those with a slide-finger closing. Sandwich bags and 1-quart sizes are the most practical. I once read a cook's comment that long-term storage in plastic food bags will "eventually impart the plastic flavor to the food inside," but I've never kept any food in a plastic bag long enough for this to be a problem. Bags sold at supermarkets come in slim, boxed rolls, which makes it convenient to take out one at a time. If cardboard is an uninvited guest aboard, it's easy enough to repackage the bags by size, one within the other. In addition to plastic bags, aluminum foil and plastic wrap have a multitude of uses for food storage or preservation. Both will insulate food to keep it warm or cold, and will discourage attack by interested insects.

Bag Mixing

One rule I follow religiously, whether cooking at home or in my galley, is to never dirty a mixing bowl when a plastic bag will work just as well. For example, you can mix together marinade ingredients and then deposit the steak, chops, chicken breast or fish into the bag along with it. It's not beneath me to resort to using a trash bag to marinate huge batches of ribs or chicken when a crowd is expected. Seal the bag well and stuff it in the icebox until you are ready to grill, sauté or bake the goods within.

PREPARATION TOOLS

Sets of galley utensils are readily available with five or six commonly used items like a large spoon, a slotted spoon, soup ladle, salad tongs, spatula, spaghetti server, pie server and other serving or cooking tools. Check camping stores for packages featuring utensils that nest or have folding handles. Add wooden spoons for mixing, a rubber spatula for scraping, a basting brush, a meat fork and metal tongs. Weigh metal items against plastic. Will you be able to use the metal spatula for any other cooking tasks if you have nonstick pans? Periodically sort through your junk drawer, and get rid of the utensils you never use.

Measurers

Space Saving Measures

Measuring devices might be considered optional. Accuracy is important in cake and breadmaking, but approximating the amounts for ingredients in less delicate dishes works just fine. To train yourself to do this, read Chapter 30. Plastic or stainless steel cups and spoons will last forever on the boat, and of course, these will nest or can be hung in the galley. Measuring spoons usually come in a set, but I've found graduated measuring spoons in kitchen shops that allow you to measure out several ingredients using a single spoon—fabulous for recipes with lots of spices.

If you do succumb to buying a set of measuring cups, select one that includes a 2-tablespoon measure since it is a perfect coffee scoop. A 1-quart or 2-cup liquid measure is convenient for small mixing jobs, and many plastics are microwave safe. A model equipped with a lid and capped pouring hole is good for mixing and storing.

Flatteners

If you frequently bake aboard and feel only your favorite rolling pin will smooth out piecrust and rolled cookie dough to your satisfaction, by all means have it on hand. For rolling and flattening, however, a smooth-sided soda or liquor bottle will work almost as well. Also try using round cans or straight-sided glasses. Items like scones, biscuits and hamburger patties can be acceptably hand flattened.

Garlic

Even if you're a sworn garlic presser and you've found one that really works, think about what a nuisance it will be to keep clean before toting it to the boat. Instead, try smashing the garlic on a cutting board or paper plate using the back of a spoon, the side of a knife, the bottom of a glass or whatever is handy.

Beaters

A wire whisk is nifty to have for mixing light-duty dishes like scrambled eggs, but a fork will work nearly as well. I've found eggbeaters and potato mashers bulky and well worth leaving at home. A good wooden spoon and a strong arm will beat any cake mix enough to make it rise; and if you cook potatoes until they are soft enough, you'll find that vigorous stirring with a fork will render them nicely mashed.

Drainers and Strainers

You'll need some sort of strainer aboard, and although the holes are larger on a colander than a mesh strainer, it will work for the majority of tasks. When choosing a colander, opt for a stainless or plastic style large and sturdy enough to hold a drained pound or two of pasta without buckling. If it will nest in a pan or mixing bowl and stand on its own when set in a sink, all the better. If you have a large pot with a separate drain basket, this will also work. For sifting flour and confectioner's sugar, or for performing other fine straining jobs, you'll need a plastic mesh strainer—plastic because metal will ultimately

To Remove Garlic Smell

While we're at it, there are a couple of different ways to remove garlic odor (and fishy smells, too) from your hands since simple soap and water washing doesn't always do the trick. The first, rubbing lemon juice on the smelly areas is a common solution, but I confess that I prefer to caress my galley sink faucet instead. I know, it might seem a bit unorthodox, but as I'm often alone in the galley, there is rarely someone standing by to snicker at me. What I do is wet my hands with cold water and then rub them back and forth along the stainless steel a few times. A chemical reaction occurs that neutralizes the odor. Try it some time and give your hands the sniff test. It really works! Garlic breath? Chew on fresh parsley, basil, fennel seeds or coffee beans; or eat lime sherbet.

rust. Some strainers have extensions that will allow them to sit comfortably over the lip of a pan or the rim of the sink.

Cutting Boards

With all the cautions in today's world about unclean cutting boards, it's a wonder someone hasn't come up with a disposable cutting surface more durable than a paper plate. The most popular

> **To Sanitize a Cutting Board**
>
> Sanitize a questionable cutting board by spraying it with a mild bleach or vinegar solution. Use one teaspoon chlorine bleach to one quart water; or use one tablespoon vinegar to five tablespoons of water.

cutting board is still a wooden one, although propylene plastic boards are touted to carry fewer bacteria, and their manufacturers claim that they won't dull knives. Knife marks trap bacteria, so avoid slicing directly on Formica countertops or on plastic plates. I've found a nice-looking acrylic cutting board impregnated with an agent that inhibits bacterial growth, so someone is finally doing something constructive about this problem.[20]

Any substantial cutting board will be awkward to handle on the boat, and when working in small spaces, there often isn't a need for a large cutting surface anyway. I have some $1/4$-inch-thick Plexiglas boards that are convenient for petty tasks, such as slicing a lime or mincing a garlic clove. I also keep on hand a small, $1/2$-inch-thick polypropylene plastic board for tougher slicing jobs. I'd love to replace it with that antibacterial acrylic board. White boards stain, so periodically soak them in a chlorine solution. I keep my few boards stacked upright behind the sink. I've read that a piece of vinyl tile also makes a good cutting board, so if you have some leftovers in your basement, give them a try.

Knives

One or two cooking knives should do the trick. If you've invested in a set of steak knives, these can be used for food preparation as well. You'll need a long-bladed knife, possibly serrated, to slice meat, bread and cake, and a small knife for paring and chopping. Keep knives well sharpened and they will be up to any task. The better the quality of the knife, the longer it will retain its sharpness. Keeping knife blades covered and protected from other items in a drawer will preserve their cutting edge. Save cardboard knife blade covers for storage, or place a knife holder[21] in a utensil drawer or upright on a wall in the galley area. A knife left lying about can become a lethal weapon if it flies off a countertop or table, so make sure it is returned to a safe spot.

Chopping, Slushing, and Picking

If you are a frequent chopper, the job will go faster with an official device. Manual choppers and slicers, electric food processors and blenders will quickly mince or puree all types of foods. To make fast work of small jobs, I've found that a mini-Cuisinart food processor or a handheld blender takes little space. The handheld blender comes with a cup-size base. A pair of scissors is by no means essential, but can be a practical thing to have aboard for miscellaneous purposes, such as snipping herbs. Do people still do that? I've always used a knife.

Blender

A blender makes a party-friendly addition to the galley for larger chopping jobs, pureeing and frozen drink mixing. There are so many models available that choosing a blender can be as tedious as finding a teenager a prom dress. Opt for a battery-operated or rechargeable unit, which will work even while at anchor. Some of these can be weighty monsters and difficult to store, so look for an unbreakable, lightweight style that has enough oomph to crush ice into slush.

Pickers

While we are on the subject of ice, be sure to include an ice pick on your galley supply list. Mount it near the icebox or freezer where it will be handy, and keep its point protected. In a gadget catalog, I once saw a floating ice pick with a cover that would travel nicely.

Lobster Picking

Other than digging into the toolbox for a hammer, I can't come up with much of an alternative to a lobster shell cracker. A standard nutcracker is what I've always used. Keep at least two aboard and store them together in a small sandwich bag. In Puerto Rico, when my captain and I were served land crabs in a local restaurant, we learned some cracking lessons, which will also apply to lobster meat. Each person is provided a wooden cutting board and a wooden dowel to roll out the meat from the claw. This works just fine, especially if the shell is not very hard. The small pinchers are then used to dig out small bits of meat, instead of a fork.

Peelers and Scrubbers

If you peel potatoes, carrots, cucumbers and eggplant, you might feel you need a potato peeler. A sharp knife will do the same job. I've convinced myself that since all the vitamins are in the skin, nothing needs to be peeled on our boat. Unpeeled vegetables, however, need to be scrubbed clean, so include a vegetable brush in your supply. Any small brush with fairly stiff bristles will do the trick. Think creatively; as long as it's clean, it will work. A nailbrush is small and will take very little storage. You can even try a new toothbrush, although it will be torture if you've got lots of vegetables to scrub. As a last resort, try using a nubby terry towel or dishrag.

Can and Bottle Openers

Every galley needs a manual can opener. Choose a double-handled style without protruding points or blades, so it can be safely used underway. Some can openers have a built-in bottle opener and corkscrew. Most bottles are now twist tops, but invariably the brand your crowd likes best will require an opener. Cheap openers will rust. Bring aboard a simple corkscrew and a church key; or mount an old-fashioned bottle opener in the galley. Keep extras aboard in case your opener walks away in an ice bag. You could also tie one to the galley, like you do the pencil at the telephone, to avoid having to attack a corked wine bottle or a can with a screwdriver; also attach one to the cooler. I came across an interesting culinary tool that packs a knife, can opener, corkscrew, salt and pepper shakers, and screwdriver all within a 5^1/$_2$-inch stainless steel case![22]

SAFETY DEVICES

Potholders

Keep one set of potholders handy to the stove and for barbecuing. Use only dry potholders. When applied to a hot pot, a wet or damp potholder conducts heat faster and can cause a steam burn. Overly plump potholders won't allow you to get a good grasp on a hot pan, and a towel or bulky cloth used as a stand-in potholder can slip and catch fire. Some people prefer oven mitts, although I've always found them awkward to use. Discard an oven mitt once it gets holes in the fingertip area. Any fabric is flammable, so avoid hanging potholders over the galley where they might dangle and catch a spark from a lit burner. I've acquired a set of washable suede potholders that not only are heat resistant, but fire retardant. These are ideal for the boat, because they are practically indestructible, and provide for a firm grip on panhandles. [23]

Aprons and Gloves

When cooking underway, protect yourself with a heavy-duty bibbed apron. Search for one that is both waterproof and heatproof. Wearing a pair of those sturdy, long armed, grilling gloves will enable you to handle anything hot or piercing without it cutting through to bare flesh.

Doneness Sensor

To be certain that food is cooked to today's safety standards, it's important to include some sort of doneness sensor in your supply list. A regular, inexpensive meat thermometer works well for roasts and thick chunks of food. An instant read thermometer runs about $30, as do the sensor forks that work the same way. I've found the sensor fork to be ungainly to use and store, and always thirsting for batteries. These types of temperature gauges are unsuited to thin foods, like burgers or fish filets; for the correct temperature to register, the thermometer tip needs to be inserted at least a quarter inch into the food. For hamburgers, try the cardboard disposable sensors sold in supermarkets. The packets are the size of a matchbook, making them easy to store (but elusive).

WIPERS AND SWIPERS

Have you ever considered life before paper towels? What did cooks do? Can you imagine having to use dishrags for all the messy stuff? No wonder few women worked in the old days; they were too busy washing rags! A good brand of paper towels absorbs better, so you'll use less. Some brands have half-sheet perforations, which discourage waste. Mount a paper towel holder in the galley area, and keep spare rolls in plastic bags to ensure they stay dry. Don't be afraid to squish them away somewhere. They make great padding for breakables.

Wet Wipes

Sanitation is always a concern when preparing food. Antibacterial kitchen wipes are practical for cleaning galley surfaces before, after and in-between meal making. Keep a small package of hand wipes near the sink as well, and sanitize your hands before handling food. Waterless hand soap is also a good solution to the no-water-dirty-hands problem.

Sponges

Sponges are handy for soaking up water and cleaning, but do confine yours to the galley. Crewmembers have a way of sneaking off with them to perform unmentionable tasks. Sponges are cheap, so keep extras handy and color-code them by use. Where space is sparse, stock up on compressed sponges that only swell to full potential when water is added. Replace the galley sponge often. Avoid sopping up raw meat juice with it or sponging down an area on which meat has been placed. Use disposable sanitary wipes or paper towels instead. If you prefer a dishrag or other device for the galley sink, replace it often or microwave it on high for 30 to 60 seconds to sanitize it. But it will be steaming hot, so remove it carefully. This works for dishtowels, as well.

Dishtowels

Dishtowels get used and abused almost anywhere they happen to be. Unfortunately, they take on the persona of an all-purpose boat rag if not guarded carefully. Provide the crew a separate bag of old towels for miscellaneous mopping, and perhaps your supply will remain intact. When using dishtowels in the galley, we tend to wipe our hands, wipe the counters or use them as potholders. By the time we are ready to wipe the water from our clean dishes, the dishes are often cleaner than the towel. I know it's difficult, but make an effort to rotate dirty towels out of the galley and into the laundry bag. If you run out, you can always resort to wiping dishes with paper towels, which is wasteful, but works in a pinch.

Dish Drainer

Unless you will be getting underway soon or feel the need to stow freshly washed dishes, allow them to air dry. This will save dealing with an unnecessarily wet towel and preserve your energy for a more productive task. If you've a double sink, use the separate sink to contain dishes. Many cooks like to use a dish drainer to help organize and aerate the plates, glasses and flatware while they dry. There are wooden and folding drainers that can be stowed when not in use, as well as small-size rubber-coated wire drainers. As many times as I've tried, I can't get comfortable with the restrictiveness of organizing wetware, so I leave mine to drain in piles atop a dishtowel.

Chapter 16
Setting the Table

Mealtime is an important part of any boating activity; it's a time for crew bonding, for socializing and sharing. An attractively served meal entices appetites and welcomes crewmembers and guests to the bounty of your table, wherever or whatever it may be.

AT THE TABLE

Most of us have some sort of table aboard that can be used for sit-down meals. There is usually one in the saloon and possibly another in the cockpit. The table types and their locations on your boat may have been predetermined by the boat manufacturer or by previous owners. If your boat lacks a table in the saloon area, peruse boat shows and catalogs to find a style that will work with your boat design. A dinner table needs to provide legroom, while being low enough to permit diners to eat without resting their chins on their plates. One of the problems with most dining setups is that the table and seating will seldom accommodate both food and people. A table for four—elves maybe—actually seats two comfortably, and so on. And while there may be enough table area, the seating is often deficient.

On rainy days dining is driven belowdecks to the saloon table, which may be fixed in place or designed to fold down as the need arises. The beauty of a fold-down table is that it can be hooked up and out of the way, freeing an area of the encumbrance. The most versatile tables are adjustable with hinged expansions or insertable leaves; or they are capable of being raised, lowered or removed entirely. Some tables can be lowered and folded to cocktail table height while others drop down to form a platform for a berth. You can expand your serving areas by adding, replacing or reconstructing table arrangements. If you have a table that's too small, consider adding a hinged extension to it. If there's no space to widen it, make it longer.

Having enough table area doesn't necessarily buy seating space. Our saloon table expands across the boat to accommodate eight or 10 people, but with seating on only the two ends, it barely works as a table for six. If this is a problem for you, here are a few ideas to consider. Can you move the cooler in place on one side? Is there a way to install a slide-out board with a removable leg underneath a berth cushion? Do you have room to store one or two folding benches or camping chairs that might be used on occasion? Those with wooden frames and canvas will last longest. Most people don't mind not having a table seat, as long as they can be near enough to join in the conversation. Look to the chart table, companionway chairs, the edge of a berth or even the seat of the commode (shut, of course). The floor will be more comfortable if you offer a cushion for the tush.

Outdoor Serving

In the cockpit, seats are up for grabs. When serving a crowd, present the food buffet style either in the cockpit or down below, and you'll find that everyone will magically find a place to settle. At anchor, a dinghy can provide overflow seating for four or more, although you'll have to pass down food to them.

Most tables for outdoor use are teak or plastic, both materials that can handle a moisture-riddled environment. On a sailboat, the cockpit table is typically installed forward of the steering quadrant. For slim spaces, choose a fold-down table. Those with hinged extension leaves are especially efficient, because they can be opened out to create a square table, as the need arises. Another way to increase your outdoor serving area is to install a small rail-mounted or rod holder-mounted fish filleting table. These 12-by-24-inch tables come with a three-sided windscreen and cost about $60. A table set up near a stern-mounted barbecue grill can hold cooking supplies or be used for buffet-style serving. For more features, try a slightly larger table that locks down to store and has tuck away leg supports.[24] In calm conditions or on a very stable boat, there may even be space to put up a small freestanding table with folding legs and rubberized feet. These are inexpensive and can be taken onto the wharf, moving the party and the mess off the boat.

Ambiance

During the day, there's no need to be concerned about creating a pleasant dining environment: the smell of sea air, the sun wrapping us with warmth and the beauty of a hoisted white sail plumped with wind is all we need for pure enjoyment. When we set aside the work portion of the day and are ready to relax, the right ambiance will turn a meal, however simple it may be, into a feast.

Soft Lights

Evening dinners in the cockpit are delightful until it gets so dark you can barely see the whites of each other's eyes, let alone find the food on your plates. Often, we require just enough light to cast a pleasant glow over the table. Look for a spot near the table where you can rig up a flashlight, a small battery-operated light or an oil lamp. Models with handles are ideal for hanging. Secure the light to a cross pole or some convenient rigging using tie wraps, sticky-backed Velcro strips or a piece of spare line. For a companionable glow, use a candle. A jar style candle is less likely to set your boat afire. Avoid those with strong scents that may overpower your dinner guests or conflict with the aroma of foods served.

Table Furnishings

Using some sort of table covering livens up a wooden table and hides an unsightly one. In the islands, charter boat cooks whip out a *pareo*, a piece of fabric like a sarong, and lay it on the table as a covering cloth. If you think about it, this makes a lot of sense. Pareos are multihued, rectangular and lightweight enough to be folded in half to fit a small table. Most pack away without wrinkling beyond control, and can be washed and line dried with little difficulty. In between, they can be worn as clothing. I also keep aboard a set of rubberized mesh place mats—they last for years—to provide bright nonskid mats for dinner plates and serving bowls. These are wrapped around bottles in my liquor cabinet whenever they aren't reclining atop a table. Placing a colorful mat underneath a small centerpiece, like a candle or jar of flowers, will spiff up any humdrum table while preventing items atop it to roam.

SERVING PIECES

When it comes to presenting foods, combine practicality with flair. Roam beachfront and discount shops with a galley eye toward attractive, unbreakable food containers. Often you can find the nicest things in the least likely places, without spending a lot of money. Zero in on nautical patterns and coordinating colors. Think about storability. Large round platters will fit in fewer places than oval ones. If you buy several matching pieces, will they stack? Are the sizes and shapes useful? Look at wooden, straw, durable plastic products and baskets. And don't ignore several-use disposables.

Platters

Flat-bottomed platters and trays can serve many purposes. I keep a decorative tray Velcro-mounted on a wall in my galley, where it makes a scenic quick grab. Years ago, I picked up a colorful, plastic oval platter shaped like a fish that I use constantly as an all-purpose serving tray for meats hot from the grill or for an array of crackers, cheeses and fruits. For dip-and-chip type servings, I set a small bowl on the platter, often a disposable one. A platter with a well to hold dips would be a nice find. When underway, wielding a flat platter will certainly result in a food-littered cockpit, so opt for a sided serving container. Here, you can dress up a metal pan by lining it with a clean dishtowel or colored napkins. When serving hot, wet foods, cover the bottom and sides of an unsightly pan with aluminum foil.

Baskets

I love baskets. They are almost indestructible, lightweight, washable and make ideal serving vehicles for almost any kind of food or meal accessory. Look for plastic mesh baskets as well as straw. If bulk is a problem, try a style that collapses flat. Unless you plan to hang up a basket, avoid space-taking Easter basket styles that can't nest. Line the basket to keep food sanitary and limit crumb escape. Plate-liner baskets, designed to support flimsy disposables, can also work as stand-alone servers. Search for an oval or rectangular flat-bottomed basket that is large and substantial enough to serve sandwiches or to hold a collection of serving items—napkins, salt and pepper shakers, condiments, beverage cans. A holder for a 9- x 13- x 2-inch casserole dish is the type of basket to watch for, as most others are too small or high-sided to function as deep trays.

Party Bowls

Often, there is a need for a crowd-size serving bowl. Inexpensive plastic bowls sold at party shops look convincingly like glass, can take a beating and make attractive onboard or dock-party serving bowls. Of course, if your large bowl needs to travel or be stored filled with chow, it will need a secure cover. Try using an extra-large, covered plastic container. A colored one makes an especially nice server.

Cockpit Drink Holders

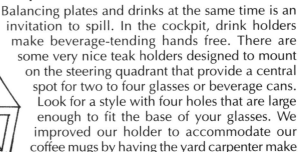

Drink Holder Altered to Hold Mugs

Balancing plates and drinks at the same time is an invitation to spill. In the cockpit, drink holders make beverage-tending hands free. There are some very nice teak holders designed to mount on the steering quadrant that provide a central spot for two to four glasses or beverage cans. Look for a style with four holes that are large enough to fit the base of your glasses. We improved our holder to accommodate our coffee mugs by having the yard carpenter make a small opening at the front of each hole for the handle.

Flip through catalogs and look at marine stores and boat shows for individual, removable drink holders that hang on lifelines, slip into a mounting in the cockpit or have suction cup backs. There is a product called Little Suckers sold at boat shows that looks like a rubber ring with an opening that will hold cans and bottles upright on just about any surface.

Drink Cozies

Chilled drink glasses, individual bottles of water, and soda or beer cans sweat just like we do when they are introduced to the warm, outside world. Years ago, we used to absorb the condensation by putting little knitted socks on their bottoms. The nautical answer to this problem is a foam drink cozy. Make it a practice to pick up these inexpensive items from different harbors, and you will have a growing collection of nonskid, protective packaging for bottles, cans and jars. In addition to the popular round foam style, there are also cozies that unroll to store flat and have Velcro closures.

Beverage Servers

While pouring juice and soda directly from bottles is fine, some circumstances call for more protected serving. High-quality plastic beverage servers with spouts and sealable covers will reduce spills, allow even small crew to help themselves, can live in the cooler or icebox, and look nicer on the saloon table than a jug.

Thermal Servers

When it is essential to keep liquids hot or cold, use an insulated server, like a coffee carafe or a thermos bottle. A well-insulated server will keep coffee or water hot all day, making it suitable for long days or nights on the water. Thermos bottles do the same job as an attractive coffee carafe, except with a slimmer profile, which also means they can be more easily stored. A wide mouth thermos is harder to pour without spilling. Be aware that part of many thermal interiors involves glass, so take care to set the carafe or thermos in a spot where it won't roll onto the floor.

Miscellaneous Table Needs

Whether set out on the table or collected in a basket or on a tray, it's customary to offer salt and pepper with a meal, butter when bread is served, and cream and sugar with coffee. Store salt and pepper in spillproof containers that will close tightly to keep out moisture. Use the same set for galley cooking that you use on the table. Avoid gadget-type shakers that won't seal well or will rust or break easily. Fancy butter dishes are nice, but many won't seal shut, making them messy to store in an icebox. I use a covered plastic container, which holds one stick of butter cut in half, stores easily and is nice enough to pass as a server. Almost any container will look fancy enough when paired with a decorative cocktail spreader. If I am entertaining, I avoid setting out butter in its original tub, as I find the advertising around the sides distracting. A sugar bowl or creamer isn't part of the average marine dinnerware set, and I can't say I've ever missed having either one. To avoid setting a large jug on the table, pour some milk (or cream) into an extra coffee cup, or use a recloseable plastic container. I'm certain Tupperware and Rubbermaid make servers and storers for both cream and sugar. If you use sugar packets or cubes, keep them in zippered sandwich bags to repel moisture and set the bag in a cup for the table.

Napkin Holders

The problem of the runaway napkin is chronic. Guests appreciate having napkins handy whenever they are offered food, but a stiff breeze can often send these same napkins flying into the drink. "Take one" holders keep napkins together. I use an inexpensive vertical holder for everyday luncheon-size napkins, and its slim line takes little space. But a more attractive Lucite holder with a depressor keeps my fancier cocktail napkins intact. As the napkins sit flat with this style holder, it consumes more storage space than an upright one.

Monogrammed Galleyware

It's always special to serve foods in or on items bearing your boat's name. You can order personalized Melamine dinnerware, paper plate, napkins, plastic glasses, Lexan polycarbonate glasses, serving trays and bowls. Find these at boat shows or have a local company do the engraving. One reliable source I can recommend is Ross Marine Ideas out of Florida.[25]

DININGWARE

Is it time to eat yet? Not quite. We still need plates, flatware and drinking glasses. The answer to the "paper or plastic" question is simple. You need both disposable and reusable dinnerware, depending on your cruising circumstances. Paper is king when trying to save on dishwater and dishwashing, but right alongside it should be a set of plastic or ceramic dinnerware that won't fatten the trash can and can be continuously recycled.

Disposable Ware

Paper plates, paper or plastic cups, and plastic utensils make cleanup a snap. They eliminate the fuss of trying to degrease dirty dishes with cold water and enable us to quickly clear the galley of clutter and food odors. They also don't need to return with us to the boat from a party on the beach. Disposable products are at their best when many people need to eat at once and a quantity of plates and utensils are needed to serve everyone. If you are on the move for several days, being burdened with extra trash may be a problem; however, one of the worst problems you'll encounter with disposable dinnerware is running out of it.

Paper Plates and Bowls

There are varying grades of paper plates. Large packs of thin white plates are cheap, but only good for serving sandwiches or other non-messy foods. More substantial paper plates cost more and come fewer in a pack, but they are more decorative and many have water-repellent finishes. If you are serving hot or wet food on paper plates, choose a firm plate that will not cave in or soak through. Reinforce flimsy paper plates by setting them on reusable rattan or plastic plate holders. Paper bowls make good throwaways for serving liquids or gooey and greasy foods that will be difficult to clean from standard dishes.

Disposable Drinking Cups and Plastic Glasses

It's easy to drink through a package of disposable cups a day if you have kids, or if you are constantly offering iced beverages to your friends and neighbors. To encourage constant sippers to use the same cup for refills, label cups with names, or color-code them by person. Clear plastic glasses, while environmentally unkind, are nicer to use than paper cups when entertaining a large number of adults; also these can be washed and reused. Buy flexible plastic glasses that won't crack. It's hard to trade Styrofoam coffee cups for paper ones, since paper cups filled with hot liquids are uncomfortable to hold, and those with handles cut into fingers. Still, most takeout places have converted over, and Styrofoam cups are getting scarce. Unless you are serving hot drinks to a crowd, it might make sense to treat yourselves to a set of nice heavy ceramic coffee mugs.

Plastic Flatware

Like paper plates, disposable spoons, forks and knives come in grades of toughness. Wimpy forks and spoons are fine for serving birthday cake or soup, but foods that need to be pierced or dug into require substantial utensils that won't give way under pressure. When you are shopping for plastic ware, know what you are buying. Wiggle the fork in its wrapper. If it moves, it's a weakling.

On-the-cheap Dinnerware

A set of dishes for the galley doesn't need to be expensive to be functional. Inexpensive plastic or Melamine (a form of plastic) dinnerware will provide the feeling of stability when you dine, and there's always a sale on them somewhere. Shop in the picnic goods department at the onset of the summer season, and you'll have some gorgeous choices. Look for soup bowls and mugs designed to hold hot liquids without cracking and leaking. With the popularity of sports drinks, there are an increasing variety of portable, spillproof and insulated drink containers available. Buy tall pastel or patterned glasses for iced drinks and stemware for wine and fancy drinks. If cups and glasses are stackable, or if the stems are removable, they won't topple and will store more easily.

Copy one of the best features of marine dinnerware by gluing circles of rubber mesh on the bottoms of platters, serving bowls, vases, pitchers, pet food bowls, candlesticks, portable CDs and tape decks, and anything else you are worried about. If you use a good fixative, the rubber mesh backing will withstand many years of use.

Marine Dinnerware

Standard marine dinnerware is also made of Melamine and shouldn't be considered microwave-safe unless it's labeled so. The major differences I can see between marine and department store dinnerware is in the patterns, styling and the nonskid properties. Most of the marine dinnerware patterns are nautical—fish, boats, seashells and seahorses—and color themes center on red, white, yellow and blue. Choosing a pattern is like registering for good china for your home. It can be purchased either by the place setting, or open stock. Select a style you love, because you will have it a long time. A boating buddy is still actively using my old dinnerware set. After 12 years of galley slaving, its only flaws are a few knife scratches and a missing rubber ring or two—and they still produce the pattern. Select a light color, as food doesn't show up well in dark dishes. For example, I have a set of navy blue bowls that can make a meal disappear at night, without taking a bite.

Marine dinnerware sets are expensive, so understand exactly what you are buying. According to 2001 prices, a set can cost upwards of $50, depending on the pattern and its properties. Make sure

Make Your Own Nonskidware

Follow this procedure to make plates, bowls, cups, glasses, trays and other items less prone to slipping.

- Purchase a roll of rubber mesh. You can find them almost anywhere and they come in decorator colors.

- Trace the base of the item onto a piece of paper to make a pattern, then use it to cut the shape out of the rubber mesh.

- Use waterproof glue to permanently bond the rubber mesh to the plastic. Avoid using your fingers to tap the rubber in place; instead use a stick or the backside of a utensil. Keep glue remover handy.

- Allow item to dry completely, upside down.

the plates, bowls and cups are the right sizes and shapes, and that your selection has the features most practical for your cruising style.

Having built-in antiskidding rings on the undersides of each individual plate, bowl or cup has always been an important distinction between marine and standard dinnerware. My old set had a beige ring inset into the underside, while my new set has a glued-on, external black rubber ring (that takes forever to dry). Beware. Some of the less expensive sets do not have antiskid properties.

Bowls
Some dinnerware sets feature extra-deep soup bowls designed to keep liquids from sloshing out while underway. An 8-inch, flat-bottomed vegetable serving bowl, which sells for less than $10, is also the right shape and size to suffice as a nonspill, offshore dinner plate. Pet bowls are another suggestion I've heard, which I find rather unappetizing. Some of the newer marine dinnerware features shallower, rounded bowls that are more familiar, but less practical for serious sailors.

Drinking Glasses
Coordinating insulated cups and glasses are made to match some marine dinnerware patterns. Heavy-footed glasses and short stemware are most resistant to toppling over. Lexan polycarbonate glasses that look and feel heavy like glass are particularly nice, although the ones I've seen don't stack, even though they are long-lasting and have thermal qualities. For serving iced drinks underway, look to nautical sources for clear plastic tumblers and for stemware with nonskid bases. Wide-bottomed, plastic or stainless steel mugs with sipping lids keep coffee hot and confined while underway and can be used for cold drinks as well.

The Real Thing
Some claim that eating a meal from ceramic dishes and sipping drinks from real glasses takes the camping feel out of a meal aboard. This, of course, is an illusion and ties into our earlier discussion about the effect of ambiance. On a boat, enjoying a meal from ceramic dishes is the equivalent of eating in the dining room, rather than in the kitchen. It signifies luxury, that the meal is in some way special.

Now, I've always been a naysayer when it comes to storing breakables aboard, since I can't push away the vision of my crew possibly hopscotching over a shattered glass. But many people whose judgments I trust aver that they've used ceramic dishes for years and have yet to break a plate. And we recently met a couple who were living aboard a 45-foot sailboat and had carried a set of delicate, fine china all over the world. So many people can't be wrong. I think I'm going to have to reconsider this breakable issue. Maybe I'll even put back aboard those special FREEDOM logo glasses or test out the durability of my old set of kitchen dishes. I *will*, however, leave those crystal water goblets and my mother's china at home. I'll never be *that* convinced.

The type of boat you have and its ability to house fragile objects will affect your decision about whether to go all the way. In the first chapter, we discussed the effect of motion on galley safety. Dishes are more apt to be safe in a large boat that suffers less motion than a small one that bobs about like a cork. If having the luxury of real dishes and glasses is important to you, keep them stable by locating them in an enclosed, midship cabinet that has been fitted with special supports designed to keep dishes stacked and cups in place.[26] Don't leave clean dinnerware stacked in the dish drain when you are underway; they'll tumble out at the first good lurch and clatter to the floor or into the sink.

FLATWARE

After years of hating my enamel-handled nautical flatware, it finally started to show signs of wear, giving me a long-awaited excuse to replace it. This time I was determined to get a set that would lie flat in my utensil drawer and use less space. The selection of stainless flatware is vast, and I found many patterns that I liked; however, one by one, I narrowed my choices down to those with flat handles. I also looked at the sharpness and length of the fork tines—fat tines don't spear well—for nicely rounded spoon bowls and serrated knives, since they cut better than standard butter knives. My old set, like my dinnerware, now lives in a drawer on someone else's boat. You can find good stainless steel flatware sets at most discount stores. At Marshalls I found a $135 eight-piece set of Oneida Stainless, complete with serving pieces, for less than $40. And there were smaller sets for half that price. Perhaps you can find a bargain on these too.

PET FEEDERS

If your dog, cat or pet pig is along for the ride, he or she will need a dinner dish and water bowl. Weighted stainless steel bowls with rubber rims will stay in place if set in a stable part of the boat. For extra staying power, place them on a rubber mat. To prevent spilling, choose high-sided bowls and keep the food and water levels low. Look through pet catalogs and in pet stores for new options, such as collapsible fabric bowls that are waterproof and come in bright colors.[27] There are bowls that won't spill, even when turned upside down, pet canteens and water bottles, and combination water feeder and food bowl units. What? You have a bird? A guinea pig? You're on your own on those!

Section Six:
Food Safety and Storage ～～～

Finally, we're ready to proceed with the food aspect of our galley. Some days our minuscule galley is so heaped with gear that it's a wonder we can squeak anything edible out of it at all. Nevertheless, the care and keeping of food is critical in a close environment teeming with opportunities for spoilage. Stay ahead of the game by practicing safe food care. Use methods of selection, storage and cooking that will ensure the provisions you put aboard will be there, ready and safe to eat when you need them.

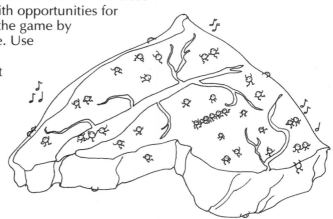

Chapter 17
Beware of the No-see-ums

There are few things worse than fighting off things we can't see. Bacteria, germs and parasites are invisible agents lurking in the shadows of our galley waiting for a show of weakness so they can pounce on our food. They're smart. They know a good thing. What could possibly be more wonderful than dining in a free restaurant with a water view? Bacteria are inventive little critters that love food just as much as we do. Protein foods in particular—meat, seafood, eggs and dairy products—are favorite munching targets that can be contaminated in no time flat. Bacterial life begins at 40°F and expires at 140°F. At their prime breeding temperatures, known as the "danger zone," these prolific no-see-ums as I like to call them become little Energizer bunnies and multiply like crazy—in 20 minutes they can double in number. I don't know about you, but to me the very idea of parasites copulating on my steak is a definite turnoff.

WHAT'S A GALLEY COOK TO DO?

It's difficult to sanitize when we lack hot water to properly clean pans and dishes, need to confine food preparation to a postage-stamp-sized space, and are saddled with a temperamental stove and icebox. We wonder, after a hiatus in our icebox, if the chicken salad is still good and if the ground beef is safe to use. Tainted food doesn't always look, smell or taste spoiled; and sometimes we convince ourselves it's okay to take a chance on serving it. It's true that supplies on a boat are limited and that there are times when we must make do with whatever is available; but dare we risk smiting our crew with the worst bout of seasickness ever?

Most bacteria won't harm us. In fact some, like those used to make yogurt, certain cheeses and vinegars, are actually helpful. Yet, their renegade cousins cause 6.5 to 33 million cases of food-borne illnesses in the United States each year.[28] Food sickness symptoms—achiness, dizziness, nausea, cramps, and diarrhea—are often mistaken for the flu and other illnesses, because most of us aren't aware that the evil no-see-ums can lay in wait for as many as 30 days before mounting their attacks. Some particularly bad guys can cause permanent health problems, even death.

Fighting Off the No-see-ums

There's only one way to be sure that bacterial gremlins aren't feasting at your saloon table, and that is to take precautions to lock them out with this simple, four-point attack plan:

1. Keep hands and surfaces clean.
2. Separate foods to avoid cross contamination.
3. Cook foods to safe temperatures.
4. Chill promptly.

Be "Mr. Clean"

New products such as antibacterial kitchen and hand wipes and waterless hand cleaners have made sanitizing countertops and hands very easy. Getting dishes clean, however, is a different story. Undissolved grease and food left on pans and dishes can make a fancy feast for bacteria. Water is always a precious commodity aboard, and hot water even more so. At times when you've no hot water, tackle this problem by heating a pan of water to boiling. Add it to your soapy dishwater or use it as a sanitary final rinse. When water is scarce as well, give your dishes a saltwater bath, as detailed in Chapter 3. Did you know that products containing salt and sodium inhibit the growth of bacteria, yeast and mold?[29] Saltwater boating offers a fine opportunity to put this information to use.

Don't Cross Contaminate

How do foods get contaminated? Easy, by swapping germs. We've been made aware of some basic food preparation taboos through the news reports on United States Department of Agriculture recommendations and findings.

The Rules

1. Refrigerator temperature should be 40°F or less. Use a refrigerator thermometer to check the temperature.

2. Never thaw food at room temperature. Thaw in a refrigerator, in cold water or in a microwave. Cook food immediately after thawing in microwave oven.

3. Wash hands with warm soapy water before preparing food. After contact with raw meat and poultry, wash hands, utensils, cutting boards and other work surfaces to help prevent cross-contamination.

4. Never leave perishable food outside of the refrigerator for over two hours. If room temperature is 90°F or above, food should not be left out for more than one hour. This includes items like takeout foods and leftovers from a restaurant meal.

5. Thoroughly cook raw meat, poultry and fish according to charts for suggested internal temperatures. Do not partially cook food. Have a constant heat source and always set the oven at 325°F degrees or higher. There is no need to bring food to room temperature before cooking.

- We know that licking a stirring spoon (or our fingers) and then using it without washing in-between passes on germs.
- We know that raw meat can hold bacteria and shouldn't mingle with cooked meat, vegetables or any other foods.

The only way to beat the cleanliness problem is to remain conscious of it throughout the entire food preparation process.

- Keep a soap-and-rinse setup available as you cook.
- Do your best to keep utensils, containers and wiping towels used for raw foods separate from those used for cooked foods.
- Heat leftover meat or seafood marinade to boiling before serving it as a side sauce.
- Avoid dipping the same knife in and out of the mayonnaise jar or other condiment containers when making sandwiches by transferring spreads into plastic squeeze bottles or purchasing them that way.
- Wash hands in between tastes and tasks using an antibacterial soap or wipe.
- Scrub cutting boards with an antibacterial dish detergent or chlorine-based cleanser, or use a disposable paper plate.
- Use paper towels to wipe dishes clean and kitchen wipes to mop raw meat juices from countertops.
- Make your own sanitizing solution by adding two teaspoons of bleach to a quart of water and store it in a spray bottle. Use this solution to disinfect cutting boards, countertops and other food surface areas, as well as to remove mildew and mold in the icebox or elsewhere on the boat.

HEED THE DANGER ZONE

These are the facts: Foods can spoil if left out for long periods, if they are not cooked long enough to kill any potential bacteria, or if they aren't kept cold enough to prohibit bacterial growth.

Cook Foods to Safety

Cook or reheat meats, seafood and eggs to at least 140°F at center. Any common cooking method will kill the bacteria on the outside of a food, such as a steak cooked rare, but a problem arises when the outside surface is mixed into the inside, such as with ground beef or casseroles blended with eggs, tuna or other protein foods. If a raw food is contaminated, it will spread this throughout. Only thorough cooking will assure that all bacteria have met a fiery demise. The most reliable way to assure a food has been cooked to its safe-to-serve temperature is to use a labeled meat thermometer or a doneness sensor.

Check Your Meat Thermometer

If your meat thermometer has been sitting in a drawer for many years, haul it out and check it against the following chart. [30] The labeling may not agree with the latest cooking recommendations, which have loosened up due to healthier farming.

Doneness Recommendations

Food Type	Degrees Fahrenheit
Ground Meat and Meat Mixtures:	
Beef, Pork, Veal, Lamb	160
Turkey, Chicken	165
Fresh Beef, Veal, Lamb:	
Medium rare	145
Medium	160
Well done	170
Poultry:	
Chicken and turkey, whole	180
Poultry breasts	170
Poultry thighs, wings	180
Stuffing, cooked alone or in bird	165
Fresh Pork:	
Medium	160
Well done	170
Ham:	
Fresh	160
Precooked (to reheat)	140
Egg Dishes	160
Leftovers and Casseroles	165

Meats

You can usually slice into a beef, veal or lamb steak and eyeball whether or not it is done to taste; these are safest to eat when cooked to medium-rare. Burgers are done when the juices run clear. Hamburger, including that made of turkey or chicken, now needs to be cooked to medium. Many restaurants will no longer serve a medium-rare or rare hamburger, and I've been pleased to observe chefs inserting doneness sensors to test burgers before serving them. Prime meats sold by a reputable butcher or offered at a top-notch restaurant are less apt to be unsafe, so in these instances you might risk serving or indulging in rare or tartar-style steaks or medium-rare ground beef burgers.

Pork

It was once recommended that pork be cooked to shoe-leather doneness, due to fear of trichinoses. The trichinosis organism is destroyed at 137°F. Modern practices have improved the safety of pork, and it is now considered safe to eat when cooked to medium. Sausages made of ground pork, turkey or chicken should be cooked to medium or medium-well, with no pink, although precooked sausages do not require cooking. Partially cooked ham should be heated to an internal temperature of 150 to 165°F, while cooked or ready-to-eat ham can be eaten as is. However, the USDA recommends that it be warmed to at least 148°F to kill any surface bacteria.

Poultry
Cook chicken, turkey and other fowl until it is no longer pink inside and the juices run clear. Dark meat takes longer to cook than white meat. Wiggle the leg or wing of a chicken. If it moves easily, this is another sign it is done. A large roast chicken or turkey will continue cooking once it has been removed from the oven and is allowed to rest, so it's okay to slightly undercook it.

Seafood
Raw shellfish carries the greatest risk of food poisoning, as does undercooked shellfish. Live clams, mussels and oysters should cook until their shells open. Discard those that fail to open or have cracked shells. Scallops turn white and firm, and shrimp turn pink when they are done. Keep frozen shrimp frozen and fresh shrimp iced until ready to cook. Cook lobsters for about five minutes per pound, until they turn bright red. A piece of fish is done when it is opaque, flakes easily and its juices are milky. Prepare a fish steak as you would a meat steak. Grill, broil or roast it at 425°F for approximately 10 minutes per inch of thickness. Restaurants now offer some firm fish, like tuna or salmon, cooked rare; and Sushi Bars have always served raw fish. Raw or undercooked fish needs to be of the highest quality and prepared by a careful chef.

Eggs
Forget about making that morning eggnog or slurping egg raw, right out of the shell. Eggs and egg-rich dishes are a medium for salmonella. Before using eggs in a recipe that will not require further cooking, such as Caesar salad, cook them until they are visibly done: i.e., when the white has been completely set and the yolk is beginning to thicken. More on eggs in the next chapter.

KEEP FOOD COLD
Arriving at the boat with questionably safe food is no way to start a vacation. It takes a consistent 40°F to stave off bacteria. Thermometers are cheap. Buy one for your icebox and keep on tossing ice in there until it holds to this temperature.

Hold That Temperature
Temperature fluctuations can cause food to deteriorate much more quickly, so keep the temperature of a cooler or icebox consistent by reducing the number of times the lid is open and shut, and by keeping it stocked with ice. With a refrigerator or freezer, limit the frequency of disconnecting and reconnecting power sources. Avoid putting warm foods in the icebox, unless you add extra ice along with them.

Transporting Foods
The safest way to get bacteria-loved foods to the boat is to load them into a cooler with enough ice to keep them cold until they get where they are going. Prepare,

refrigerate or freeze meats and such in advance. Never take a partially cooked pan of lasagna or any other casserole to the boat with plans to finish it there, unless you plan to invite the no-see-ums to dinner. Pack frozen foods together so they will keep each other solid. At the boat, stash the cooler in a shady spot until you can unload it.

Freezing and Defrosting

Freezing slows molecular movement, causing bacteria to take a nap, so frozen foods consistently kept that way will remain safe to eat; although over time flavors may deteriorate and food may develop white dried-out patches, called freezer burn. Freezer burn isn't dangerous, but it will make meat tough and food tasteless. If you are not sure your boat freezer has been behaving, perform the Ice Cube Test outlined in Chapter 7.

Setting frozen meat, fish and egg- or cheese-laden casseroles out on a countertop to thaw is risky, as the defrosted juices will attract our fiendish foes. Whenever possible, allow the food to gradually defrost in the icebox or cooler. If you forget to do this in advance and need to rush the task, immerse the item in cold water. Leave steaks and roasts in their original packaging so they won't get waterlogged, and change the water frequently so it doesn't get warm. If you have a microwave oven aboard, defrost the food in it just before cooking it. Once an item is thawed, the no-see-ums will be waiting to pounce and multiply, so handle thawed foods as any other perishable food.

Cool Down Hot Foods

Package leftovers you are comfortable saving to cool quickly. Maximize surface area by dividing large quantities into shallow plastic containers, freezer-weight plastic bags or foil packets. Pre-chill large quantities of very hot food in a separate cooler before dropping it into the icebox or refrigerator. Situate food where it will chill the quickest, over or under a bag of ice or near the coils or holding plate of the cooler, icebox or refrigerator; and where it won't add warmth to adjacent foods. Maintain the temperature of your cold storage device by either lowering the thermostat or adding fresh ice.

SAFE SERVING

It's impractical to expect boaters to run around like Nurse Nancy, taking the temperature of everything to be eaten or served. But it *is* important to pay attention to how long particular dishes are left out and how they are displayed. Avoid leaving hot or cold perishable foods out for more than two hours, one hour in hot weather. Keep foods hot longer by covering them with a lid, foil or plastic wrap. This will also stave off disease-bearing insects. To keep salads and deli meat platters safe in 90° weather, serve them on ice. Create a simple ice nest for your bowl or platter by putting some ice cubes in a shallow baking pan or in a Ziploc-style bag. At a boat party where several dishes are going to be left out buffet-style, set out only the amounts you feel will be eaten. Keep extra food ready to go—on ice, or hot in the oven or on the stove. Instead of adding more food to a dwindling casserole, remove it from the table and set out a fresh one. Either reheat or chill the leftover food. Toss out questionable leftovers.

LIFE IN THE ICEBOX

In my experience, foods last half as long in an icebox or cooler than in a refrigerator or freezer. I suspect this is due to the temperature fluctuations we discussed earlier. To give you a head start toward making the toss or serve decision, I've adapted the USDA cold storage guidelines, based on home refrigeration systems, for the average boat icebox. Your unit may vary to the good or bad of these, depending on how efficiently it operates and how well insulated it is. Mark your own adjustments to the chart and keep it handy as a reference.

Cold Storage Guidelines

Item	Freezer	Refrigerator	Icebox	Yours
Bought deli salads	don't freeze well	3-5 days	1-2 days	_____
Hot dogs, opened	2 months	1 week	3-4 days	_____
Hot dogs, unopened	2 months	2 weeks	1 week	_____
Lunch meats, pkgd	2 months	3-5 days	2-3 days	_____
Deli-sliced ham	freezes, watery	3-5 days	3 days	_____
Deli-sliced turkey	freezes, watery	3 days	1-2 days	_____
Deli-sliced roast beef	freezes ok	3 days	1-2 days	_____
Soups and stews	3 months	3-4 days	2-3 days	_____
Ground meat	4 months	1-2 days	1 day	_____
Bacon	1 month	7 days	3-4 days	_____
Steaks, chops, roasts	4 months	3-5 days	2 days	_____
Fresh chicken, turkey		1-2 days	1 day	_____
Meat leftovers		3-4 days	1 day	_____
Restaurant meals		3-4 days	1-2 days	_____
Sauces, i.e., spaghetti		6-7 days	2-3 days	_____
Leftover sandwiches		2-3 days	1-2 days	_____
Fresh milk		6-7 days	2-3 days	_____
Juices, opened		7 days	3-4 days	_____

Note: See the next chapter for more information on storing perishable foods.

HELP ON THE WAY

I recently read that a Canadian firm is developing a plastic food wrap that will change color if the food is contaminated with dangerous bacteria. Toxin Alert's wrap will contain antibodies that stick to the inside of the wrap and are activated when it touches spoiled food. It is expected to be as affordable as today's supermarket sandwich wraps. The USDA has also approved the use of low dosages of radiation to kill bacteria like E. coli, which is found in meats, and salmonella, which is found in eggs. If you are either looking to buy products that have been treated this way, or to avoid them, look for the Radura symbol that must be displayed on all irradiated products.

ON A PERSONAL NOTE

I've read boating articles where food safety is made light of, saying that the USDA guidelines are "overly strict," and that it's okay to leave leftovers out for snacking later on. My views tend to swing to paranoia because I've studied the subject, and if the precautions and statistics were meant as scare tactics, they certainly worked for me. I can only present here the approved way to maintain food safety in your galley or in your kitchen at home. Knowing a few critical facts and exercising vigilance and old-fashioned common sense gives the cook a basis for decision making, perhaps even risk-taking. It's your galley, your crew and your responsibility. You are the cook.

Chapter 18
Perishables

In addition to fending off the no-see-ums, it's important to stock your galley with foods that will last the longest and taste the finest. Select the freshest foods you can buy, grow or catch, and then manage their storage and safekeeping like a doting parent.

MEAT SELECTION

Generally, we purchase meat from a butcher, whether he or she is behind the counter at a meat market or in the back room slicing and packaging cuts for the supermarket case. Meat products are highly regulated and supervised by the USDA, which assures buyers that all meat has been inspected for wholesomeness and that its processing and distribution meet sanitation and safety standards. Even so, every once in a while harmful bacteria—E. coli, salmonella—creep in and spoil a batch of meat, causing widely advertised hysteria.

Tenderness and Grading

Love meat tender? Most folks do. The chewability and palatability of meat depends on the age of the animal, its species and how it has been fed and raised. Beef, veal and lamb are graded against standards set in the industry for tenderness, juiciness and flavor. These desirable qualities have a great deal to do with the amount of fat marbled throughout a piece of meat, as well as the meat's location and function within the animal. Meat is muscle. Less stressed muscle, such as tenderloin, loin, sirloin and ribs, will have a fine, close-grained texture. Well-exercised muscles, such as the neck, shoulders and leg, are leaner, more coarsely grained and generally chewier—like chuck and shoulder cuts. It's both comforting and distressing to realize that the happy free-range chicken we pay extra for at the market might be a tough bird because it's been allowed to exercise more than its sad sidekicks, who had the misfortune to be raised in confined quarters, under controlled conditions.

Package labeling can be confusing. Meat labeled as "kosher," for example, certifies cleanliness, not quality, and the fact that the meat has been processed in accordance with rabbinical law. Although the USDA has set labeling standards, the grading and labeling of meat is not mandatory, even in the United States. Some large meat packers and supermarket chains have developed their own grades, which are used in place of or in addition to USDA grades. Beef, veal and lamb are usually graded, while pork is not. You might encounter contrived variations such as, butcher's choice, top choice, high choice or star.

USDA Label guides for beef, veal and lamb

Highest quality: Prime

Very good: Choice

Good: Good or Select

Mediocre or poor: Standard, Commercial, Utility, Cutter and Canner

The lowest grades are rarely seen in retail markets. If you encounter nongraded meat, as you might when shopping in a rural area or in a foreign country, this does not necessarily mean it won't be tender or tasty. The best shopping strategy here is to look for well-shaped cuts with clean, pure-looking fat and compact, evenly-grained muscle.

PREPARING MEAT

Different cuts from the same grade or same animal will vary as to how they need to be cooked. Cuts that are tough and coarse require special handling to become tender, while those that are buttery and soft can be grilled or roasted as is. As a rule, the larger and leaner a piece of meat, the longer it will keep. Fatty meats, like pork, ground beef and sausage, for instance, will spoil quickly. Leave fresh meat in its original packaging when you store it. The plastic wrap used at the supermarket allows meat to breathe. Meat wrapped in butcher paper should be stored with the paper loosened for ventilation.

Always give raw meat the once-over before cooking it. The surface should be moist, not slimy, and it shouldn't have an "off" odor. Keep meat chilled right up until cooking time. To help chicken and pork last longer and to reduce the chance of cross contamination, precook it and freeze it before relegating it to the icebox.

Poultry

The most common birds we'll feast on aboard are chickens, but poultry includes a variety of other fowl, such as turkey, duck, quail and ostrich. Assuming your poultry comes from the supermarket, like mine does, your choices are there before you, encased in plastic wrap. Check the sell date on the package, and avoid poultry whose hour is nigh. If the package contains an unusual amount of liquid, feels sticky or has the faintest off odor, the contents are suspect. Most chicken arrives frozen and is left to slowly defrost in a chilled meat case. Store chicken in the original packaging in the coldest spot of the cooler, icebox or refrigerator, as you would other meats, and use it within two days or freeze it. (Meat that has been refrozen will still be safe to eat, but it will have diminished in flavor, texture and overall quality.)

Cold Cuts

Curing uses salt to retard bacterial growth in preserving pork products, which we boaters use in the form of bacon, hotdogs and deli meats. Some packaged cured meats do not require refrigeration, but check the label or ask the butcher if you are not sure. When in doubt, send any meat to the cooler. Vacuum-packed and standard deli roast beef, turkey and ham products, like Hormel and Boar's Head brands, while not cured, are processed and contain added preservatives. Store-baked items do not. When meat is sliced, it increases the amount of surface area subject to spoilage, and as a result sliced deli meats or cold cuts will not keep as long as a fully-cooked roast. Lunchmeats are so common to boating excursions that most of us have learned the signs of spoilage—slimy, sticky surfaces and funny smells. Roast beef will turn dull and grayish after a day or so, but it will still be safe to eat as long as it doesn't get that fluorescent glow. When in doubt, use it is as fish bait.

Once you have amassed a collection of cold cuts for a trip, use them in order of spoilage: store-baked turkey and roast beef first, deli-cured roast beef and turkey next, and ham last. Stacking together packets of meats in a shallow, sealed container seems to keep out air and help them last longer. If you do this, be certain each type of meat is wrapped individually in leakproof casing, so one won't infringe on the other.

I have found that, if fresh, leftover cold cuts can be tucked into the freezer and used another time. Outer wrap them with foil or freezer grade plastic wrap and mark the package with a date label. Defrost cold cut packets in the cooler, icebox, or refrigerator and use them right away. You'll find meats like roast beef, turkey and ham will still taste fine, although they may be a little watery from the freeze and defrost process. To avoid a soggy sandwich, blot off the excess water with a paper towel before using the meat. Do not refreeze leftovers.

SEAFOOD

Clams, mussels, shrimp, crab, lobster and freshly caught fish are synonymous with being on the water. It's great sport to land a fish and cook it for dinner, to wade in low waters and dig for clams, or to pull luscious fresh mussels off the rocks. And what seagoing kid hasn't dropped a string off the dock holding yesterday's baloney as bait to snare a crab? But there are times when we must settle for the thrill of the hunt, because if the water is polluted, so is its bounty.

Caught Fish

Seafood taken from polluted waters can make a person very sick, and coastal U.S. waters are not always very clean. There are more toxins in the water than ever due to bacteria-riddled raw sewage that is routinely dumped in our waters by industries and boats. If you plan to go fishing, call your state fisheries department beforehand to find out which waters are safe fishing and shellfishing grounds. Under the National Shellfish Sanitation Program, administered by the Food and Drug Administration, the government tests the waters in harvesting areas and closes those found to be highly contaminated. When you drop the hook over the side, if you are not certain the water is untainted, take a photo of the fish and throw it back in.

Bought Seafood

Begin by purchasing all seafood from reputable sources. Be wary of buying shellfish sold off the backs of pickup trucks in shore areas. Although it may seem fresh, there is a chance it may have been taken from contaminated waters. To protect yourself, ask to see either the shipping tag or shipping number of the shellfish. All shellfish caught in approved waters must carry such a number. If you are at a shoreline restaurant and suspect the fish was caught locally, the same caution applies. Your safest menu choices are entrees where the fish is well cooked and served piping hot.

Fish Finding

When perusing the fresh fish display, turn your nose up at those with a strong fishy odor, as they are past their prime. If whole fresh fish are looking back at you with bright, clear, shiny eyes, they're fresh. Scales should be shiny and cling like a slinky, sequined ball gown to the skin. The gills should be bright pink or red. Choose steaks and fillets that are glistening and moist, with no drying or browning around the edges. Poke the flesh. It should feel firm and spring back.

When buying packaged fresh fish from the supermarket case, check the sell-by date, and if it's expired, leave the fish there. Seafood that has been flash-frozen and kept that way is usually top quality, as this process quickly transforms freshly caught fish or shellfish to a rock-solid zero degree Fahrenheit and locks in color, moisture and flavor. Frozen, prepared seafood items, like crab cakes, should be solid and odorless. Avoid buying packages that are above the frost line in a store display freezer, and choose those that are clean, tightly sealed and contain fish that is free of ice crystals, freezer burn or any signs of thawed juices. At the deli, don't buy cooked seafood products that have been kissing raw fish in the display case. Smoked seafood should have a pleasant, smoky odor. Keep smoked seafood products refrigerated and use them within 10 days.

Shellfish Selecting

All shellfish—mussels, clams, and oysters, shrimp, crab and lobster—must be sold alive, and can live for weeks out of water if properly cared for. Freshly caught lobsters and crabs can be kept alive in a bucket of saltwater until you are ready to cook them. If you have purchased them from a market, cook them the same day; but in the meantime, keep them chilled. Look for feisty lobsters and crabs that move their legs and snap their tails when picked up. Sluggish ones will lack flavor and be mushy when cooked. Pasteurized crabmeat will last under refrigeration for up to six months, but once it's been opened, use it within three to five days. Pasteurized products should not be frozen.

Make certain clams, mussels and oysters are still living before committing them to the pot. Tap the shell of slightly open mollusks and ditch those that don't clam up, because they are goners. Healthy, freshly shucked oysters and scallops will have a clean, salty odor and be surrounded by a clear, slightly milky or light gray liquid. Shucked oysters should be cooked within one week, so check the sell-by date when purchasing containers from the market.

The quality and safety of seafood deteriorates if it isn't kept cold, so make fresh fish and shellfish your last market stop, and then get them on ice as quickly as possible. Before cooking, rinse seafood under cold water to remove surface bacteria.

DAIRY DO'S AND DON'T

Check the expiration or sell-by dates on all dairy products and bring to the boat only those that are current. Use borderline dairy products at once, with the exception of yogurt. As a rule, all dairy products need to be kept cold to slow the growth of bacteria.

Milk

Fresh milk spoils quickly, especially with inconsistent chilling, and will only last a couple of days in an icebox or cooler. If you need to have a supply for children, or your breakfast cereal or coffee, keep several kinds of milk and milk substitutes on board. Canned, vacuum-packed milk, such as Parmalat, can be stored indefinitely, although once it has been opened, it will only keep about three days. Try the chocolate flavor! Refrigerator case nondairy creamer cartons will keep one to two weeks after being opened, and can be frozen. Powdered milk and nondairy creamers keep for a long time, as long as they have moisture-proof and insect-resistant packaging.

Yogurt, Cheese, and Butter

Yogurt makes a healthy portable snack or breakfast food. Like sour cream, it uses good bacteria to gain its distinctive flavors and properties. Yogurt that's up to one week past its prime is fine to eat, although it will be more acidic. Cheese can survive without refrigeration as long as it doesn't get moldy. Blue cheeses are supposed to be moldy, but check out the veins. They should be blue or green. If they are off-color or you see furry spots, get rid of the cheese. Hard cheeses, such as cheddar or Parmesan, can last for up to six months. If a piece of hard cheese becomes moldy, cut off the moldy areas plus a half inch of the cheese around it before eating it. Softer cheeses will fend off mold without being refrigerated if they are wrapped in muslin that has been dipped in vinegar. Brie, cottage cheese, cream cheese and other spreadable cheeses should be tossed out uneaten if they develop mold.

I've always treated butter as I do fresh milk and kept it cold, but some say butter does not require refrigeration. I'm sure the USDA doesn't agree. When butter has spoiled it will become rancid. Use your best judgment. Warm weather will escalate spoilage. Long-term cruisers use canned butter, which can be found in specialty stores and, like canned milk, will last indefinitely.

Eggs

The shell is an egg's coat of armor. If it is cracked, damaged or dirty, the egg will spoil more quickly. When cracking an egg, take care that the outside of the shell, which may contain bacteria, doesn't touch the fresh egg. If the egg you need for a recipe is suspect, crack it open into a separate bowl to check it before adding it to the mix. As an egg ages, the yolk flattens and the white portion becomes clear and thin. A stale egg will smell like damp grass or straw. The smell doesn't always tell. Good eggs will sink to the bottom of a pan of water, while a rotten egg will float on the surface.

Eggs deteriorate much more quickly at room temperature and when exposed to air, than when kept covered and chilled. If you plan to keep eggs for more than a week, remove them from their cardboard carton. Cardboard draws moisture and will escalate spoilage. Plastic egg holders will keep eggs fresh longer and also protect them from breaking. Don't wash eggs until you are ready to use them or to prepare them for long-term storage. If you opt for egg substitutes from the dairy case, you will need to pay attention to sell-by dates. You might be surprised to know that if kept consistently chilled, unopened egg substitute cartons can last for months—and they are unbreakable!

There are many theories on storing eggs for long keeping. The petroleum jelly method calls for washing and drying the eggs to remove surface bacteria, and then sealing the pores with a thin layer of the jelly. Some say that dipping eggs in vinegar will retard bacterial growth. The key is to start with fresh eggs that have never seen the inside of an icebox. Sometime, it would be fun to run an experiment and test the various preservation methods against spoilage time.

Fresh, unwashed eggs that have never been refrigerated will last (without refrigeration) for a few weeks if kept in a cool, dark, dry place; and a week or two longer if refrigerated. I've found supermarket eggs to survive for several weeks under refrigeration. Cooked eggs should be cared for as any other cooked protein food: kept cold.

CONDIMENTS

Understanding the what, why and wherefore of storing condiments (and canned and dry goods) will help keep these foods ready to eat when you are; because ultimately, all foods are perishable.

There are many schools of thought on refrigerating common sauces like catsup, mustard and mayonnaise. The labeling on the jar cautions us to "refrigerate after opening." And I have always thought that mayonnaise in particular required refrigeration, as it is made with eggs, which attract bacteria. But after playing the hide the mayo game with a Caribbean charter boat chef—each time I spotted the mayo on the counter, I hurriedly stashed it in the icebox; only to find it taken out again the next time I looked—I began to question this. The answer is that mayonnaise *doesn't* need to be refrigerated, and neither does any other condiment that contains preservatives.

According to the American Dietetic Association, commercial mayonnaise, salad dressings and other favorite sauces are usually made with salt, lemon juice, and vinegar or other preservatives that slow bacterial growth. In fact, in mayonnaise-based salads, it's often not the mayonnaise that poses the risk but the eggs, chicken or tuna used. This doesn't, however, mean that these items can be treated with complete neglect. One problem is that many condiment containers offer wide-mouth access to what's inside, leading to cross-contamination. There is also a tendency to "double dip" a spreading tool, depositing whatever else was on it in the jar as well. By chilling your condiments, bacteria will be kept at bay from these other foreign food items. The new pull-top, plastic serving containers for common condiments go a long way toward eliminating this problem and make them safer to store aboard without need of refrigeration.

KEEPING FRUITS AND VEGETABLES

All produce is safe to eat, regardless of whether it's been kept cold. Certain fruits and vegetables stay fresh longer if they are kept in a dry, cool spot or refrigerated. Refrigeration may slightly alter the flavor of some types of produce, but it will prevent fruit from ripening further and keep vegetables crisper. Take care to keep produce away from areas in the icebox where it is apt to freeze or get knocked around.

Warm Weather Spoilage

When the weather is warm and humid, fresh fruit will ripen and spoil more quickly. Grapefruit, oranges, lemons, limes, melons and apples will last for about three weeks; unripened kiwi fruits, mangoes, pears, papayas and bananas will last about two weeks; peaches, apricots and plums will need to be eaten within one week; and berries need to be eaten right away. When fruit starts to spoil, make an effort to use it as soon as possible. Cut off the bad parts, and the rest will be fine to eat.

Select Produce to Last

Hard fruits like apples and pears won't bruise or spoil as quickly as more delicate fruits like peaches, plums, grapes and berries. Purchase firm, blemish-free produce that is free of signs of deterioration. White dots on citrus fruits signify the onset of mold. When you buy fruit, consider its degree of ripeness and match it against the length of your stay. Certain produce, including tomatoes and avocados, continue to ripen after picking. Store green tomatoes wrapped loosely in tissue paper or newspaper and you can enjoy them for three or four weeks. Some varieties of tomatoes are bred to keep longer. My Dad loved his garden, and tomatoes were his specialty. Each fall, before the first frost, he removed all the plants laden with green or ripening tomatoes and laid them on a long table in the basement; we enjoyed garden tomatoes until Christmas.

Longevity Tips for Unrefrigerated Produce

- Wrap vegetables and fruits loosely in paper to allow them to breathe and to prevent moisture from forming.
- Store in a cool, dark place.
- Check frequently. Remove spoiled or over-aged items and turn the others over.

Caring for Produce

Green beans, broccoli, carrots, cucumbers and mushrooms will last almost a week without refrigeration, but broccoli will yellow in a day or so. Garden carrots will survive a couple of weeks if you cut off the tops and wrap them in paper. But store-bought carrots will wilt after a day or two and lose their crunchiness, although they will taste okay if cooked. Wrap unrefrigerated cucumbers individually in paper and store in a cool, dry spot. Keep loose mushrooms about a week without refrigeration by storing them in a paper bag; mushrooms squished in cartons won't last as long.

Both celery and lettuce have high water contents and will lose their crispness unless they are kept chilled and moist to replace evaporated water. Keep celery about a week without cold storage by standing the stalks upright in a beverage container with a small amount of water. Change the water and periodically wipe the base of the stalks to keep them from getting slimy.

Lettuce is perhaps the most delicate of veggies and the hardest to replace when you're craving crunchy greens. Enjoy it while you have it. The less you do to it, the longer it will last. A freshly picked head of lettuce may keep as long as a couple of weeks without refrigeration if stored with the core removed and wrapped in paper in a cool dark place. Once it has been washed or chilled, however, it will wilt within a week if not kept cold. A firm head of iceberg lettuce will last longer than leafy lettuce. Remove the core by twisting it out to allow air to circulate inside the head of lettuce. When lettuce starts to lose its crispness, perk it up by steeping it in cold water. Pre-washed and bagged lettuce purchased cold from the market needs to be kept that way, although its days will still be very few. Long-term cruisers find that growing sprouts helps alleviate the need for lettuce in some instances.

The sweetness of fresh corn deteriorates so rapidly that it should be eaten as close to being picked as possible. Refrigeration will slow the process of the sugar turning to starch, which is what makes the corn tasteless. To store ears of corn for a day or two at room temperature, leave on the husks and place the ears in a mesh bag or hammock.

Good Choices for Dry Storage

Many kinds of vegetables can live aboard for several months without refrigeration, as long as they are stored in brown paper bags or wrapped in newspaper, which will allow them to breathe. Long keepers include onions, potatoes, cabbage, all the winter squashes, brussels sprouts, cauliflower, carrots, cucumbers, radishes and bell peppers. Refrigeration will alter the flavors of potatoes, winter squash, tomatoes, onions, garlic and bananas.

Fresh potatoes will keep for up to six months—an entire boating season—if you don't wash them, keep them dry and ventilated, and store them out of the light. Washing and refrigerating potatoes will reduce their longevity to two months. Sort through your cache of potatoes periodically and toss out the wrinkled ones. If eyes have sprouted, cut them off, along with the green portion, which is toxic; the remainder of the potato will be safe to eat. Onions will also keep for several months if stored like potatoes; however, don't allow potatoes and onions to cohabitate, or they will both deteriorate faster. A clove of garlic or a piece of fresh ginger root will keep for months when stored in this same manner.

Prepare to Store

Wash fruits and vegetables in batches and rid them of surface bacteria and chemicals by dipping in a mild acid bath of two tablespoons of table salt and the juice of one-half lemon in a basin of water. Dunk the items, rinse with clear water, then allow them to drain in a colander or on paper towels. Using a combination of clean seawater and lemon juice will work equally as well, as long as this mixture is rinsed off. For long-term storage of fruits and vegetables, add a drop or two of chlorine bleach to the wash water (in place of the salt-lemon combination) to be sure they are free of parasites or bacteria.

With the exception of water-based vegetables, like lettuce and celery, drain and dry items before storing them in a plastic bag to keep them from getting moldy. Store each kind of vegetable in its own container as not all of them get along. Place a few paper towels at the bottom of plastic containers and plastic bags to absorb excess moisture. There are two products made to neutralize the ethylene gas released by produce to help keep it fresh longer. Try using Evert Fresh "breathable" bags to help extend the life of certain kinds of fruits and vegetables, as well as Green's Extra Life cartridge, a small round disk sold at the supermarket, which can be placed in the icebox or refrigerator along with produce. I had wondered why my potatoes were going moldy in the Evert bags, until I realized that potatoes weren't on the recommendation list at the back of the pack. It pays to read!

Soft Fruits and Berries

Soft fruits and berries can be protectively stored in quart-sized, or larger, plastic containers. Cut fruit doesn't keep well, so it should be eaten within a day. Packaged berries, grapes, tiny tomatoes, or mushrooms from the market will last longer if you allow them to stay in their original container, unwashed. Stash them in a dry spot in the icebox or on a cool countertop where they will be less apt to mold. As needed, rinse them out by the handful and pat dry with a clean paper towel.

CANNED FOOD

We probably have some canned items stored on our shelves at home that are almost as old as we are. Canned foods can be stored almost indefinitely without fear of them spoiling or becoming toxic, unless they were not originally processed properly or the seal has been broken. The "best-if-used-by" date on the can ensures nutrient quality up to that date. Throw out immediately any tin or paperboard can that is bulging, swollen or leaking. Glass jars that don't "pop" when you open them may have a damaged seal or a crack in the glass. In flexible pouches, a leak in the manufacturer's notch used for easy opening or a slash in the packaging may also mean it has been contaminated.

Canned food is, incidentally, just as nutritious as fresh food. While fresh produce deteriorates, the nutritional content of canned goods stays constant. Fruits and vegetables destined for canning are picked at their peak and processed a short time later. Flash freezing and other new processing technologies assure that nutrients are preserved. Canned foods tend to be higher in salt and added sugar, and, like any cooking procedure, canning can cause some loss of heat-sensitive and water-soluble vitamins. However, the heat processes used release more antioxidants, like beta carotene and lycopene. There are low-salt, low-sugar alternatives for diet watchers.

DRY GOODS

In warm climates, remove foods that come stored in paper or cardboard boxes and place them in sealed plastic containers. The glue in the boxes can attract and harbor a variety of insects. Also, cardboard holds moisture, which could eventually cause the box contents to go stale or become soggy and impart an odd taste. Plastic jars with screw lids, Tupperware, Rubbermaid Super Seal and other tight-seal containers are all good repackaging options. For short-term storage and in cool climates, simply place the entire factory-sealed package into a zippered plastic bag to protect it from moisture and keep it fresh. If you have a weevil problem, add a few bay leaves to flour or cornmeal to discourage them.

Chapter 19
Planning Ship's Stores

Whether you are a pleasure boater or a serious sailor, the one thing you will always need to have on board is an ample supply of nutritious, tasty foods. The best-laid plans often get waylaid, changed or trashed completely. Your trip may take longer than expected, or you may arrive to find there's neither a market nor a restaurant nearby.

The smart cook pads the pantry with a just-in-case supply of foods. One night in our early years of boating, long before the advent of the cellphone, I learned my lesson when some friends were no-shows at a quiet little cove for dinner—and they were the ones bringing the steaks. Ever since, I have kept the makings for a backup dinner aboard, no matter how short our trip. (We've also learned to avoid last-minute surprises by monitoring a prearranged VHF marine radio channel whenever we are traveling with or meeting friends.)

Careful planning helps avoid overstocking, which can crowd space for other gear. Load up on foods that you routinely enjoy and that may be hard to find or expensive to buy at your destination. Canned and bottled beverages are heavy to tote by foot, so start a trip with a large supply and, if you've space, leave leftover sodas on board. Having a good supply of bottled and canned beverages aboard can be a lifesaver on a long passage in the event of a problem with the fresh water supply.

PLAN SUPPLIES

There are two types of foods to keep aboard: perishables—the short keepers that we'll call our A Team; and non-perishables—the long keepers that we'll refer to as our B Team. A combination of these two types of supplies will provide the most desirable meals; however, it's the long keepers on the backup team you'll resort to in a pinch.

Why Perishables?

Fresh foods—breads, fruits, vegetables, dairy products, meats and seafood—are the stars on our A Team; nice-to-have, but apt to desert you in your hour of need as they require lots of fussing over if they are to keep fresh. Perishables, while preferable to canned or boxed foods, are just that—perishable. Lettuce wilts and browns, bread goes stale and develops mold, milk curdles and sours, and meats and seafood get slimy and become contaminated. Here's where the B Team marches in to save your dinner.

The Backup Troops

Canned, dry, bottled and boxed foods that can survive in a boat locker almost indefinitely are the bottom-line basics. The comfort in knowing that the B Team is waiting in the wings is key to any sort of cruising, whether it is an overnight stay or a weeklong voyage. Should your lunchmeat spoil, open a can of tuna. A supply of canned or boxed lunch and dinner items, such as a large jar of pasta sauce and a pound of linguini, can save you when unexpected company stays on or the weather is miserable. If you and your crew like to wing it, it's even more imperative to have ample staples aboard to free you to take off whenever you feel like it, to sail as long as you like, and to pull in wherever you wish, without concern about shore provisioning. You may not dine on filet mignon, but you won't go hungry either. One of our most memorable times aboard was the stormy night we shared cans of Dinty Moore's beef stew and Brown Bread, a bottle of red wine and memories with old friends—better than any restaurant meal we could've had, anywhere!

STOCKING UP

If you've been cruising for a long time, you may already have a sense of what food items work best for you. But if setting up food supplies is new to you or your present method often leaves you caught without, take a minute now to rethink your strategy. There are a couple of ways to tackle provisioning: amass a base of B Team supplies in advance, and then add A Team perishables as needed; or stock as you go.

Use the Universal Supply List at the end of this chapter as a checklist for choosing your seasonal or long-term stores. Stocking food supplies as you go is a practical strategy for those with small boats or who are light-duty sailors. Start with a bare galley and then use menu-planning (see upcoming chapters) as a means of accumulating a base of nonperishables— soup and instant oatmeal, crackers and chips, teas, coffee, sugar, hot chocolate, juices, sodas. Although this method requires that you continually plan, weed out and shuttle supplies to the boat, it is functional and space efficient; and will provide you the exact items you need for a particular stay.

With either full or stock-as-you-go provisioning, you'll find that as long as you keep abreast of what's on board and what is needed, you will always have the supplies on hand to make a meal or more afloat.

PREPARE TO STORE

Think small. Try to avoid bringing large sizes of a product to the boat unless you've got a place to store it and will use it over the course of the season or boating excursion. The contents of small containers are used up more quickly with less chance of spoilage. Discard bulky, excess packaging whenever it makes sense. Use zippered plastic bags to repackage and size items for their stay aboard. Condense the contents of cardboard boxes. Divide snacks into serving size bags. Pre-measure or premix dry ingredients. Scoop small amounts of herbs and spices into labeled bags, and then keep them together near your cooking area in a larger container or bag. Keep unopened items in the coolest, driest place possible. Once they have been opened, encase the remains in plastic.

MANAGING THE TROOPS

Keeping a boat well stocked for both emergency meals and ongoing preparation needs isn't much different than keeping cupboards supplied at home. Any of these processes will keep things flowing smoothly and save you from being browbeaten when the gang is craving those chocolate cookies forgotten at home.

Standard Upkeep

Follow this general procedure to help keep a running supply of provisions aboard.

- Keep a small pad and pencil with you or tack up a sheet of paper in the galley.
- Each time, before you depart for home, assemble a list of food supplies you'll need to buy or bring for next time. Note the nonperishable foods you already have on the boat, so you won't duplicate them. Include sizes and quantities needed.
- If you are a Pricilla Planner type, create a master checklist and make several copies to keep on board. Fill out one each time you leave so your return list will be complete.
- Create your shopping list from your inventory and replenish items that are low or needed.

Heavy Duty Inventory Control

If you are going on a major trip, it may be crucial for all to know what supplies are on board, where they are located and whether they are raw, cooked or need further preparation. Keep a supply inventory, organized either by food type or by location.

Supplies by Type

This sample chart, based on the menu in Chapter 29, exemplifies inventory by food type; it served me well on a two-week passage to Tortola.

Supplies by Location

If you are organizing supplies, but don't intend to be in charge for an entire trip, it's important to let stand-in cooks know what is available and where it is located. For this situation, creating an inventory by location works best. Save the cook from unearthing the freezer only to find that the bacon is in the icebox, or from unloading an entire dry locker to find the spaghetti is stored elsewhere or used up. Create your list, then cut it up and mount it near the appropriate area. Here's an inventory I wrote for a combination offshore-onshore passage between Rhode Island and Florida. I like to draw a line through items that are used, and edit counts.

Inventory Worksheet and Item Locator (for Major Trips)

Qty	Category	ITEM	LOCATION	STATUS	USE FOR/REHEAT METHODS
	Meat/Dinners				
1		turkey breast	freezer	cooked	sandwiches/dinner
1		honey baked ham	refrigerator	cooked	sandwiches/dinner
16 (2 pkgs)		stuffed clams	freezer	precooked	appetizers/microwave
2 pkgs		hot dogs	freezer	raw	lunch
6 indiv		Dinty Moore's stews	cupboard	canned	lunch/dinner-microwave
1		lasagna	freezer	cooked	dinner-reheat oven
8		tuna fish	cupboard	canned	lunch
2		chicken cacciatore	freezer	cooked	dinner-reheat micro/oven
	Fruits/Vegs				
1		peaches	cupboard	canned	for peachtree pork dinner
5		tomatoes	hanging basket	fresh	misc.
	Dairy				
1		sugar packets	over stove		
2 doz		eggs	refrigerator	fresh	breakfast/lunch
	Bakery goods/sweets				
4		sliced bread	freezer		lunch/breakfast
1 box		asst. chocolates	snack cupboard		snacks
	Packaged Foods/mixes				
2 boxes		rice mixes	cupboard	raw	dinner-stovetop
	Spreads/canned goods/snacks				
1 jar		peanut butter	cupboard		misc.
	Condiments				
1		mayonnaise	cupboard		
1		soy sauce	behind stove		
	Beverages				
4 lbs.		coffee	over stove/port shelf		
	Paper goods/Misc.				
6		paper towels	behind upper cushion/port		
	Cleaning Supplies				
1		dish detergent	behind sink		
	Linens				
10		dishtowels	top drw/port side v berth		

Inventory Worksheet for Major Trips

Supply Inventory by Location

Freezer (mount over freezer)

Ice   2 blocks, 1 bag

Cooked Foods:

1 pkg. Lloyd's BBQ ribs (for 2)
1 homemade chili (for 4)
1 homemade Chicken Chardonnay (for 4)—add rice
2 pkgs. homemade meatballs and sauce (1 pkg. serves 4-6)—add pasta
1 shredded BBQ chicken (for 4)—for sandwiches
6 stuffed clams
1 pkg. Heat and Serve bacon
1 whole cooked chicken
2 lbs. mild chicken wings
2 pkgs. Japanese appetizers

Raw Foods:

4 sandwich steaks
1 lb. bacon
25 hotdogs
4 strip steaks
1 lb. ground beef
$1\frac{1}{2}$ lbs. chicken breasts
2 lbs. ready-to-cook shrimp

Other:

2 boil-in-bag peas (for 2)
2 boil-in-bag broccoli (for 2)
$1\frac{1}{4}$ lbs. butter
1 orange juice concentrate
12 bagels
12 English muffins
1 Sara Lee pound cake
1 container homemade cookies
1 loaf Italian bread
1 loaf garlic bread
1 pkg. tortillas
1 pkg. pita bread
1 loaf sliced whole wheat bread

Large Dry Locker (mount next to locker)

Breakfast Foods: (shelf 2)

Dry cereal—1 large box, 1 pkg. indiv. asst. boxes
1 box oatmeal packets
1 box cereal bars
1 box pancake mix
1 bottle maple syrup
2 boxes soymilk
2 boxes Parmalat
1 box sugar packets
2 lbs. ground coffee

Dry food and mixes: (shelf 1)

1 box Bisquick
4 lbs. linguini
1 bag bow tie pasta
1 box instant mashed potatoes
2 boxes boil-in-bag rice
5 boxes crackers

Jars and cans: (shelves 1 and 2)

1 pickles
2 small olives
1 chickpeas
1 artichokes
2 cans tomato sauce
2 cans strewed tomatoes
4 microwave, indiv. containers asst. stews
2 cans Dinty Moore stews
1 can Brown Bread
2 cans Hormel chili
4 cans soup (for 2)
4 pkgs. Ramen noodles
1 pkg. indiv. applesauce
1 pkg. indiv. fruit
1 jar pesto
1 mustard
1 mayonnaise
1 relish

I made similar notations for the contents of the icebox, snack cupboard and areas where beverages, spices and paper goods were stored. Once we arrived, it was easy to reprovision.

THE B TEAM

B Team members are the Green Berets, the nonperishables that can tough it out almost anywhere and still get the job done. Your only concern here is that their sleeping quarters are dry and that overweight jars and cans of liquids are tucked away safely, as low as possible on the boat. Protect glass soldiers further by wrapping them individually in bubble wrap, encasing them in old socks, or cushioning them with rolls of paper towels or toilet paper. If you have a squared area for storage, it will be easier, because boxes, cans, and bottles can sit evenly. Set a folding plastic milk crate in an odd-shaped locker to make the bottom level.

Store Supplies by Function

If your nonperishable B Team members are stored as if they just tumbled from a grocery sack, you'll have trouble calling them into action. Develop your own system, but group them by meal type or use, so you can quickly locate what is needed. Whenever possible, store goods nearest the place of access.

This is how I have my B Team housed:

In dry storage cupboard or locker: Meal making supplies
Breakfast items (pancake mix, syrups, honey, cereals, granola bars, jams and jellies, boxed muffins)
Lunch items (canned soup and stew, canned tuna fish, peanut butter)
Main dish items (pasta, rice, spaghetti sauce, mixes, canned ham)
Unopened bottled condiments (mayonnaise, mustard, catsup, barbecue sauce, soy sauce)

In a separate dry locker near the companionway:
Snacks and hors d'oeuvres (chips, cookies, crackers, canned salsas and pesto, nuts)

Handy to the galley:
Mixed drink items (tea, coffee, beverage mixes and concentrates, hot chocolate mix, boxed milk)
Sauces, marinades, salad dressings

Handy to the stove:
Dried herbs and spices, (salt, pepper, parsley flakes)

CLOSE OF SEASON REMOVALS

When hauling out the boat for a long winter's rest, we must decide what stores can remain aboard. Cold temperatures create condensation and moisture in a closed-up boat, so be sure cardboard boxes and paper goods are wearing protective plastic bag coats or have been left wrapped and unopened. Remember that when liquids freeze they expand, and if there is no room for this, the contents will explode all over your beautiful boat. Be certain to remove soda, beer, water jugs and canned goods from boats stored in areas of the country with temperature drops below 32°F.

Dry goods such as herbs, spices, teas and coffee are usually fine to leave aboard, as long as they are well wrapped. One fall, I left aboard a package of Pepperidge Farm cookies. They were still fresh in the spring. This company lines its cookie bags with foil, ensuring a long life.

Universal Basic Supply Checklist

Review the following list of commonly used foods. Add items unique to your recipes, or those integral to your meal making. Use the items you have checked off as a starting point in deciding which supplies might earn a spot in your basic pantry. Divide your selections into two groups: perishables and nonperishables. Storage is always an issue, so limit your supplies to those that you will use for several recipes or have other practical uses aboard.

Fats/Oils
Vegetable oil/olive oil
Butter or margarine

Baking items
Cornmeal
Corn syrup
Baking powder
Baking soda
Cornstarch
Flour
Nuts
Raisins (boxed or snack packs)
Chocolate bits
Flavoring extracts

Baking Mixes
Biscuit mix
Cake, muffin, brownie mix
Icing mix or canned icing
Pancake mix

Sugar
White granulated, Brown
Honey
Maple syrup
Molasses
Sugar substitute

Herbs
Basil
Bay leaf

Capers
Cilantro
Dill seed
Dried rosemary
Dried parsley
Garlic (fresh, powder or salt)
Marjoram
Dried tarragon
Dried thyme

Spices
Allspice
Black pepper
Cayenne
Cinnamon
Celery seed
Chili powder
Cloves
Coriander
Cumin
Ground or fresh ginger
Nutmeg
Oregano
Paprika
Poppy seeds
Poultry seasoning
Salt
Seasoning salt
Sesame seeds
Spice blend

Sauces and Condiments

Barbecue sauce
Ketchup
Mayonnaise
Mustard (Dijon, yellow, dried)
Salad dressing
Soy sauce
Steak sauce
Tabasco sauce
Vinegar (white, wine, balsamic)
Worcester

Canned vegetables

Corn
Green beans
Baked beans
Tomatoes (paste, puree, sauce, stewed)

Soups

Variety, canned, dried mixes
Stews (Dinty Moore's), chili
Broth, chicken, beef
Dry soup mixes

Other

Breadcrumbs
Cereal, oatmeal
Chips (potato, corn, pretzels)
Crackers and cookies
Canned fish (tuna, salmon, anchovies, sardines, shrimp, clams, crab meat)
Canned meats (chicken, ham)
Canned brown bread
Cocktail dips and spreads
Dried beans
Fruits, canned snack-size
Gelatin, prepared snack packs
Jelly, jam
Olives (green, black, cocktail)
Onions (fresh, canned, dried)
Pasta
Pickles
Potatoes (fresh, boxed)
Peanut butter
Pudding (mixes, prepared snack packs)
Rice (white, brown, packaged mixes)
Spaghetti sauce

Beverages

Beverage concentrates
Coffee
Juices
Milk (evaporated, canned whole, nondairy creamer)
Hot chocolate mix
Tea

Fresh

Breads and rolls
Cheese
Deli meats
Dinner meats
Eggs
Fruit
Milk
Seafood or shellfish
Vegetables

Frozen Goods (for the freezer)

Extra butter or margarine
Extra bread and rolls
Bacon
Cakes, pies, breakfasts goods
Prepared dinners
Packaged vegetables
Meats
Seafood

Section Seven:
Things to Think About ~~~~~~

There is much to consider that will impact food choices when provisioning. You will need to find out about your trip and crew and figure out your responsibilities. This introductory section to menu planning will help you define and accept your cooking style and accumulate the details necessary to create workable menus for trips of any kind.

Chapter 20
Who's Cooking?

So, you're the cook. Are you happy about it? Whether you've inherited the job by default or by choice, you undoubtedly have questions about the extent of your responsibilities. What exactly are they? How do they fit in with your cooking abilities? Are you organized or disorganized? Ambitious or lazy? Are you comfortable in the galley or would you rather be somewhere—anywhere—else? It's only natural that your personality and skills will travel with you to the boat.

To help you understand your *modus operandi*, check off any of the following items that you agree with. There are no wrong answers. No prizes will be awarded.

1. Your canned goods are organized in alphabetical order.
2. Mealtime is whenever anyone is hungry.
3. There are three casserole meals in your freezer right now.
4. The galley sink is a good place to wash out underwear.
5. Your grocery list is on a sticky note.
6. The grocery store is a place to buy beer and soda.
7. This is your second time through reading this book.
8. Dinner is just a phone call away.
9. Your freezer is so stuffed with Lean Cuisine that the door barely shuts.
10. You are on a first-name basis with the clerk at the nearby convenience store.
11. You can't break the habit of coupon clipping.
12. You're short at least one ingredient each time you cook.
13. There are items in your refrigerator sprouting fuzzy green things.
14. Your idea of making dinner is to add water and stir.
15. The only menu you are aware of is the one a waiter hands you at a restaurant.
16. Fresh vegetables come in cans and frozen boxes.
17. You'll decline a dinner invitation because you've already defrosted the supper meat.
18. You only need to go to the grocery store once a week to keep supplied.
19. You know what you'll prepare for dinner two weeks from Thursday.
20. You break out in an itchy red rash when you get anywhere near the galley.

Chef Personalities

Pricilla Planner

Lazy Lucy

Last Minute Louie

Clueless Karl

Pricilla Planner

If you checked off questions 1, 3, 7, 11, 17, 18 and 19, you are a Pricilla Planner type. Pricilla is not comfortable unless everything is well organized. A person with this profile might prepare weekly menus in advance of heading out to the grocery store; cook double portions of favorite dishes and freeze half for another time; and serve meals at the same time each day. Pricilla runs a tight, organized galley that is the envy of her dock buddies.

Last-minute Louie

A Last-minute Louie might've answered yes to questions 2, 5, 10 and 12. Will you prepare your own mixes or buy them from the market on the way to the boat? If so, you're a Louie-in-progress and may care less about cost than saving time and work. It's common for this personality type to be rushed and forget to buy important items like ice and the steaks for grilling. Too often, Louie makes a second trip to the store.

Lazy Lucy

A Lazy Lucy type may have checked off questions 8, 9, 13, 14 and 16. Lucy knows how to cook and can do it if need be, but feels it's a bother. Such a personality can often be found sunning in the cockpit sipping a cold drink or on the cell phone ordering pizza. Sounds good to me!

Clueless Karl

If questions 4, 6, 15 and 20 describe how you feel about cooking, then you are blessed with Clueless Karl genes. A Clueless Karl type isn't aware that the boat even has a galley. You don't want him as your cook, because his most common comment will be, "Well guys, what shall we do for dinner"? There are times when playing "Karl" is not a bad idea!

YOUR JOB AS COOK

As the person on stomach patrol, the cook's job is to stop hunger by doling out good food as needed. A meal for the crew doesn't necessarily need to be prepared from scratch or cooked aboard; it can be bought or ordered out. The main thing is that it is wholesome. Some of us revel in preparing a meal, while others hate it. And we all have days when we don't want to think about food, touch it, smell it or even *say* it out loud. Here are some pointers to ease the job and give you peace of mind.

No Need to Be the Galley Slave

If you guard the galley like a ferocious watchdog, everyone aboard will feel it's off limits, and the result will be that you'll become their unwilling servant: "Get me this, get me that!" Others can certainly make the coffee, toss together sandwiches for lunch, do the dishes, watch a pot or take over and make the entire meal. Having a stand-in cook is particularly important if you tend toward seasickness.

Think of yourself as a supervisor. Many hands make light work is an old adage that still rings true, and galley chores are no exception. Ask for assistance when you need it; that's what the crew is for. Familiarize everyone with the galley, so they too can comfortably maneuver about it.

Don't Be a Martyr

The crew always enjoys a special meal, but they'll appreciate it just as much if you've produced it easily. Spending the entire cocktail hour holed up in the galley may result in a homemade potato salad your crew will rave over and a pork roast that's pure heaven; but they would rather have enjoyed your companionship than feel guilty about your slaving ways. The temptation to please others is always there, and if we succumb we deserve exactly what we get—lots of praise and a sour disposition. I don't know about you, but I get in a foul mood when I have denied myself pleasure, even if it was my choice in the first place. Fortunately, there are some easy solutions to some of the more burdensome aspects of galley life.

Lower Your Standards

Perfection is nice, but "decent" is okay too. Drop your standards until the crew starts squawking. Chances are they will barely notice that the meals aren't so fancy or that you have prepared a dish differently. With so many distractions in boating, food only needs to be there to taste good.

Convenience foods—including bought-and-brought meals and precooked foods—are the foundation of good boating meals, so guiltlessly take shortcuts. Use your creativity to figure out how to accomplish a task with the least amount of effort, using as few supplies as possible. Dress up store-bought potato salad with a spring of parsley or paprika, and it can pass off as homemade. Canned stews and chili can look and seem elegant if served with flair. Scoop out small round loaves of bread and use them as bowls—fewer dirty dishes. Top any entree with a dollop of sour cream, a sprinkle of grated cheese or a capful of rum and few will care how the meal got there.

Simplify

Simplicity breeds contentment. Do, but don't overdo. This whole boating thing is a sport, and it's supposed to be fun. We go to the boat to get away from stress, not to wallow in it. Use your head, not your hands, and reduce the work in meal preparation.

- Choose foods that need little fussing to taste good. A tasty, tender piece of meat or fresh fish doesn't need a fancy sauce. Just sprinkle on herbs and spices, and save the messy mixtures for another time and another place. Fruit, even canned, tastes fine with little or no embellishment.
- Find easy ways to prepare food. Leave skins on potatoes; don't peel carrots, cucumbers, and summer squashes. Cut chopping time in half by making larger chunks. Slicing an onion into wedges, instead of dicing it, won't impact the flavor of the stew.
- When using a recipe, read it over and think it through. Can you eliminate a step without sacrificing the result? For example, when making a long-cooking dish like a stew, chunks of meat, onions and mushrooms don't need to be browned first. Toss everything in together, and at the end of an hour or two, everything will be wonderfully cooked.
- Recipes using a large number of ingredients spell W-O-R-K. Consolidate seasonings and eliminate the pinches of this and that. Instead of using three kinds of onions, use more of one; or eliminate the washing and chopping entirely by substituting dehydrated onion flakes.

Organization is Half Your Work Done

Trade cooking odors wafting from the stove for the smell of salt air, and pot watching for kibitzing with the crew. By doing as much as possible at a convenient, earlier time, you too can be in the cockpit sharing a cocktail with a magnificent sunset. You certainly deserve it! Make the most out of whatever you do. Be realistic about the amount of time you have available, and try to keep your chores organized.

- Begin preparation by amassing all the ingredients and utensils you will need for the first segment.
- Order your tasks to avoid small bottlenecks. If you will be baking, preheat the oven before beginning, so it will have reached the correct temperature by the time you are ready to pop in the biscuits. If you are cooking food that requires a large pot of boiling water, like pasta or lobsters, start the water heating first and use the wait time to work on other preparations—make the salad, heat up the sauce or cook a vegetable.

- Do your chopping all at once. Chop enough onions to sauté for your main dish and to toss in the salad. Wrap up extras and store them in the icebox for use in tomorrow's stew or salad.
- The more clutter you have about, the more frustrated you will be. Clean up as you go. Mixing in plastic bags instead of bowls will save space. Wipe down counters and stow items as you finish with them.

One thing to remember as we proceed is that as a cook you have a responsibility to yourself as well as your crew. Shape the tasks at hand to suit your personality. Give yourself permission to take liberties with your job. You'll be more fun to be around when you're dancing in the cockpit than grumbling in the galley.

You're now ready to think about where you are going and who will go with you. Put on your Pricilla Planner hat and let's go!

Kitchen Afloat proverb
        Haste makes work.

Chapter 21
Define Your Mission

Are you taking a day trip to drop anchor and go swimming for a few hours, or planning to dock at a marina overnight? Perhaps you are on an extended trip and will hop from spot to spot for a week or two—or just keep going. Are you flying to the Caribbean (lucky you) to pick up a charter boat for a week or more of spoiling yourselves? Or are you anguishing over how you'll deal with an offshore passage? Any of these situations are apt to either put you in the galley preparing meals aboard or in a dinghy headed to shore to dine out. The volume and type of provisions you will require will depend on your cruising style and destination plan.

PUT ON YOUR THINKING CAP

Before you start provisioning for a cruise of any type, begin by defining your time aboard with the following questions. Each one leads to a trail of others, which will get you thinking, which is exactly what you need to do first.

How Long Will You Be Aboard?

The length of your trip will affect the quantity of food you will need, the overall cost of your provisioning, and even the type and number of people that are able to travel with you. While most people are available for a daysail, longer trips often conflict with work schedules and other non-sailing events. If you are stocking for short hops or have children aboard who often require small snacks, prepackaged foods and individual portions may be your best option. The longer you plan to be away from shore, the more nonperishables you'll need to stock. On an extended trip or an ocean voyage, having aboard enough basic staples to create dishes from scratch—canned meats and vegetables, herbs and spices, flour, sugar and other baking needs—will provide the most flexibility.

Where Are You Going?

Once you have a destination plan, you will be able to judge whether you'll need to fully or partially provision for your stay aboard. A long passage obviously requires complete provisioning, while short hops that offer reprovisioning and dining opportunities require fewer supplies. Find out about your intended harbor. Consult the waterway guide for the area, talk to friends who have been there before or ask personnel at the harbor's marina about area provisioning. Next, make decisions about docking and dining. A slip will provide you with dockside power, which allows boaters with few facilities aboard to cook using portable electric fry pans, microwave ovens and electric coffeepots. On a mooring, you'll be reliant on your boat's cooking facilities and independent power.

Foreign Ports

It is particularly important to understand what supplies may be available when traveling to a foreign port. If you are chartering a boat, consult the company's provisioning department or contact the local charter office. A main port of entry like Bermuda typically caters to boaters and will have plenty of places to reprovision. If you are traveling to a duty-free destination like St. Thomas where rum is cheaper than bottled water, wait to stock up on the alcoholic beverages until you arrive, but bring soft beverages.

What Are Your Cooking Facilities?

Facilities, or lack of them, will limit the amount and type of food you will feel comfortable preparing aboard, as well as the size of the crowds you will want to feed. Frozen foods won't keep on a boat without a freezer, and stocking bulk quantities of staples will be a waste of space if you won't consume them over a boating season.

Where and When Will You Cook

Your choices are to cook underway or at dock. On long trips, it's almost impossible to avoid preparing food underway, but on short excursions, the average galley guru finds it simplest to save extensive preparation until reaching port. Once there the cooking might be done in the galley or in the cockpit on a barbecue grill. In the cockpit, meats and seasonings need to be set in a platter for the grill, and table settings need to be handed up and out. If your meal is moved ashore to the marina wharf, parking lot, beach or picnic area, you'll need to pack food, beverages and dining supplies for travel.

COUNTING HEADS

This might include the captain (unless you are jockeying for that role as well!), the kids (hopefully yours) and assorted guests that you've invited along. The number and profile of the individuals cruising along with you will affect where you choose to go, how much and what type of foods you will take with you, the amount of money you will need to spend on food, and whether you will dine on board or ashore.

The more people you entertain on board, the more complicated mealtime becomes, so think about this before you invite the entire front office to go sailing with you. It's fairly obvious that you will need twice as much food for four people than for two. This is one area where age and sex are important. While children may be satisfied with a peanut butter and jelly sandwich, an adult will scream like a banshee if you call this "dinner." Men, notoriously, have heartier appetites than women, and drink more beer. If you are hosting teen-age boys, there will be no need to be concerned about spoilage because all the snack food, sandwich supplies, breads, milk, soda and juices will fly out of your storage areas and into their mouths. If your children are babies or toddlers, they will have special needs and may eat at different times than the adults aboard. Older children, who are more self-sufficient, will normally share mealtime with you, unless they are out romping with their friends.

CATER TO SPECIAL NEEDS

Just as at home, to maintain good health and harmony it's important to use common sense and heed dietary constraints and food fetishes. At today's saloon table it's almost a guarantee that you'll have seated at least one person who can't or won't eat something being served. If you know a person well enough to invite to your boat, take the time to find out if he or she has any special needs. Also, understand that even when queried about likes and dislikes, people unintentionally commit the sin of omission. When stocking for an offshore passage, I ran my menu past each crewmember. Even so, once we were underway, I encountered resistance. "Oh, I hate onions" or, "I can't stand mayonnaise and mustard mixed together." No matter how well you query, the I-forgot-to-tell-you's will happen, so being armed with easy alternatives is always a good plan.

Specify beforehand if you haven't the facilities for elaborate preparation aboard. Ask for suggestions for buying the proper items, or have the person bring his or her own supply of special foods to supplement your menu. If the person is joining you as crew on a passage and isn't being paid for the pleasure, you owe it to him or her to do your best to accommodate them.

Dietary Intolerances

When purchasing food for the boat, read the labels to ensure that the *one* item a crewperson cannot abide isn't buried within the ingredient list. Folks that have definite intolerances to lactose, gluten and sulfites suffer nasty aftereffects like diarrhea, bloating and vomiting. Some people have greater degrees of these food allergies than others.

Milk Sickness

Don't plan to serve a macaroni-and-cheese casserole to a lactose-intolerant guest. Include a humus hors d'oeuvre along with that cream cheese dip. Offer coffee creamer, 100-percent lactose-free milk, or soy milk instead of cow's milk for their cereal or coffee, and then use it in recipes[31]. There are also a variety of soy-based, lactose-free cheeses that work quite well in sandwiches or atop burgers, and can replace real cheese in many recipes. Yogurt with active acidophilus will help a mildly intolerant person digest a dairy product. Its effect lasts for three or four hours.

Gluten

As gluten is a primary ingredient in flours and in many types of pasta, a gluten intolerant person can't eat most bread products and cereals. When reading labels, avoid products containing wheat and wheat starch, oats, barley, rye, modified food starch, hydrolyzed vegetable protein, malt flavorings, distilled vinegars, emulsifiers and stabilizers.

Sulfites

Sulfites are additives used to prevent certain foods from browning, and they are added to beer, wine and other fermented food to slow the growth of bacteria. The sulfite-intolerant will need to avoid these items, so have plenty of juices and soft drinks available, and pay attention to the labels on packaged foods you'll use in meal preparation. For you, red wine drinkers, two aspirins at bedtime helps stave off the wine headache you'll no doubt wake up with in the morning.

Diabetes

Diabetes is a complicated illness related to maintaining a balance of glucose in the diet. It's important to talk with the sufferers about their needs and to be certain you have the correct food on board. Some are on pill medication, while others must administer injections to control the disease. With even the mildest cases, diet control is essential.

Food Allergies

There are specific foods, such as peanuts, strawberries, corn, chocolate and shellfish that are known allergens. Food allergies need to be taken seriously. In some severe cases the body reacts to an allergen by producing a histamine reaction. Symptoms can range from itchiness and giant hives to internal swelling, which can cut off breathing and become life threatening.

The Veggie People

One can't expect a vegetarian to eat a ham sandwich, so add extra vegetables and fruits to your provision list for the trip. Your veggie friend will be happy—and the rest of the crew can always use the extra fiber in their diets. Many vegetarians will eat chicken or fish, but draw the line at red meats. A vegan doesn't eat anything that comes from an animal, and won't touch eggs, milk or anything made with dairy products. A true vegan isn't wearing leather shoes or belts either.

Fussbudgets

I've seen some folks who call themselves vegetarians wolf down spareribs and only eat certain vegetables. These are actually closet fussbudgets. Do your best to stock foods they enjoy, but be sure to consider a portion for them in your regular planning, lest they change their mind and scarf down yours.

MAKE NOTES

Not all of us remember the right things, and we tend to return to places we didn't like, seldom realizing what we've done until we've been seated and consumed our first mouthful. I keep a trip journal—this is not the captain's logbook—in which I record anything of interest that occurs during our trip. I include information such as favorite restaurants, places to shop and special area appeals, as well as the names of restaurants and markets that served us tough chicken or pungent seafood. Use a spiral notebook or a fancy nautical journal; it doesn't matter as long as you are comfortable writing your thoughts in it.

Section Eight:
Menu Planning

Putting together meals for a trip is like walking a tightrope; it's a balancing act to provide enough of the right kinds of foods at the right times to keep energy and spirits soaring. It's helpful to understand how various foods work within our bodies before moving on to create pleasing, appetizing and healthy meals. Once you've mastered the technique of menu making, you will find that planning meals for any type cruise will be a snap.

Kitchen Afloat proverb
No fuel, no fire.

Chapter 22
Calories Count!

Stamina. Vitality. Strength. Performance. Whether you are racing or just cruising, you are using energy, which requires fuel—food in the form of calories. When we're busy, it's easy to ignore hunger pangs and skip meals, snacks and drinks (and to think maybe we need to lose the weight anyway). But what we may not realize is that by doing so, we are also impacting our ability to think, perform and react. Those of us operating a boat need to be alert and capable of responding to any and all situations.

The yin and yang of eating is balancing our personal "fire" by feeding it enough of the right kinds of fuel. There are foods that provide sustained energy and those that afford a needed quick spurt that won't last. If we don't take in enough calories to meet our energy requirements, we'll peter out like the Energizer bunny's competitor. On the other hand, extra calories get stored in our fat cells. (And we all know where those are located!) Learning how to balance foods to create menus for trips is one of the more interesting facets of meal making.

GUIDELINES

Statistics show that in 1999 potato chips, French fries and iceberg lettuce—one of the least healthy greens—accounted for more than a third of the average American's daily vegetable intake. With the latest medical research unveiling so many dos and don'ts, and the growing popularity of funky diet books, it's no wonder that so many of us are confused about what constitutes healthy eating. The need to be thin is so popular today that there's focus on eating less, but what we really need to do is eat *right*.

Healthy eating is a combination of choosing the right quantity of the right kinds of foods and consuming them regularly throughout the active part of the day. The time-tested diet plan recommended by the USDA has always been the benchmark for nutrition with its famous Food Pyramid. In 1992 the USDA realigned the old food pyramid by reducing the recommended quantity of protein foods and adding more grains, fruits and vegetables (See chart on p. 152). Both pyramids tell us to avoid too much of the good things: flavor-carrying fats and comforting sugars that constitute calories with little nutritional value.

150

Healthier Choices

It's reassuring to know that respected health groups are working very hard to educate the masses on proper eating for disease prevention and overall vitality. The New American Plate Plan, developed by the American Institute for Cancer Research, puts emphasis on sensible eating and weight control as a means of preventing health problems, promoting increased servings of produce and whole grains, and fewer of meats. In the ideal American Plate, plant foods fill two-thirds of a plate and meat the remaining third. "Plant" food means colorful vegetables—the more colorful the better. It's been proven that the chemicals that give plant foods their color—carrots, beets and blueberries—are actual disease fighters.

The Healthy Eating Pyramid from the Harvard Medical School concurs with the more-vegetables-and-complex-carbohydrates-less-meat-and-dairy theory; the Healthy Weight Pyramid from the Mayo Clinic stresses breads, grains, cereals and produce along with exercise. These and other findings from reputable sources are the exact antithesis of the faddish Atkins Diet—abundant with proteins and fatty foods and low on carbohydrates and produce—which, although it results in weight loss, causes nutritionists to cringe.

How Food Affects Us

All foods produce energy in different ways. For this reason they are classified into three groups: proteins, fats and carbohydrates. Let's go back to our metaphor of the fire. Protein foods are the large logs that take several hours to burn and keep a fire roaring contentedly. Proteins supply amino acids, which build, repair and maintain muscle, skin and connective tissue throughout the body. They also provide energy when carbohydrates and fats are in short supply. Meat, seafood and dairy products are sources of protein as are some vegetables, such as beans and soy, which supply heart-healthy fats as well as fiber—a nutrient essential for maintaining good health. Too often the protein in meats is combined with fat; even lean meats can have as much as 50 percent of their calories from fat.

Fat makes a fire sizzle and sparkle, like kindling wood, but it isn't long-burning. In addition to supplying energy, fat performs other important jobs like transporting nutrients throughout the body and keeping skin supple and hair shiny. Fat is found in foods we love, but the problem is it loves us so well that it tends to hang around. Think cellulite. Saturated fat is that which is derived from animals, such as meat and dairy products. Opt for unsaturated fats from vegetables and nuts like soy, peanuts and corn to keep cholesterol levels stable. Learn to choose lean meats and low-fat or fat-free foods. Use low-fat cooking methods and go easy on fatty dressings, sauces and spreads.

Sugars and starches make up the carbohydrate group, our body's preferred source of energy—the medium-size logs that help our energy fire to stay hot and lively. Sugars are simple carbohydrates found in fruit, honey and table sugar, while starches are complex carbohydrates found in grains, vegetables and certain fruits. Complex carbohydrates break down into sugar during digestion. All digestible carbohydrates act to provide energy to our brains, muscles and nervous systems.

USDA RECOMMENDATIONS

Even though there are now a variety of food pyramids from which to choose, I'm going to use the USDA's version as a basis for our menu planning, as it's an old standby. To adapt the USDA Pyramid to any of the other pyramids we discussed, simply add more servings of produce and grains and cut back on protein and dairy foods—and get more exercise!

The USDA Food Pyramid

At first glance, it may look as if the USDA expects us all to chow down like ranch hands after a full day on the prairie. But slow down, little buckaroos and don't get too excited. The notable issue here is not the *number* of servings, but the *size*— who ever said that size doesn't matter? Serving size is the quantity of a particular item recommended at one sitting. One big blob of mashed potatoes might seem a normal serving, but the USDA may count it as two or more carbohydrate or vegetable servings. People must have eaten like birds in the good old days when the chart was first developed. To keep both your energy and metabolism levels consistent, choose foods from all the groups in the ratio recommended, and spread them out through the day to deliver a constant stream of energy to the body.

Use Fats, Oils, and Sweets Sparingly

Oils, fats and sugars are present in potato chips, pickles, candy, cookies and almost anything enticing. Occasionally, it's okay to drop off the wagon, as long as there are no major health concerns, like diabetes, high cholesterol or obesity. Market shelves are stocked with "free" stuff—sugar-free, fat-free, lactose-free, salt-free and cholesterol-free, which makes it easy to cut back without deprivation. If boating has become your life style or your summer is a perpetual vacation, then you may opt for the healthier alternatives.

USDA Food Pyramid
Fewer Fats & Sweets

2-3 Dairy

2-3 Meats

3-5 Veggies

2-4 Fruits

6-11 Grains

Suggested Daily Servings

Dairy: 2-3 servings/day

1 serving dairy:
1 cup milk or yogurt
$1^{1}/_{2}$–2 ounces cheese

Two to three servings a day for milk products, cheeses and yogurt are manageable on a boat. One ounce of cheese is the size of your thumb. Dairy items need special care, as they must be kept cold to remain fresh, so it's tempting to cut down on these. You will need milk for cereal, coffee and as a beverage for young children. Some dairy products are also protein-rich. Low-fat cottage cheese is a more healthful breakfast food than yogurt, as it contains twice the protein. Buy single-serving containers of fruit-flavored cottage cheese and yogurt for convenient on-the-water snacks. Boost food value by substituting milk or soymilk for water in instant oatmeal, pancake or biscuit mix and when reconstituting soups. Add cheese to a sandwich or sprinkle it on pasta, rice or salads.

Grains: 6 to 11 servings/day

1 serving grains: 1 slice bread
$^1/_2$ cup cooked pasta, potatoes, or cooked cereal
3 ounces ready-to-eat cereal

Bread, cereal, pasta and rice—these fillers hold the rest of our menu together. Six to 11 servings a day may seem like a lot, but if you consider that you will probably have at least one serving per meal or snack, you can make the six mark with no problem. A half-cup portion is the approximate size of a closed fist. A sandwich will use up two servings of grain, while a bowl of spaghetti might use up to four servings. Bread is one of the first things to go stale or moldy on a boat, so as a backup plan, have a package of Pillsbury refrigerated bread, which will bake up in just 10 minutes. Also try vacuum-sealed tortilla for wraps, pita bread, and canned brown bread. If we stretch it, I suppose we could also consider cakes, cookies, crackers, sugary cereals and flavored rice cakes as grains.

Meats and Beans: 2 to 3 servings/day

1 serving protein group: 3 ounces meat or fish
1 egg
$^1/_2$ cup beans
2 tablespoons nut butter or $^1/_3$ cup nuts

Sizzling steaks, lobster, clams on the half-shell, fried chicken, bacon and eggs—only two to three servings a day of these goodies, and they are *small* ones at that. Three ounces is only the size of a tape cassette or a deck of cards, so that large juicy steak you inhaled at dinner likely filled most of your protein (and fat) requirement for the entire day. Half a cup of dried beans, peas or lentils can count either as one protein serving, or it can cross-over into the vegetable group.

Unless you are a confirmed vegetarian, sticking to these guidelines is tough to handle on vacation. I'm still back in the Dark Ages where I feel a meal is incomplete unless it contains a healthy dose of protein. When it is eaten in moderation, extra protein—especially of the nonfat variety—is not harmful and isn't likely to cause undue weight gain. Unlike carbohydrates and fats, protein will fill body-building needs before it is either expended as energy or stored as fat. My suggestion is that, unless you are living aboard your boat, serve your crew whichever protein foods they enjoy. You can all return to a healthier diet at the end of the cruise.

Vegetables and Fruits
This is the hard part, but worth the effort. With fresh, frozen and canned fruits, vegetables and beans so prevalent, planning meals and snacks around these foods isn't difficult. Vegetables and fruits contain antioxidant vitamins, which neutralize free radicals, nasty byproducts of the oxygen in the air around us. Free radicals can wreak havoc with our DNA, escalate the aging process and contribute to heart disease, cancer and other life-threatening diseases. These demons sneak in through holes in the earth's protective ozone layer and are transmitted to us via the sun and wind. As boaters, we are constantly exposed to free radicals, so it is even more important that produce be an important part of the diet.

Vegetables: 3 to 5 servings/day

1 serving vegetables:	$1/2$ cup cooked or raw
	1 cup raw, leafy vegetable
	$3/4$ cup juice, like tomato or V-8

It takes planning to offer three to five daily servings of green and yellow vegetables on a boat. To meet the challenge, clean and chop up crudités in advance of your trip, since you'll most likely go into avoidance mode once you're underway. Once prepared, it will be easy to offer raw vegetables as side snacks with lunches, as appetizers in the evening, or alone any time during the day. Celery sticks, baby carrots, broccoli florets and sliced green and yellow peppers and cucumber make good nibblers. Growing your own sprouts aboard will assure you have a constant source of fresh, crunchy greens for sandwiches and salads. Sneak grated vegetables like zucchini and carrots into salads and other mixed dishes like mashed potatoes or lasagna. Add extra vegetables to pizza, omelets, sandwiches, stir-fry meals, dips and spreads. Does anyone remember the I Hate vegetable line of frozen foods that hid green beans, peas and carrots inside French fried potatoes? It was the only way I could get my kids to eat anything green! Make the food enticing, and it will tempt tasters, even finicky ones. Remember, the sliced tomato you put in sandwiches and salads you are considering a vegetable is really a fruit.

Fruits: 2 to 4 servings/day

1 serving fruit:	1 piece medium fruit or one wedge melon
	$1/2$ cup chopped, cooked or canned fruit
	$3/4$ cup fruit juice

It's not as hard to fill the fruit requirement as it is to concentrate on vegetables. Fruit is delicious, refreshing and abundant during the summer months. Although fruit contains essential fiber and vitamins, especially antioxidants, the USDA limits their intake to two to four servings a day. I suspect this is to control sugar and carbohydrate intake. Fruit contains fructose, a natural sugar.

SEASONING

Salt has been given a bad rap, even though it is as essential to our health as water. When we sweat, we lose salt as well as fluids, and these need to be replaced. This isn't too difficult as salty snacks like potato chips, hotdogs and pickles are all stuff we crave when we are having a good time. Our problem with salt is that too much can create an imbalance in our systems and lead to health problems. If you are a salt-lover, remember that, like sugar, it is an acquired taste, so if your doctor advises you to cut back, it will be less painful if you do it gradually. I have used Salt Sense for years. It looks and tastes like regular salt but has one-third less sodium. Switch over to salt substitutes or experiment with spices and herbs. Condiments, spices, sauces and salt enhance the flavors of foods and some, like ginger and garlic, even have some medicinal value. Spike cooked carrots with ginger, sweet potatoes with cinnamon, or spinach with nutmeg.

THE 8-CUPS-PER-DAY STORY

1 serving: 8 ounces or 1 cup

Drink heavily, preferably water, as the body most easily absorbs it. A drink here is defined as any liquid you can pour down your throat from hot tea to icy lemonade. We can survive for days without food, but not without fluids. Liquid consumption is particularly essential on the water because the sun, wind and salt air are dehydrating.

Our body has a continuous thirst for water, but rarely tells us about it until our hydration level is dangerously low, i.e., when we feel thirsty. Once you get into the habit of drinking water routinely, you'll find that you will always be thirsty, which means your system is in balance. In situations where you've worked up a sweat hauling up the anchor or churning the winch, be sure to replace lost fluids by drinking extra water. Some of us drink coffee, tea, coke, beer and other beverages; these beverages actually have a diuretic, or dehydrating effect in spite of their being fluids. Cheating on fluid consumption at home may be okay, but in a boating environment it can be debilitating.

As cook, you not only need to have fluids in the form of water and other non-dehydrating beverages available to your crew and guests; but you need to watch that they drink them. I suggest having aboard twice what you think you will need. Allow 64 ounces of water or other nonalcoholic liquids per day per person. This equates to eight 8-ounce cups or glasses (many are 10 or 12 ounces), or at least $4^1/_2$ beverage cans in the standard 12-ounce size. There is a tendency for some folks to avoid drinking when they are on a boat because they don't want to deal with using the head, especially underway. Instruct each new person aboard on the operation of the head to make certain he or she will be comfortable maneuvering belowdecks.

Bottled or Canned Beverages

These are easy enough to bring, although they are burdensome and can create a disposal problem. You will want to have juices aboard, especially if you have children. Vegetable and fruit juices meet daily nutritional demands in addition to providing fluids. It's always a safe bet to keep aboard a supply of super quenchers like Gatorade, which boost hydration. Individual cans or boxes are perfect for the boat.

If it's quantity you need, bring a 48-ounce jug of juice to get started. Wash out the jug and refill it with reconstituted dry or liquid juice concentrates. Concentrates are great because they last almost forever and take a small amount of space. It's a good rule to use water to quench thirst, instead of alcoholic beverages.

Alcoholic Beverages: in moderation

1 serving: 1 12-ounce can beer
              1 8-ounce glass wine
              $1/2$ shot 80 proof hard liquor

No civilized boater would be without a proper bar, so it's okay to keep your boat well supplied. However, alcohol and boating make a dangerous cocktail. Save offers of beer, wine and hard liquor for times when everyone is lounging about at dock. Alcoholic beverages are dehydrating, and hot sun and winds elevate this effect. Alcohol enhances the negative effects of most seasickness remedies and conflicts with some medications.

Taken in moderation, wine and beer do have some redeeming value as they contain trace amounts of nutrients. Wine also aids digestion and acts as a mild, natural sedative. An analysis performed by the Hawaiian Department of Health indicated that a modest amount of booze may protect mental functions in the same way it wards off heart problems: by boosting good cholesterol and preventing blood clots and harm to the brain's blood supply.

However, there are other helpful ways to avoid heart disease and to relax. The USDA recommends that, if you choose to consume alcohol, you limit it to one alcoholic drink per day for adult women, and two for adult men. Heavy drinking is linked to social problems and violence as well as many health problems including high blood pressure, strokes, heart disease, certain cancers, birth defects and liver diseases. It also impairs judgment and encourages alcohol dependency.

Alcohol is absorbed more quickly on an empty stomach, so offer a snack along with that round of cocktails. Have a sip, don't gulp. Slow your pace and limit your intake by alternating alcoholic with nonalcoholic drinks. Lite beers contain less alcohol, and there are some very good nonalcoholic beers available. I just read a recipe for a reverse martini—heavy on the white vermouth and whispery on the gin—which was touted as a sneaky way to prevent dinner guests from weaving to the table. Right!

THE BOTTOM LINE

In planning healthful meals and snacks for your boatload, balance the amount and types of foods you provide with physical activity. Plan a varied menu that includes plenty of grains, vegetables and fruits, and try not to go overboard on fatty foods, salty snacks, sweets and alcoholic beverages. Once you get the hang of it, you'll find the act of meal planning will come naturally.

Chapter 23
The Balancing Act

One of the most trying parts of being a cook is deciding what to serve, and it's a lonely task. The only time your crew will care about the menu is if the entree plunked in front of them looks nasty. And should you ask what they want, I'll wager you'll either get suggestions for a complex or funky dish you wouldn't dare try onboard or hear the usual, "I don't care, anything will be fine." But they *do* care, and so should you.

CREATING MEALS

Use the USDA Food Pyramid to develop good meals and snacks for your crew. Begin by putting together one meal, and then graduate to a plan for an entire day, weekend, or longer. Start with a protein food, then pair it with foods from other groups—grain, fruit, milk—to balance the flow of nutrients and supply both instant and long-term energy. As the body converts protein foods into energy more slowly than those from other food groups, everyone will be less hungry after having a snack or meal that includes it.

It's easy to start balancing meals once you realize that common protein-carbohydrate combinations are as familiar to us as meals at McDonald's. Think about famous duos like hamburgers and fries, hotdogs and beans, pork chops and sweet potatoes, chicken and rice. Taste, texture and balance—it's almost automatic.

The Perfect Dinner Plate

1 part Meat
3 parts Veggies & Grains

The Ideal Dinner Plate

When you create a meal, consider the dinner plate as one entity. Fill one-fourth of it with meat or seafood, and allot the remaining three-quarters of the plate to grains and vegetables. Add a glass of milk and fruit for dessert, and you have a comprehensive meal representing all food groups.

Why a Menu?
Creating a menu in advance of a cruise or passage will not only prevent your crew from keeling over with fatigue, but also help you rescue calm from the chaos that often accompanies mealtime aboard. With a plan, your provisions will be precise and you'll get a head start in preparation. Best of all, when plans change or the seas are unfriendly, you can pull a rabbit out of your chef's cap by discovering new ways to use the foods on hand. Think of your cruising menu as a loose guide to ensure you have an ample supply of the right kinds of foods for a particular stay. Well-thought-out menus and provisions assure that you will be self-sustaining. I guarantee your crew will love you for it.

HOW TO PLAN A MENU
Make an effort to dispense foods from all groups throughout the day. The old three-meals-a-day-plan with small snacks in between still works. Snacks are important to maintain energy levels and stave off hunger. Dip raw vegetables into cottage cheese, yogurt and peanut butter; or make up a trail mix with nuts and dried fruits.

General Menu Planning Tips
- Work out several days' worth of menus at a sitting so you can deal with the big picture. This will make it easier to locate weak spots. Foods should vary from meal to meal, and from day to day. Plan for leftovers that can carry over into other meals.
- Consider each meal in relation to the others served during the space of one day. Are all of the USDA food groups represented in their recommended quantities?
- Abide by the likes and dislikes of the crew. There's no sense slaving over a dish most of your crew won't eat.
- Consider the season. Cold weather sharpens appetites and brings on cravings for warm, hearty foods. In warm weather, we tend to eat lighter and more frequently—cold salads, drinks, less structured meals. No matter what the temperature, try to serve one hot meal a day. Warm food is satisfying and soothing, both psychologically and physically.
- Consider potential sea conditions. If you will be cruising in rough waters, plan quick-to-grab individual snacks and simple heat-and-eat fare.
- Suit the meal to the occasion. No one wants to tackle a bony piece of meat or fish or a tough chop while balancing a plate on his or her lap. Food should be bite-sized or tender enough to cut with a fork.
- Be artistic. An all-white or all-brown meal, no matter how nutritionally balanced or tasty, is drab and unappealing. Think of the dinner plate as a canvas, and paint it with brilliant colors, textures, shapes and flavors.
- Balance flavors and food types. Avoid serving too many rich foods in a

single meal. Same goes for bland ones. Complement a spicy food by pairing it with a bland one; a tart taste with sweet; crunchy with soft and mushy.

- On a tight budget? Save money by serving dishes prepared with less costly cuts of meat. Marinate London broil to tenderize it instead of serving filet mignon. Spread a small quantity of meat thin by using ground meat to make spaghetti sauce or chili instead of hamburgers. Many pieces serve more. Two chicken breasts will feed four people if sliced and combined in a Caesar salad or used in a chicken dish. Convenience foods can be very costly. Save money by preparing your own meal kits to take to the boat.
- Create a spreadsheet similar to the one below and use it to work out daily menus and to verify that the day's plan is nutritionally balanced.

Build In Flexibility

Think through your food choices and plan for a default. If barbecuing will be in question, select a versatile meat or fish than can be just as easily sautéed in a skillet belowdecks as grilled. Chicken breasts can be sliced lengthwise into chicken fingers to cook quickly in either a pan or on a grill. Ground beef makes a base for a

Daily Menu Planning Worksheet

| DATE: | | GROUP | | | | | | FUN | |
MEAL	FOOD	GRAIN	VEG	FRUIT	DAIRY	PROTEINS	FOODS	DRINKS
BREAKFAST								
SNACK								
LUNCH								
SNACK								
COCKTAIL HOUR								
DINNER								
DESSERT								
TOTALS								
USDA REC.SERV/DAY		6 TO 11	3 TO 5	2 TO 4	2 TO 3	2 TO 3	NA	64 OZ.
*Count large portions as double servings and small portions as partial servings								
** Beverages: preferably, water. Also fruit juice or millk for children.								

skillet meal; and fish can be turned into seafood stew. Prepare something ahead that can be served cold, such as sandwiches and pasta salads, or choose soups and stews that can easily be reheated or warmed. Some cooks won't leave port without a canned ham!

CUSTOMIZE YOUR MENU

By writing out a meal plan for several weeks in sequence, you'll be able to adapt your favorite dishes into workable galley plans. The menu you develop for boat stays should be in sync with your family's eating style at home, and include many of the favorite dishes and foods you all enjoy. Here's one way to do this.

Begin by analyzing the meals you currently serve at home with an eye toward each dish's appropriateness for the boat. Perhaps favorite recipes can be simplified or prepared in advance and frozen. Can you substitute canned ingredients when fresh ones are not available? Does a recipe include bulky or uncommon ingredients? Can you pare down the number of ingredients or make substitutions without ruining the dish?

Obtain a spiral notebook and keep it in a convenient spot in your kitchen at home. Early spring or a month or two before the onset of boating season, begin to jot down the foods you serve. No need to be too detailed. Include takeout foods, supermarket convenience foods, and note restaurant meals. Assign one page per day. For example:

Week No. 1 Monday: Breakfast: bagels, juice
                       Lunch: turkey sandwiches
                       Dinner: ground beef casserole, salad, bread

          Tuesday: B: Yogurt, juice, coffee, milk
                       L: Chicken soup, salad
                       D: Ordered pizza

...and so on

Use spare space on each day's page to jot down notes or thoughts about the practicality of a specific food or dish. Circle items you feel will work especially well on the boat. The true test of a meal is when you attempt it aboard. Review your recipes for versatility. Can leftovers be recycled into sandwich makings or a salad? With a meal of pasta in a hearty meat sauce, the sauce might reappear as Sloppy Joes on buns for lunch. And don't just douse the whole batch of pasta with sauce, since you can use the leftovers as a basis for a cold pasta salad or side dish.

Select dishes that will be most appealing for the time of year. You may want to save that pot roast for winter dinners at home, but a bowl of beef or chicken stew—homemade or canned—will be most welcome on raw, rainy days aboard. What foods did you serve with a particular entree? Was the meal balanced nutritionally? How might it fit in with other meals on a particular day? You might, for example, add carrot sticks, fruit and milk or cheese to that simple turkey sandwich lunch. Add rolls, biscuits, dumplings or canned Brown Bread to a one-pot stew to sop up the sauce. Finish with a green salad and a glass of milk, or serve a milk-based dessert—pudding or yogurt—to complete the meal.

Don't feel you need to strike from your list of considerations takeout Chinese food, pizza, burgers and fries, Kentucky Fried Chicken, Boston Market meals or any others eaten in or out. If you expect to seek out a particular type of food during your trip, leave some space for it in your trip meal plan.

If an occasional meal is unbalanced, basically tasty but unhealthy, it's okay, as long as you consider it within the framework of the other meals served on a particular trip. For example, if you know you will be ashore for lunch, make an effort to balance breakfast, dinner and snacks. Fruits, vegetables and grains will offset the fats found in burgers and fries. Chinese food is loaded with salt, so lighten up on salt-laden foods for the day; replace the chips or salted nuts with crisp celery sticks or plain crackers. Your crew may still hunt down the chips and nuts, but you can relax knowing you've done your part by having healthier options on hand.

In your notebook, cross off items that won't work and circle or highlight items that will. For a neater record, rewrite your preferred options onto separate sheets. When you are finished you should have accumulated a base list of main dishes, side dishes and snacks that you can consult whenever you are pondering "what to have for dinner."

Once your base plan is in place, it's easy enough to alter it as you go. Packing for the boat will become almost automatic, and you'll find yourself only writing out an actual menu for major trips. A collection of your most versatile and seaworthy dishes will emerge, which you'll use repeatedly.

Kitchen Afloat proverb
Practice makes provisions.

Chapter 24
Plan a Weekend Menu

It's been a horrendous week at work and the one thing that's kept you sane is the thought of getting down to the shore to feel the lilt of your boat beneath you. Sometimes, you are content to do little more than putter; but usually you're primed to cast off your dock lines to explore new destinations and hone your boating skills. Alas, but your trips are short spurts and before you realize it, it's time to head home for another week of work. If this sounds familiar, you may recognize yourself in this section, as we work through the thought processes involved in provisioning for a weekend aboard.

ALL ABOARD!

TGIF! We've packed our gear into the car and hurry down to the marina to catch the sunset. We'll arrive about 6 p.m. and need to be home Sunday evening to prepare for a meeting on Monday. We know that three meals per day are the norm, so for each full day we'll assume we will need three meals per person. Multiply the number of full days by three, then decide the meal count for the partial days. Add in the snacks afterwards.

Here is how a weekend on the boat might go on a per person basis.

Friday Night	6 p.m. to 12 p.m.	1 meal, 1 snack
Saturday	7 a.m. to 12 p.m.	3 meals, 4 snacks
Sunday	7 a.m. to 5 p.m.	2 meals, 2 snacks

For the purposes of illustration, let's assume you'll all be aboard for the entire stay and that you and the rest of the crew will sleep between midnight and 7 a.m. If you were traveling overnight, you would need to include additional snacks for the period from 12 p.m. to 7 a.m. Once you have formed the habit of counting meals and snacks, you will find it easy to plan for any length stay.

CREATE A SIMPLE MENU

Using the information we discussed in the last two chapters, let's create a simple menu and then test it out on a weekend cruise. As you will notice, I allotted an extra snack on Saturday to allow for the late dinner hour. If you were dining earlier, this would not be needed.

Sample Weekend Menu

	Arrive 6 p.m.	
Friday	Dinner	Cold chicken
		Potato salad
		Carrot and celery sticks
		Beverage (soft drink, juice or milk)
	Snack-dessert	Brownies
		Beverage
Saturday	Breakfast	Cereal and sliced bananas with milk
		Juice, coffee, tea, hot chocolate, milk
	A.M. snack	Fresh blueberries
	Lunch	Turkey sandwiches w/tomato, lettuce
		Potato chips
		Carrot and celery sticks
		Beverage
		Cookies
	P.M. Snack	Crackers and cheese sticks
		Beverage
	Cocktail hour (6 p.m.)	Cucumber slices with crabmeat dip
		Beverage
	Dinner (7 p.m.)	Grilled fish
		Broccoli
		Rice
		Rolls
		Tossed salad
		Beverage
	Snack-dessert	Leftover brownies and pudding cups
Sunday	Breakfast	Blueberry pancakes and bacon
		Juice, coffee, tea, hot chocolate, milk
	Snack	Fresh pears
		Beverage
	Lunch	Ham and cheese sandwiches
		Celery and carrot sticks
		Potato chips
		Beverage
	Snack	Mixed nuts
		Beverage
Depart 5 p.m.		
	Dinner	At home

Okay, you caught me! I've sneaked in a bit of realism. Let's face it. A few junk foods are essential to our feeling of well-being, just as are the healthy ones. As you can see, there is nothing too fancy to be concerned about. Many of these items can be purchased or made in advance, reducing the time you'll spend sweating in the galley. Grill chicken aboard or buy it rotisserie-cooked from the supermarket. Make the potato salad at home or pick it up at the deli when you shop for the cooked chicken and lunchmeats. Buy the brownies and rolls ready-made, pick up the re-frigerated and bake variety from the dairy case, or make them from scratch. Use traditional bacon or the pre-cooked variety. Toast frozen pancakes, buy a shake-and-pour mix or pre-measure your own ingredients at home. Use the most perish-able foods first. Notice that we first ate the cooked chicken, then the turkey. The ham lasts the longest, so we saved it for the last day. With one- or two-week menu planning, factoring in longevity becomes even more vital.

DOES IT PASS THE USDA TEST?

Just for fun, let's see how Saturday's menu matches up to the requirements on the food pyramid. This is what we'll need per day: 6-11 servings grains, 2-4 servings

Daily Menu Planning Worksheet

MEAL	FOOD	GRAIN	VEG	FRUIT	DAIRY	MEAT & FISH	FUN FOODS	DRINKS
BREAKFAST	CEREAL WITH BANANAS/MILK	XX		X	1/2			2 OZ
	JUICE			X				4 OZ
	COFFEE, TEA, WATER						X	8 OZ
SNACK	FRESH BLUEBERRIES			X				
	BEVERAGE**							12 OZ
LUNCH	TURKEY ON WW BREAD, LETTUCE, TOMATO	XX	X			X		
	POTATO CHIPS						X	
	CARROT & CELERY STICKS		X					
	BEVERAGE							12 OZ
	COOKIES						X	
SNACK	CRACKERS AND CHEESE	X			X			
	BEVERAGE							12 OZ
COCKTAIL HOUR	CUCUMBER RINGS WITH CRABMEAT DIP		X			1/2		
	BEVERAGE						X	12 OZ
DINNER	GRILLED FISH					X		
	BROCOLLI		X					
	RICE	X						
	MULTIGRAIN ROLLS	X						
	TOSSED GREEN SALAD		X					
	BEVERAGE							12 OZ
DESSERT	BROWNIES						X	
	PUDDING				X			
	TOTALS	7	5	3	2.5	3	5	74 OZ
	USDA REC.SERV/DAY	6 - 11	3 - 5	2 - 4	2 - 3	2 - 3	NA	64 OZ

*Count large portions as double servings and small portions as partial servings
** Beverages: preferably, water. Also fruit juice or millk for children.

fruit, 3-5 servings vegetables, 2-3 servings dairy, 2-3 servings protein.

We did it! And on the first try too. I suppose we could even twist the truth a little and include brownies as grains, potato chips as vegetables and bacon as a protein. We're allowed to do that on vacation.

CREATE A TRIP PROVISION LIST

We discussed provisioning in an earlier chapter. If you chose to pre-stock your larder, you may have many of the items needed to complete our practice weekend menu. However, I promised you a sample stock-and-go plan, so here's one that also works through needed galley supplies.

Create a provision list by going through each menu item and listing the ingredients needed. Include garnishes like parsley, which can make a dull dish sparkle. It's easy to omit a utensil, seasoning or plate, so add these to your list. Having a list ensures that you won't forget a critical ingredient, like the barbecue grill for Saturday night's fish dinner.

Separate your weekend provision list into these three categories:

1. Bring to the boat: Check off items you have at home. If necessary repackage items into smaller containers, and then set them aside to be taken to the boat.
2. Have on board: Cross off any items that you know are already on the boat. (For the purposes of this exercise, let's assume you have nothing aboard.)
3. Buy: Items left over will become your grocery list.

PLANNING LOGIC

Let's work through our practice menu day-by-day to be sure we've accounted for everything we'll need to implement it.

Friday Night:
You've bought this entire meal ready-made from the supermarket. None of it needs to be heated, so all you will need is a means of keeping the perishable items cold. Don't forget to bring trash bags, as well as water for cleanup and personal use.

Buy	Bring to the Boat
Chicken (cooked or raw)	Pre-chilled cooler
Carrots and celery (ready-to-eat)	Trash bags
Brownies	Have on Board
Potato salad (unless making it)	Dinner plates
Soft drinks	Forks and knives
Milk	Napkins, or wet wipes
Paper towels	Washing water (boat tanks)
Ice	Paper cups (optional)

Saturday:
You will need one or two saucepans. One will suffice to make morning coffee or tea and to cook the broccoli in the evening. Add a second saucepan if you need to cook the rice and broccoli at the same time. Cook the longest-cooking item first—in this case the rice—and keep it warm while you cook the vegetable. One skillet is also needed to cook the pancakes on Sunday. In case of bad weather, you might need the skillet to sauté the fish indoors, instead of using the barbecue grill.

Your heat sources are a two-burner stove and a barbecue grill. Pack a potholder so you can handle hot cookware. Drinking water is needed to make coffee, tea and the rice. If you can't drink your boat's tank water, add bottled water. To wash dishes, pans and utensils that aren't disposable, you will need dish detergent. Use paper towels to dry the items, or pack a dishtowel.

Bring butter, margarine or cooking spray to use for cooking the pancakes, and seasoning for the fish, rice and broccoli. Bring salt and pepper in a moisture-proof container and leave it aboard for next time. Make or buy your favorite fish marinade, then seal the amount you will need in a leakproof plastic bag. For other dry seasonings, especially those you will use another time, repack some from home in a small container you can leave aboard. If you like a squeeze of lemon or lime on your fish or in your rum and Coke, add a fresh lemon or lime to your list.

<u>Buy</u>
Cereal
Bananas
Milk
Fruit juices
Coffee and tea
Coffee creamer (optional)
Sugar (optional)
Drinking water
Blueberries
Sliced turkey
Sandwich bread or rolls
Tomatoes
Lettuce
Potato chips
Cookies
Crackers
Cheese sticks
Beer, wine, cocktail mixers, and other alcoholic beverages (optional)
Cucumber
Crab dip
Fish

Fish seasoning
Fresh lemon
Broccoli (fresh or frozen in bag)
Rice (boil in bag or box)
Dinner rolls
Salad dressing
Pudding cups
<u>Bring to the Boat</u>
Mayonnaise
<u>Have on Board</u>
Bowls
Spoons
Coffee pot (optional)
Coffee filters (optional)
Two-burner cooktop
2 medium saucepans
1 skillet
Potholders
Barbecue grill
Charcoal and lighter fluid (optional)
Matches
Salt and pepper

Sunday:

If we are making the pancakes ourselves, we'll need a skillet; frozen pancakes can also be reheated in a skillet or a toaster oven if you want to bring one aboard.

Buy

Frozen blueberry pancakes or pancake mix

Butter or margarine

Maple syrup or other topping

Pears

Sliced ham

Sliced cheese

Pickles

Bring to the Boat

Mustard

Have on Board

1 skillet (already listed) or toaster oven

Now, all you need to do is create a grocery list and find a well-supplied store. See Chapter 25 for smart shopping strategies.

TEST YOUR MENU

Hold off shopping until you can test this menu against your activities to be certain you've built-in enough flexibility and serving options. So far, we've discussed preparing and serving a weekend menu with the boat at rest. As you well know, however, stays on the boat are always somewhat of a surprise. Realistically, the foods you choose to serve at any given time will depend on the weather, sea and other travel conditions. So, let's complicate things a bit and see if our menu can tolerate change.

Arrive Friday Night: three-hour sail to Block Island

Planned menu: Cold chicken

                             Potato salad

                             Carrot sticks

                             Canned or bottled beverage

On Friday evening your plans are to go to Block Island, Rhode Island, for the weekend. It can be a four-hour sail or a one-hour motor trip, depending on your boat. Our meal of cold chicken is just the thing. I would serve it once we have cleared the harbor and are on course to Block Island. Fix the plates in the galley with each person's portion of chicken and potato salad, complete with utensils. Set the roll of paper towels or package of wet wipes and a trash bag in a secure spot in the cockpit. Use sturdy plastic or paper plates with lips or shallow bowls to prevent food from spilling over. Wrap and rechill leftovers, and put plates and utensils that need to be washed in the sink to deal with once you arrive.

If the seas are feisty, hand the chicken pieces up in a single, sturdy basket or pot that can be easily passed from person to person. Everyone can eat it off the bone and then clean their hands with paper towels or wet wipes. The bones can go overboard if you are far enough from shore. Save the potato salad for another meal, but pass around the bag of carrots. Fat-laden foods can be heavy on the stomach in rough seas, so use your discretion about serving the brownies. Read more about "meals in motion" in Chapter 26.

<u>Saturday Sail to Long Island</u>
Planned Breakfast: Cereal and sliced bananas with milk
                       Juice, coffee, tea, hot chocolate

Suppose you decided to get up Saturday morning and set sail from Block Island to Three Mile Harbor, Long Island, a two- to four-hour trip depending on boat speed. You want to be there by lunch, so you will eat breakfast underway.

Breakfast Underway
The waters are often calm early in the morning, so you will likely be safe sending prepared bowls of cereal, already fixed with the sliced bananas and milk, up into the cockpit. If you purchased individually boxed cereal, you can eliminate washing a bowl by slicing the boxes open along the perforations at the back. Serve juices in individual cans, boxes or plastic bottles. Pass up fixed coffee cups. When dealing with any liquid in the cockpit, it's important to be sure it will not spill. Avoid using open cups and glasses, and set drinks in a holder or a slip-resistant spot.

Bouncy seas again? Pass up the cereal boxes and eat it dry, along with whole bananas. The peels can go overboard as long as you are out of sight of land. Cereal in larger pieces—like Quaker Oat Squares and Crackling Bran O's—makes a good, late-morning finger-food snack as well. Wash it all down with cups of milk.

<u>Saturday Lunch: *still underway*</u>
Turkey sandwiches w/tomato, lettuce
Potato chips
Carrots and celery
Beverage
Cookies

At lunchtime we are still underway, and all stomachs aboard are growling. Meals seem to come around quicker when you are on the water, and noshing is a fine way to pass the time on a tedious trip. If you were smart, you made sandwiches while the coffee was perking, in anticipation of a late arrival. Otherwise, calm your crew with a snack until you reach shore, or venture below and try to rustle up something despite the bounce.

When you prepare a meal underway, omit some of the niceties and keep tasks simple. Tomatoes can be a nuisance to slice and may slip messily out of a sandwich. To enjoy them underway, place wedges in a small bowl and pass it around. Cherry and the tinier grape tomatoes are very versatile, but devilish to trap. If their containers spill they will roll around like a splatter of tiny beads. Dessert? Pass the bag or box of cookies.

<u>Saturday Dinner: on anchor</u>
Grilled fish
Broccoli
Rice
Rolls
Salad
Beverage

It's a gorgeous night, and you're enjoying cocktails and hors d'oeuvres in the cockpit. The captain has fired up the grill and will cook the fish, so all you need to worry about is fixing the vegetables and rice. Open up the cockpit table and send up the plates. When the fish is done, bring the rice and broccoli into the cockpit and serve them out of their pans. Hot pans will need to be placed on a folded dishtowel or a padded potholder. After dinner, put on a pot of coffee or tea to go with dessert or have another cocktail and watch the stars light up the evening sky.

If it's dinnertime and you are *still* underway, you picked an awfully long trip to complete on a weekend. Check your heading, because Three Mile Harbor is a scant four-hour sail from Block Island, unless you're tacking your way over. It would be a juggling act for the unseasoned boater to prepare and serve our planned meal while on the move. Using a grill in anything but the calmest waters would be foolish; and making this meal requires coordinating and handling up to three pans worth of hot food.

So, let's change our menu to something easy. If you have leftover potato salad and chicken, send it up cold. Otherwise, put out some crackers and cheese, or make more turkey sandwiches. No more turkey? Dip into the ham intended for Sunday lunch. If you knew before you left that you would be traveling through the dinner hour, you might have swapped meals and had the fish dinner on Friday, saving the chicken for Saturday. What should you do with the unused fish? If you feel it will spoil, cook it the next morning. Have it for breakfast or chill it and make fish sandwiches for lunch (and take home the ham). If you feel it will last, cook the fish later in the day and enjoy it for Sunday evening's dinner.

<u>Sunday: returning home</u>
Pancakes and bacon
Juice, coffee, tea, hot chocolate

Hopefully, you've hit landfall by now and are enjoying a lovely morning at anchor. You've earned a big breakfast. If your engine is running, though, I guarantee that unless the captain is merely charging the batteries, you'll be moving soon. If you don't have time for the planned, leisurely pancake repast, drag out the cereal again and offer blueberries. If you went to shore or took the dog in for his constitutional early this morning, you might've picked up some fresh muffins or pastries. These are always a treat and can be handled underway with one hand, as long as you don't mind a few crumbs. If you've got frozen pancakes, toast them and send them on up instead of toasted bread.

If you departed after breakfast for home, lunch will likely be taken underway. Make the sandwiches before you leave and tuck them in the icebox, individually wrapped in foil and collected in a basket or large plastic bag. Leave chips in their bag and pass around the pickle jar, along with a fork, toothpicks or a pickle plucker—yes, there is such a thing.

Ham sandwiches

Pickles

Potato chips

Beverage

Ahoy, you should be pulling into your homeport before long. If you survived thus far, you're pretty much ready for anything. Longer trips are just extended weekends!

Kitchen Afloat proverb
  All that glitters isn't food.

Chapter 25
Smart Shopping

Time to go shopping? Do your best to find a well-supplied market that will allow you to get everything you need for your cruise in one stop. Start your shopping with a cartless stroll through the aisles to find out what is available—no need to buy anything yet.

NEW PRODUCTS

The shelves are brimming with why-didn't-they-think-of-it-sooner conveniences. Use your "galley eyes" to envision the many ways you can use some of the newest ideas. You may opt to buy an item, or simply copy the concept. There are a dizzying array of packages and modes for each food. You can stand in the aisle for hours just contemplating what kind of vinegar to buy! Choose from the different cans, bags, boxes, squeeze bottles and rip-open bubble packs. Even staples like flour now come in resealable plastic bags. Canned soup and tuna, in addition to boxed mixes, are available in vacuum-sealed foil pouches and bubble packs, which are easy to store aboard.

Meal Kits and Prepared Foods

The aisles abound with new forms of instant meals, in addition to the familiar add-water-and-serve variety. Entire dinners like spaghetti with meat sauce are packaged ready to microwave or heat stove-side in provided containers. Taco kits have been around forever, but the appetizer portions of chili-and-cheese dip and chip combos are new.

In the produce section, you'll recognize the salads-in-the-bag display that has ousted many a head lettuce from the shopping cart. These packed-to-go, triple-washed treats make a salad for four or can be used by the leaf for sandwich fixings. Complete salads that include dressing packets, croutons and other trimmings are being made even more tempting with the additions of cooked chicken and even the bowl. Also in the produce section, look for ready-to-eat celery (some with dip), carrots, packaged coleslaw mix, pre-peeled and sliced onions and potatoes, and ready-to-cook vegetable mixtures with sauce packs. Bear in mind that prepared produce is a poor pick for long trips.

Vacuum-packed to Last

Isn't vacuum sealing wonderful? Now we can buy fresh beef, pork tenderloins and other meats that not only stay fresh longer, but can be tossed about like footballs without making a drippy mess. Processed or fully cooked foods may last for over a month if kept refrigerated, and many items can also be frozen. Check the sell- or freeze-by date and match it to your trip length. Cold cuts and cheeses packaged in this manner are a boon for extended cruises. I've found that the roast beef and turkey are a bit tasteless, but the ham and cheese products are just fine.

Stop by the fully cooked, processed meat department where the ham and bacon live. You can buy precooked bacon that doesn't need to be refrigerated except during a heat wave. Lloyd's barbecued products are staples on my boat. A rack of prepared, ready-to-warm beef or baby back ribs cost little more than buying them raw. Also peruse the seasoned, cooked and packed-to-last chicken choices, as well as the many ham products. We brought a whole, cooked Tyson chicken on our last cruise, froze it for weeks, and found it tasted even better than store chicken when reheated. Tyson also packages cooked chicken pieces that make a dinner base or can be added to salads. The small, sealed packages of cooked half hams and turkey breasts keep quite well and are versatile.

Fresh Meats, Too

In the refrigerated meat case, you'll find that fresh steaks, tenderloins and chicken pieces are also being vacuum-packed. Sealed in this manner, meats will stay fresh longer than they would if packaged in the standard Styrofoam tray, and they won't leak smelly juices into the icebox. Also find pre-seasoned and pre-marinated meats, as well as kits for preparing such delights as chicken fajitas and chicken Parmesan.

Eat and Goes

Today, healthy snacks and quick meals come individually wrapped in containers small enough to fit in a pocket or purse. Aboard, these make quick grabs that can be doled out whenever needed for an energy boost. Find cereals prepackaged with a serving of milk and a spoon in the dairy case, in individual travel pouches or in bar form. Try yogurts with spoons built-into the lid or in a freezable, squeeze-to-eat package. Snacks like crackers and cheese, chips and salsa, humus and crackers, peanut butter and jelly, tuna salad and crackers, and graham crackers and applesauce come in one-portion sizes with tiny plastic knives.

Food for kids can be food for adults, too. Check out quick-fix meals and lunchbox fare. Individual soups, stews, hot cereals and meals like macaroni and cheese come canned in microwaveable containers; some have metallic bases that can sit in boiling water for reheating. There are cheese sticks, mini puddings, Jell-O packs, fruits and drinks like Parmalat milk and vacuum-boxed juices for kids with a straw (plain, 100-percent juices—orange, apple, grape—are buried among the sweet combos for the young ones). The list goes on as new, great-for-the-boat items pop up daily.

Wise Buying

With such a mind-boggling array, decision-making can be difficult. Match your needs to the product. Balance time and convenience with money spent. Pre-prepared and precooked items will cost more, as they are more labor-intensive, but they require less preparation time and leave fewer leftovers to contend with.

Some staples are ultra-practical to keep aboard because they have uses other than for cooking. Use vegetable oil for everything, even in a salad. It also is a safe lubricant for plastic, fiberglass or moving metal parts. White vinegar cleans many boat surfaces, is invaluable for dissolving built-up minerals clogging hoses and drains, and also works for freshening head odors. Fresh or bottled lemon or lime juice is a delightful way to revive a tired fish or chicken dish, spike a cocktail, or degrease and deodorize sticky cooking hands. Baking soda goes beyond cooking and baking to deodorize and clean an icebox and remove stains without the harshness of commercial cleansers—it even douses a fire!

EXPEDITE SHOPPING AND LIST-MAKING

Any major shopping excursion deserves a well-thought-out list. Your list will include items that need to be replenished, as well as those required to execute your meal plan. In the last chapter, we created a menu and from it a "buy" list. Now, let's organize this supply list to speed up your trip around the grocery store.

If you make it a habit to organize your grocery list by food type or department, you'll find your shopping will stay on track and you'll be able to quickly locate all the items on your list, no matter what size or type of market. Every store is divided by department: meats, dairy, produce, canned and dry goods, delicatessen foods, health foods, baby foods, drugstore items, cards and books. Use these categories to set up your shopping list. This is what I do.

Take a small piece of paper or the back of a 3 1/2-by-6 1/2-inch envelope—stash coupons inside—and mark headings.

This process has served me well since I began doing it as a young bride, and it has become automatic. Whenever I plan a store trip, I begin by setting up an envelope or similar paper with headings, write in items I am low on, and then supplement the list with other items needed, perhaps to complete a recipe or a planned meal. By the time I'm ready to shop, my grocery list is accurate and complete.

Grocery List Layout

List Layout (front)	
Meats	**Dairy**
chicken	milk
Fresh	**Frozen**
tomatoes	broccoli
onions	waffles
bread	
Dry	**Canned**
rice	tuna
cereal	soup
cookies	coffee

List Layout (back)
Household
paper towels
Lysol spray
toilet paper
Other
West Marine-new tote bags
Fish market-clams
Pharmacy-sun lotion

DEVELOP A GROCERY LIST

In Chapter 24, we developed a list of items to buy for our weekend menu. Now, let's figure out how much of each item we need to buy, based on our trip plan.

Serving Sizing

Buy only quantities you can use without waste or that you can comfortably store onboard. If you have done any amount of cooking, you may already be adept at estimating how much of each item you'll need to buy. Most recipes give the number of portions, not the number of people they will serve. Appetites vary. You might allot a half portion for a child and a double portion for a teenaged boy or robust man. Some will go for seconds; others will pick like pigeons.

Read the Label

The label on an outer package will list suggested serving sizes and other details about a particular food. By law it must include the net weight, all ingredients and a breakdown of calories, fats, proteins, carbohydrates, and sodium content. Look for low numbers under "total fat "and "sodium," and high numbers under "protein." Ingredients are always listed by quantity in descending order.

The number of servings per container is based on what the USDA lists as a serving size. This information is nice to have when deciding how much of an item to buy. I always find it interesting to see how many potato chips or fun-size chocolate bars are considered a serving. Once I have checked, I feel deserving of *at least* that amount.

Apply the Law of Averages

Dieticians have learned that the most accurate way to compute large quantities of food is to multiply out the average size serving, although some find these servings skimpy:

Allow a quarter pound helping of meat per person
Allow a half cup portions of vegetables per person

Factor In Your Common Sense

My Italian heritage has instilled in me the compulsion to overfeed my guests, so I tend to allow more generous portions than these. I've adapted the grocery list for our sample menu to reflect the amounts that I would buy for four adults. Naturally, you'll want to apply your own thoughts as to what is acceptable for your crewmembers.

Sample Grocery List

Let's assume our sample crew consists of two adult couples—two men, two women. Based on our practice weekend menu, our final shopping list might look like this:

Meats

2 small chickens (cooked or raw)

2 pounds fish

1 pound sliced turkey meat

$1/2$ pound bacon

1 pound sliced ham

$1/2$ pound Swiss cheese

2 pounds potato salad (unless you are making it)

Fresh

1 large container blueberries

1 bunch bananas (about 6)

1 lemon or lime

3 tomatoes

1 bag carrots (ready-to-eat or whole)

1 bunch celery (prepared or whole)

1 head lettuce (or prepared salad in a bag)

1 head broccoli (or 2 packages frozen)

1 family size batch home-made brownies (or 1 dozen purchased)

1 loaf sliced bread or 8 sandwich rolls

6 dinner rolls

Dairy

1 quart milk

1 pkg. individually wrapped cheese sticks

1 container butter, margarine or cooking spray

Frozen

2–3 bags ice

2 packages green giant bubble pack Broccoli

Dry

1 regular size box cereal (or 1 package of assorted, individual boxes)

1 box sugar (individual packets)

2 bags potato chips

2 boxes or bags cookies

2 boxes crackers

1 package pancake mix or frozen pancakes

1 packet boil-in-bag rice-serves four

Canned

2 48 oz bottles or cans juice, or 3 packages (6/per pkg.) individual juices

1 pound coffee and/or 1 small box tea

1 small jar mayonnaise

1 package (6/pkg.) individual pudding cups

1 small bottle maple syrup

1 jar pickles

1 small jar mustard

24 cans soda

2 large jugs water

1 12-pack beer, 1 bottle wine

Dry Goods

Paper dinner plates and bowls (optional)

Plastic spoon, knives and forks (optional)

Paper napkins

Paper towels

Dish detergent

Charcoal, lighter fluid, matches (optional)

Vary Your List

Now that you've got the consummate grocery list, it's time to be flexible in putting it into action. Use the list as a base, but be open to new ideas. Keep an eye out for store specials or foods that are in season. You may plan to buy broccoli, but find that the spears of asparagus on sale are more appealing. By the time you're through, your menu may be greatly altered. No matter. As long as you are substituting like items rather than adding or deleting essential ones, the show can go on.

PACK SMART

There is no need to shuttle the same food supplies about. Organize your packing procedure to move items as little as possible. Keep coolers and totes handy to loading and unloading areas.

At the Market

Just before your market trip, stash some boat bags and a cooler packed with a few frozen gel packs or a bag of ice in your car. Take a few minutes as you load your groceries into your car to re-sort them into the totes and cooler. Don't do extensive bag sorting at the supermarket checkout counter, unless you are ready to ignore the nasty glares and comments of all the other folks behind you in line. If you are going directly to the boat, there's no need to remove anything from your car. If you don't have a car or the means of transporting large quantities of supplies from the market to the marina, ask the marina to put you in touch with a local cab service. Some marinas also offer courtesy cars for guests.

At Home

As a rule, I keep spare boat bags both near the door of our garage and in the kitchen. As I gather needed items, I add them to the nearest bag or set them by the door. Avoid overloading bags to the point where they can barely be lifted. Distribute beverages and other weighty items among several bags, and use nonbreakable plastic bottles, cardboard boxes or puffy bags of chips to cushion glass bottles. Do this, and you will find that by the time you are ready to depart for the boat, much of your packing is done.

A WORD ABOUT SMALL MARKETS

There's nothing like a mega-supermarket for getting the job done; but for interim shopping, relish the homey feel of a small market. Yes, it costs more to shop at a small market; and they offer fewer brands, sizes and products than a full-scale market. But often you'll come across a hidden jewel, sparkling with friendliness, services and only the best kinds of foods. Joe the butcher may cut prime meat to order, grind his own hamburger and advise you on the best deals of the day. Clyde at the deli counter may use secret family recipes to tempt you with salads, interesting sandwiches, made-to-order-pizzas, or gourmet-cooked dinner foods; and Mary's bakery goodies make you drool. Eggs and produce may come from local farms and be the freshest tasting in the area. You maybe able to call in an order and pick it up later, or have them deliver it right to the marina for you. If you are in a strange harbor, ask around. You may be surprised to find that the best provisions can be had from that tiny hole-in-the wall market, less than a quarter mile away.

FOREIGN SHOPPING

We travel to foreign lands to experience them; and what better way to do this than to learn about their cuisine. Here's an opportunity to try new dishes, take advantage of locally produced foods and interesting spice combinations, and become intimate with the skills needed to negotiate a sale in a land where English may be optional and the money system a mystery.

The best way to learn how to shop in a strange country is to befriend a trusted local person and have him or her escort you to their favorite markets. I've found it best to not look too much like a tourist and to comply with the customs and dress of the area. In some countries, bare skin is frowned upon. If no one's thighs are showing, wear slacks, a skirt or a dress. Stay away from flashy clothes and expensive jewelry that flaunt wealth, and be conservative about displaying wads of cash. Leave the camera at the boat or hide it in your shopping tote.

Some countries love bartering, and their vendors expect customers to argue for the best deal. Do your part, and both you and the vendor will part ways with smiles. If you are accustomed to dollars and cents, trying to figure pesos, EC's, euros and bahts under the gun can be daunting. Bring along a calculator, so you can quickly convert the local price into an amount you can understand before agreeing to a purchase. In Cancun, we were appalled to find that we had paid $80, not pesos, for a bottle of very fine tequila. Other countries also use the dollar sign, so it pays to verify with a shopkeeper whether or not the prices are listed in *U.S. dollars*. In some instances, it may be vital to understand the weight system. Knowing how to calculate pounds and ounces doesn't necessarily prepare you to estimate in metrics.

Island Time

When you pull into a small island, prepare to accept whatever is available. If there is a market on the island it may be small and supplies extremely limited. If eggs didn't arrive on the boat and no chickens are on the island, you'll simply have to do without. Not all islands are capable of producing their own food, so many rely on a delivery boat to keep supplied. Learn where and when the boat comes in, because that is the time to get the best selection. Tortola is a larger island in the British Virgin chain, yet we found that it too suffers delivery problems. Produce arrives in Tortola once or twice a week. On Tuesday the tomatoes are pale and need to ripen. If you go back on Friday, those same tomatoes may be there, over-ripe and picked over; or the bin may be empty.

Locally grown produce is cheap and in abundance, but avoid the temptation to overload on it. You may get 1,000 bananas for $2, but unless you're very creative, it's unlikely you'll consume that many in two weeks. Even using your most creative culinary skills, the crew will know that their dinner is banana in disguise.

Larger islands and quality provisioning companies will obtain meats and canned and packaged foods from the States or from their mother country. In the British Virgin Islands, you'll find many English products. In Tahiti the products will be from France or Europe. Most of the best meat comes from the United States, and you'll often find it in the freezer cases of other countries. Local meat is sparse, and its availability depends on the types of animals that roam the islands. At a local market in Tortola, I found few choices.

Part of the appeal of an island is its lazy ways. Relax and enjoy the wait, and in time you'll have your supplies. If you are in St. Vincent and the Grenadines, you are apt to be approached by boat people, who motor about the various harbors offering delivery services to cruisers. They'll gladly bring you fresh lobster, bakery goods, produce and local crafts priced very reasonably. Wouldn't it be nice to have that kind of service in our U.S. harbors?

Okay, your cart has been filled to overflowing with goodies, and they're stowed safely away on board. It's time to go cruising!

Chapter 26
Meals in Motion

Should you embark on a lengthy trip or an overnight sail, it's almost certain you'll be doing galley time in a bouncing boat. There are many times when the seas are relatively calm, making galley work a rewarding diversion. But the weather is fickle and can change in a blink of an eye. Step outside. Feel the wind. Look at the sky. Listen to the weather report, and be prepared. Plan your meal-making strategy in accordance with the wind and sea conditions—the rougher the weather, the simpler the fare. Stow the galley, plan and prepare foods during calm periods, take safety precautions and be alert to signs of mal de mer.

SECURE THE GALLEY

Begin any departure with a well-organized galley. Clear extraneous gear off the countertops, and put away the porcelain cups and that fancy copper teapot. Wedge a cooler under the table, tuck the drip electric coffee pot in the corner under a pillow, stash the toaster in a locker and plop the vase of fresh flowers in the sink. Keep the breakable glasses, bottles and cups in your cupboards apart by stuffing dishtowels, potholders or place mats in between them. Tie down swinging baskets and lamps with a length of line. If you expect tumultuous seas, you need to be fastidious about stowing and securing everything. Lids, floorboards, cabinets and drawers will fly open and loose items that normally stay intact will flip off shelves. Hard-stow anything breakable and pad it well.

GET READY TO GO

I expect you have planned a menu and have a good selection of stores aboard. Doing as much advance preparation as possible is particularly helpful if you expect a difficult trip. If the winds are howling and the boat is sloshing about at rest, belowdecks is not going to be a good place to spend much time, unless it's flat on your berth. For a day trip taken under normal sea conditions, have snacks available, make sandwiches, see that the cooler or icebox is stocked with soft drinks and plenty of water, and place any other items you may need during your trip in the get-ready position. In boisterous seas, limit trips below by setting up a cockpit cooler.[32] Fill it with enough beverages, sandwich fixings and snacks to last for the duration of your cruise; or until you expect conditions to improve. Be certain to include plain crackers, ginger ale or Coke, a selection of seasickness remedies and frozen gel packs or ice to keep items chilled. Keep the cooler intact by lashing it in place.

Get a head start on overnight or longer trips by making your first day an easy one. Acquaint the crew with the whereabouts of the power bars, peanuts and cookies, and clearly mark lockers and cabinets with content lists. Set up the coffee pot; make the first day's breakfast and lunch, pack and amass individual snack bags, and have a bland, starchy casserole waiting in the icebox to be warmed for dinner.

MAKE WISE CHOICES

Consider not only what you will provide, but also how you will serve it. Choose foods that are easy to manage, and serve them in individual portions. For example, if you plan an early start and will be breakfasting on the move, your menu might include packaged juices, granola bars, yogurt, hardboiled eggs, fresh fruit and whole-grain muffins. Opt for one-pot meals that can easily be eaten with one utensil. Avoid serving items like a chicken breast or steak that need to be cut up to be eaten.

To reduce spilling and sloshing, serve nonchunky soups in insulated plastic mugs instead of bowls, since these can be held in one hand and sipped. Take a tip from offshore sailors, who eat their meals out of soup bowls, and avoid serving flat plates full of salads, sandwiches, and chips. Go for the one-handed sandwich that won't easily fall apart. Substitute hotdog rolls or sandwich wraps—closed at one end burrito style—for sliced bread and serve them wrapped in aluminum foil. Foil holds its shape and supports food better than limp plastic sandwich bags, plastic wrap or waxed paper. When you are finished, crush crumbs and papers into a foil ball for the trash.

When McDonald's came out with its line of shaker salads, little did the company know it had developed the ideal solution to serving salad aboard a moving boat. If you're a frequent Mickey D'er, wash and save the shakers for your trip; otherwise, partially fill tall, lidded plastic glasses with greens and other veggies. Adding any handy protein food—chicken bits, shrimp, tuna, cheese, or nuts—will elevate a simple salad to meal fare. Just before serving, add dressing and shake to mix.

Lightweight items like napkins, paper plates and potato chips will float about like butterflies unless they are anchored. Leave chips in their original bag to pass around or stow snuggly between two addicted passengers; or switch to pretzels or something healthy like carrot and celery sticks. Serve beverages in cans or plastic bottles with pull-to-sip tops, or use lidded, nonbreakable mugs or glasses with wide or nonslip bases. Keep a container of wet wipes available for cleanup afterwards. Mount a small plastic bag in the cockpit to hold trash until you can conveniently dispose of it.

Noshing Belowdecks

In foul weather, it may be necessary to have a snack or quick meal belowdecks—a feat for those with iron stomachs and good coordination. Wind will not be a problem, but the boat's movement will be more pronounced. Sit in a secure spot, as close to amidships as possible. Keep your hands wrapped around your sandwich, soda or bowl to keep it from shifting and spilling, or place it on a rubberized placemat and guard it closely. Concentrate on one item at a time. Shuffling between bites of a sandwich and sips of soda won't work unless you've located a snug holding spot for these items. Remember, overturned foods and drinks make for treacherous floors.

A DOZEN WAYS TO SAVE THE COOK

To prevent injuries, review these safety measures for galley-slaving underway.[33]

1. Anticipate the items you will need before beginning meal preparation. Assemble and organize them in a secure spot to keep them from rolling around. Locate and position cooking pots on the stove to avoid last-minute searches.

2. If you have a pressurized alcohol stove, fill it with alcohol while the boat is calm to avoid unnecessary spills.

3. Wedge yourself in a secure spot to maintain your position in the galley. Stand with both legs balanced and slightly apart. There will be a rhythm to this to which you will attune. In rough weather, lash yourself to the galley with a safety harness to keep from sliding or falling. To lower your center of gravity, do as much preparation work as possible sitting down.

4. If the boat is heeling, secure cooking supplies on the down side, so they won't slide onto the floor and drop onto your feet.

5. Work tight. Keep as few things out on the countertop as possible. Reseal and recap jars and boxes. Stow them away or keep them in the sink until conditions improve.

6. Think antiskid. Often you can purchase rubber banding that will slip around the base of an ordinary glass, cup or jar to make it nonslip. Buy a roll of rubber mesh matting and cut off a length to fit your preparation area or set down rubber mesh place mats.

7. If you are fortunate enough to have a microwave oven, line it with a rimmed holding container to catch splashes and spills when it gets tipsy underway.

8. If you plan to spend much time stove-side, wear a heat-resistant, waterproof apron to protect your body from being scalded from a hot spill and use potholders or oven mitts that grip well.

9. To prevent accidents, avoid dumping large amounts of hot pasta into a colander. The same goes for soup into bowls or heated sauces into another pan or container. Instead, use a strainer, slotted spoon or soup ladle to lift out and transfer small portions of foods into the receptacle.

10. If you are heating liquids, secure pots and pans with oventop clamps or fiddles. Fill pans only halfway to prevent boiling liquid from slopping over onto the boat and you.

11. Food in the oven? With the gimbaling on you'll need two hands to manage food removal: one to keep the gimbaling stable and the other to deal with the food. The oven will be hot, so do this carefully. If both hands are needed to tend to the food, lock down the gimbaling function, strap yourself in so you won't fall forward and go for the goods while timing the opening of the oven door with the roll of the boat. Good luck!

12. Line the countertop nearest the stove with a sheet of corkboard to make a heat-resistant haven for hot pans and casseroles.

NURSING SEASICKNESS

Tending to a seasick crewmember isn't exactly the cook's responsibility; it's everyone's. Seasickness is a byproduct of boating, and anyone who claims to never get sick is either fibbing or hasn't yet experienced the right conditions. Even my sea-hardy captain turns sickly green once in a while. Men, in particular, have a problem admitting it, even as they are bending over the lifeline in the throes of it all. Seasickness can attack when you least expect it; and it's much easier to prevent than to cure.

Avoid Unfriendly Foods

It's true, old sailors never set out to sea without having had a hearty meal. An empty stomach creates air and stomach acid, which invite the queasies when mixed well and shaken. Eating crackers often helps calm the turbulence, since crackers expand inside the stomach and absorb aggravating acids. High-fat, high-fiber and acidic foods will often upset an already finicky digestive system. To avoid a messy cockpit, keep it light and simple when the seas are up. A greasy breakfast of bacon, eggs and hash browns will sit in the stomach and rock-and-roll before exiting over the side. On a Tahitian charter, all five of us upchucked our way to Bora Bora when we encountered uncomfortable, post-storm seas after having downed healthy servings of butter-fried French toast and bacon.

In heavy weather, the smart cook offers starchy comfort foods like baked macaroni and cheese, bland soups and stews, crackers, carbonated drinks and tea. Keep the crew hydrated, but avoid citrus juices and coffee. One of the worst situations is beginning a trip with a hangover; all that goes down will invariably come back out—and it won't be pretty. On an extended trip, the first day is normally one of adjustment, so expect that appetites will be small and queasiness likely. I usually plan a chicken and rice meal, which sometimes gets reduced to servings of plain rice. Pasta is also a good solution, but omit any extra butter or oil.

Nausea-friendly Foods to Keep Aboard

White rice
White bread
Water crackers or saltines
Chamomile tea
Ginger ale
Ginger cookies
Coca-cola

Recognize the Symptoms

Motion sickness is caused by inner-ear disorientation, disturbing balance and leading to nausea. People react differently to this, resulting in a variety of symptoms that are often mistaken for other ailments such as dehydration, migraine headaches and laziness. A mildly seasick person may not experience nausea. Be suspect of any person aboard who is unusually quiet, yawning, pale, lying down or claiming to have cold sweats or feel lightheaded or "spacey."

Those in the Throes

Folks on the edge need to be out in the fresh air, so if possible have them stay on deck. Clean up messes quickly, positioning the sick one on the lee side (if conditions are safe) and provide them with a bucket and damp towel. Be kind when anyone aboard is green in the gills and steer the conversation away from the inevitable war stories about "the time when…"

And whatever you do, don't talk of food!

Natural Remedies

There are as many suggestions for curing motion sickness as there are for stopping the hiccups. Not everyone gets seasick in the same way, so it is only natural that people don't respond universally to stock treatments. Here are some ideas.

- Hand over the helm. For some, the concentration and distraction is enough to wash away the nausea. This works particularly well in dicey sea conditions.
- Watch the horizon or a fixed point to stabilize the inner ear. The problem is finding a fixed point that doesn't have everything around it in motion. It doesn't work for me, but it may help you.
- Ginger has no known side effects and has been proven to delay and reduce seasickness symptoms. All that is needed to avert nausea is a quarter teaspoon of any form of ginger: ginger ale, ginger cookies, ground or candied ginger, ginger root, ginger tea or ginger capsules.
- Topical herbal oil blends can be dabbed discreetly behind the ear, like a wonderfully scented perfume. I have found that Motion Eaze[34] counteracts the lethargic type of motion sickness (to which I am prone). This is important, because most remedies are geared to quelling nausea. This

oil can be applied and reapplied at any time, and takes effect within 10 or 15 minutes.

- One of the newer solutions, which I've yet to test but is supposed to be fast-acting, is an herbal-based mouth spray, developed for pilots, that contains ginger, vitamin B6 and a small amount of antihistamine.[35]
- Acupressure electronic magnetic pulse bands[36] work by applying pressure to a spot (the Nei-kuan point) on the inside of the wrist that is related to the body's nausea trigger. I've used acupressure bands for years. They are inexpensive and can help control borderline cases of motion sickness. I have found the electronic model works pretty much the same; however it is less comfortable to wear, requires more precautions and is costly. Both devices can be used in combination with other methods.

Prevention

"Do you get seasick?" Ask this question of anyone new you invite aboard. Some are ready to admit to it, while others will wait and see. When the subject is addressed at the onset of a trip, the power of suggestion may take over, so do your asking in a neutral spot well before the boat sets sail.

Those who are subject to motion sickness will normally come armed with an arsenal of prescription or over-the-counter remedies—or, they won't come at all. In addition to prescription drugs and the scopolamine patch, the pharmacy shelves offer several choices, many of which claim to cause less drowsiness than the remedies of yore. I keep aboard supplies of Bonine, since some boaters swear this one works the best, and Dramamine. In order to work, most drugs need to be taken about an hour in advance of departure, after which the medication will remain in the body for 12 to 24 hours. Alcoholic beverages exaggerate the sleepy side effects, so if you know a crewmember is on "the pill," don't be too quick to offer him or her a beer.

Once you find something that does the trick for you, stick with it. As a preventative measure on iffy days, I use a spot of herbal oil behind my ears or don sea cuffs as we are leaving. When I expect to sail in heavy waters, I take a half pill or less of an OTC motion sickness drug to head off a problem without rendering me useless. If conditions are particularly bad, I put on the cuffs and do the oil dab as well. I tested the new scopolamine patch on my last trip, and of our crew of four, I was the only person with an appetite for dinner the first evening out. I was thrilled until, after two days, I developed some side affects—a mild headache and some edema. So I think I'll stick with my original methods. It's a good practice to save the literature on any drug you take, so you can refer to the fine print when oddball symptoms occur.

Section Nine:
Provisioning for Special Trips

Having a block of time to spend aboard is one of the finest delights for any sailor, and taking a vacation of a week or more is a luxury. Those looking for a challenge may try a simple overnight sail or take on an offshore passage, but the majority of boaters are content to relax and cruise in vacation mode. In areas of the country where winter chills force us to put the boat away along with our summer clothing, many of us seek solace by embarking on a winter charter in tropical climates like the Caribbean.

We've thought through the logistics of our destination, crew and facilities and understand how to balance a meal. Now it's time to apply everything we've learned. In this section, I'll try to help you cope with the provisioning of and planning for all of these scenarios by sharing with you my thoughts and experiences.

Chapter 27
You're on Vacation!

Hooray! We've got some vacation time! Whether you own a boat, rent one or sail on someone else's, you are a recreational boater. Cruising vacations are times to rejuvenate while sharing the sport of boating with others. When it comes to food, this may translate into loosening the belt and gorging on sinful foods that might otherwise be turned down, or relaxing with easy-to-fix meals and snacks. With this style of boating, flexibility is key.

TRIP MANAGEMENT

Don't take the pleasure out of cruising by over-challenging yourself. Divide your trip into manageable legs, using charts and waterway guides to locate comfortable, convenient waystops. Balance your trip as you might your meals. Pace it to allow a blend of the quiet and natural with the bustle of more commercial harbors, so that everyone will return satisfied. Arrange to be at your furthest destination halfway through the trip, so your return leg can be just as enjoyable. If you travel an eight-hour day, make the next day a short one. Factor in layover time to avoid battling foul weather to get home. If you are new at cruising, join with fellow boaters to form a flotilla. Stretch your wings. Learn to navigate at night. Plan an offshore passage.

FLEXI-MENUS

Menu planning for harbor-hopping vacations can often be more of a challenge than provisioning for serious sailing trips, as frequent stops and sporadic jaunts are part of the fun. Trips of varying durations and with different types of destinations will be jammed together within a short season. They may even involve some nonboating activities like touring, biking and beach-bumming. This means you'll need to constantly rethink your menu for appropriateness and adjust your provisions accordingly.

Consider a multi-harbor trip as several weekends strung together. The best-planned vacations are a mix of both onboard and onshore dining. A harbor-hopper's menu needs to be adaptable and not necessarily as precise, especially if you've planned periodic stops at harbors where you can find a restaurant or easily replenish stores of bread, produce, dairy and meats. Once you've charted your float plan, gather information on each harbor you plan to visit, so you will know what to expect. Based on this, you will be able to estimate the number and type of meals needed aboard. Begin a trip by stocking enough fresh food to last until the first harbor where you are certain you can reprovision. Also be sure to load your dry lockers with sufficient nonperishable boxed, canned and bottled goods.

Most of the time, we travel on our own with our family or a crew of close friends. If we are lucky, we own the boat as well. Familiarity simplifies provisioning for a trip of any kind, because you've already worked through problems like how to get the funky oven lit, where to stash the bread so it won't get squished and how to estimate the life span of a bag of ice in the icebox. In addition, having the same crew means you know how much to buy and which foods will be enjoyed.

JOIN WITH OTHER CRUISERS

Attending a boating regatta or rendezvous or traveling in the company of other boats as you might in a club trip or flotilla adds a few twists to menu planning and provisioning.

Rendezvous and Regattas

It's great fun to attend a planned gathering of fellow boaters, meet new people, test skills and learn from talks by experts. Boaters come from afar, and there may be anywhere from 10 to 80 boats in attendance. Most boat manufacturers put on such events in conjunction with a local sales office. Once you sign up to attend, you will be provided an agenda that spans the event, usually held over a weekend. Typically, these take place at a major harbor, where restaurants and groceries are available. For planning purposes, this is how such an event might go:

- Arrival and check-in evening: Cocktail hour; dinner is either a potluck supper or on your own
- Mornings: Coffee and pastries along with meetings and seminars
- Lunches: Sandwiches, which you will make to bring to the day's events
- Last evening: The finale is often a cocktail party followed by an award dinner

Potluck

When a potluck dinner is on the agenda, be prepared to contribute a dish of some sort—a salad, casserole, dessert or appetizer. For a large event, I've found it easiest to make something at home and reheat it for the party. Or better yet, choose a dish that can be tossed together at the last minute without needing to be rewarmed or cooked, or that can be served cold—a chicken Caesar salad, for example. If you need to prepare your contribution aboard, start early lest you be left behind tending your creation while the captain and crew join the others for cocktails under the tent. Remember that it can take over an hour to warm a cold pan of lasagna! Too often we've arrived at large gatherings to find the heartier fare gone. For this reason, I try to bring a one-dish meal rather than a side or dessert, and it doesn't go on the table until we arrive. Affix a name label to the bottom of the dish and be sure to include a serving spoon or tongs. You'll be taking a dirty bowl back to the boat, so add a trash bag to your travel tote.

Club Trips/Flotillas

Learn about yacht club events through billboards at your marina or club newsletters. The trip may be a weekend jaunt or an extended cruise. Such trips involve fewer people than regattas or rendezvous, and usually center around an informal event like a gathering on the beach, a lobster-fest or clambake, a BYO food and booze communal barbecue, or an out-to-dinner night at a local restaurant.

Prepare for Parties

Any cruise becomes a flotilla when several boats travel together, keeping contact along the way and meeting at prearranged harbors. Having the expertise of more seasoned boaters is always a comfort when the fog rolls in or the seas get rough. Typically such trips include an informal group party, so pack up the makings of a side dish or dessert to contribute and come prepared with ideas and ingredients for attractive appetizers for the inevitable cocktail hour. With our flotilla group, with whom we've cruised for many years, we host cocktails or dinners aboard round-robin style. This means having a supply of libations to offer along with some extra snack food. An unwritten law of the sea is that when invited to another's boat it's customary to bring a bottle of wine, a six-pack of beer or an hors d'oeuvre of some sort. Arrive on any boat with your first drink in hand, and your host and hostess will love you.

Pack Versatile Foods

There are certain items I've learned to take along on each trip, because they are versatile enough to work as either a snack or a meal. Friends are always delighted to see a warmed plate of wings or ribs, and I've used chili as both a fast meal and a hot cocktail-hour dip served with pita or tortilla chips. Hotdogs keep well, are easy picnic fare, provide a hot lunch on a cool day and work as a snack when cut up into circles and arranged on a pretty platter with toothpicks and a spicy dip—anything but plain-old mustard. We seldom eat bacon at home—too many calories and too much cholesterol—but I almost always pack some for vacation. On a leisurely layover day, I guarantee that at some point the smell of frying bacon will emanate from a nearby boat, and your crew will want some. Besides, leftover cooked bacon makes good BLTs or can be tossed into salads or soups.

Fancy spreads and sauces make tasty marinades or sauces for a block of cream cheese or a wedge of Brie and, if used sparingly, can turn a basic sandwich into a gourmet treat. As one boating buddy says, "It's all in the presentation." My fruit basket often includes a ripening avocado, which I can slice up on a sandwich, add to a salad or turn into a cocktail-hour guacamole dip. Leftovers will keep a day and, when spread on a sandwich, will liven up deli ham or turkey. See Chapter 30 for more ideas. Other fresh items I routinely pack are a few onions and enough potatoes for a side dish—baked potatoes or potato salad. Hotdog and hamburger rolls and soft tortillas for wraps also find many uses aboard.

Meals and Snacks

As sandwiches are the mainstays of a boating vacation, I provision for enough lunchmeat to last three meals. Dinner meats and seafood are the hardest to keep, so I am careful about what and how much I bring. For example, when we go to Cuttyhunk, I know we will be in port in time to buy fresh lobsters or seafood from the dock. But as an emergency meal, I might bring a pound of frozen ground beef, which could be used as a base for spaghetti sauce or to make hamburgers.

Advance Tactics

Select a few boat-hardy recipes and keep the needed ingredients on hand so you can pull a special creation out of your galley for any occasion. I get a head start on the trip by making or buying basic items in advance. Our first day out is always a long one, so we get an early start and have breakfast underway. I often boil some eggs to have on hand as an easy-to-eat protein source. The shells can go overboard. Leftover eggs make deviled eggs or can be used to enhance salads or sandwiches. Pack a cake of some sort that can be dressed up with fruit and Cool Whip or canned frosting for an unexpected celebration.

Add an Herbal Touch

Often I purchase an inexpensive herb plant to bring along. Last year's was an oregano plant; the prior year, I took basil. I tuck the little plant in a snug nook in the galley and water it when I think of it. Throughout the trip, I snip away, adding bits to season whatever I am preparing. Fresh herbs taste superior to the dried ones and make a decorative garnish that is unexpected on a boat.

SAMPLE FLOTILLA MEAL PLAN—10 DAYS, 6 BOATS

The partial menu below will give you the gist of the planning process involved for the trip our flotilla takes to Cape Cod each summer. Because I know what to expect at each harbor, I can shop from harbor to harbor and plan local specialties into my menu. By researching your destination, you too will know when and where you can supplement your boat provisions with local seafood, produce and onshore meals. You will note that there are only two days during this trip that require that all meals be prepared aboard. Since much of the provisioning is done on the fly, take your notes with you to remind you of your original plan and help you to adapt to deviations. Once you have laid out your itinerary, focus on provisioning for those days you will spend most time aboard. Plan to obtain fresh supplies every few days. This will allow you to change plans without feeling guilty about meat festering in the fridge. (It took me a few years to figure this out.)

Day 1: Noank, Connecticut to Cuttyhunk, Rhode Island (8-hour sail)

Breakfast and lunch aboard. Buy lobsters at Cuttyhunk for dinner. This port has limited facilities, but is known for its fresh fish and lobsters. Cuttyhunk Shellfish Farm provides shrimp, oysters and clams throughout New England and has a traveling raw bar that services the harbor and is for us a highlight of this stopover. The island is dry, so BYOB or you will be too.

($2^1/_2$ meals, 2 snacks)

Breakfast underway: Muffins, hard-boiled eggs and coffee. Put remaining coffee in a thermos if you wish to sip it for a while after you leave. Also, make and store sandwiches for lunch.

Snack underway: Crackers and juice

Lunch underway: Roast beef on roll with lettuce and tomato, fresh pears, beverage

Snack after arrival: Cookies, beverage

Cocktail party with group: Get shrimp, clams from Cuttyhunk Raw Bar

Dinner on board: Take dinghy into Old Squaw and order extra-large, cooked lobsters. Make a fresh green salad to go with them. Serve rolls. Save leftover lobster meat to sauté in butter for sandwiches or to make into an appetizer.

Day 2: Layover day at Cuttyhunk

(2 meals, 3 snacks)

Breakfast: Ashore at Cuttyhunk Fishing Club

Lunch: Make turkey sandwiches, carrot sticks, chips and sodas for the beach (will need a traveling cooler). At beach, collect mussels from rocks to prepare for appetizers

Appetizer/ Dinner: Party on the beach. Steamed mussels cooked in pot over fire on beach. Also bring pretzels and dip. We'll grill hamburgers and hotdogs. Contribute hamburgers and rolls to party. Bring large bowl of pasta salad. (If it rains, we will move the party to one of our boats.)

Day 3: Cuttyhunk to Martha's Vineyard (4-hour sail)

Replenish fresh supplies if needed. Breakfast and lunch aboard. Dinner ashore.

(2 meals 2 snacks)

Breakfast at Cuttyhunk harbor: Muffins or cereal with fruit, juice and coffee

Lunch underway: Ham sandwiches, pickles, chips, beverage

Snack on arrival: Beverage, apple

Appetizer to bring: Leftover lobster on bed of lettuce with homemade dip

Day 4: Martha's Vineyard to Nantucket (4-hour sail)

Breakfast and lunch aboard, dinner ashore. No large market within walking distance.

(2 meals 2 snacks)

Breakfast: Bagels with peanut butter and jam, coffee, juice

Lunch: Tuna sandwiches with tomato and lettuce, carrot sticks, chips, beverages

Snack: Pears, beverage

Appetizer on board: Crackers, cheese and summer sausage with hot mustard

Dinner ashore

Day 5: Layover in Nantucket
Replenish fresh supplies. Supermarket in harbor area. Breakfast and dinner aboard, lunch ashore.

(2 meals 2 snacks)

Breakfast: Bacon and eggs, bagels, juice, coffee

Snack: Apples, beverage

Appetizer for party: Spicy chicken wings with blue cheese dressing and celery stick, purchased at supermarket on shore (bring wet wipes), beverage

Dinner aboard: Grilled steaks, grilled zucchini halves and pasta salad (leftover from Cuttyhunk party). Dessert is pound cake with whipped cream and fresh strawberries, beverage

Day 6: Nantucket to Hadley Harbor (7-hour sail)
Begin of return to Noank. No facilities at Hadley. All meals aboard.

(3 meals, 3 snacks)

Breakfast: Yogurt, muffins, juice and coffee

Snack: Dry cereal, beverage

Lunch: Roast beef sandwiches with lettuce and tomato, pickles, cookies, beverage

Snack: Apple, beverage

Appetizer for party: Make-do shrimp cocktail

Dinner: Grilled chicken, homemade parsleyed potatoes, carrot and celery sticks, bakery brownies

Day 7: Hadley to Newport (3-hour sail)
Breakfast and lunch aboard, dinner ashore.

(2 meals 2 snacks)

Day 8: Newport to Block Island (4-hour sail)
Breakfast and lunch aboard. Dinner ashore.

(2 meals 2 snacks)

Day 9: Layover at Block Island
Replenish fresh supplies if needed. Breakfast on board (delivered by Aldo's Bakery boat). Lunch ashore. Dinner aboard.

(2 meals 3 snacks)

Day 10: Block Island to Noank (3 hours)
Return to home port. Dinner ashore or at home.

(2 meals, 2 snacks)

Kitchen Afloat proverb
If it sounds too good to be true, it isn't.

Chapter 28
It's a Rental

Congratulations! You're flying to some beautiful Caribbean Islands where you'll be chartering a boat. On this type of cruising, it's common to bring our vacation attitudes along with us and hope that everything will be in place to meet our needs. This isn't always so, unless you've chosen a crewed charter with a hired cook. You may be traveling as a family or with a group of friends. Either way, as the host you're in charge. You've got everything figured out except the food thing. The charter company offers provisioning, but some friends who went last year swear it's better and cheaper to do it yourself. What should you do?

SELF-PROVISIONING

Doing your own provisioning always sounds like fun. You envision your gang happily promising to bring favorite foods, and then once you arrive, you'll all pile in a cab to a local market to buy the rest. At first, it seems like a food-gathering fest, the preliminary step in a fun-packed vacation. Several discussion sessions, however, will sow seeds of regret in most, as the amount of planning and physical labor involved in self-provisioning unfolds. As we have always traveled with other couples and the expenses are divided, I can say that self-provisioning entails more work than I care to do on a vacation. However, if my husband and I were footing the entire bill and responsible for feeding our family, I might feel differently.

There are several benefits to handling your own provisioning. You can control costs by selecting markets with the best prices and quality foods. If you are bringing foods from home, you can save additional time and money by preparing meals in advance and by shopping for sales at familiar markets. The down side of self-provisioning is that there is more to worry about and do.

If you opt to do your own provisioning, either by choice or by necessity, begin by planning a menu, using the process we discussed earlier. Sit down and arrange your itinerary, as you might on a harbor-hopping vacation. Decide how many nights you will dine out and at which harbors it's likely you'll partake in meals ashore.

Shop On Arrival
If you plan to defer shopping until you reach your vacation destination, it's helpful to be familiar with its offerings. Contact the local charter company by fax or e-mail

and inquire about the proximity of local markets. If you are planning to cruise among small island groupings, using the charter company's provisions will save much grief and unnecessary disappointment, as choices may be limited and costly.

Combo Plan: Pack, Ship, and Shop

Prepare and freeze meals to bring along. One expert suggests cooking a double recipe of each meal at home and freezing the extra batch in disposable pans.[37] Use the packing method described for long-term cold storage in Chapter 5. Ship by carrier, or check frozen supplies as luggage at the airport. To ship, place foods in a well-taped Styrofoam cooler, labeled "ship's stores." Omit your return address to avoid having the melted mess greet you at home. Should you decide to check the cooler as luggage at the airport, don't pack it with dry ice. If the box does not arrive with your flight, sit tight. There is still hope. Last year our cooler bag of meat, all specially flash-frozen at the butcher shop, turned up one day late and, amazingly, was still solidly frozen.

In the event your supplies don't make it, carry your original shopping list, menu and extra cash, so you can replace lost foods. Once you arrive, you may need to take a cab to purchase fresh fruit, vegetables, dairy products and bakery goods. Major charter companies often have provisioning facilities on the premises, so it's possible you can pick up what you need there.

CHARTER COMPANY PROVISIONING

A reputable charter company can provide a greater variety of high-quality food than you can find at local markets, since it will import foods to appeal to a variety of palates. Many companies offer several levels of provisioning, as well as captain and cook services. Choose from full, split or custom provisioning. Your charter package should include menus, supply lists and costs for each of these arrangements. Menu plans are based on a one-week charter, so if yours is two weeks long, expect to receive the same items, doubled.

Menu-driven Provisioning

This is a good and easy way to be supplied, especially if you're a first-time charterer, since it eliminates some of the confusion in getting settled. The charter company charges for provisioning on a per-person basis. Full provisioning means you will be provided with enough food to eat all meals aboard. Split provisioning is the most popular, as it allows for a few nights of restaurant dining. It includes enough food for a week's worth of breakfasts, lunches and snacks, as well as three or four dinners.

With menu-driven provisioning, there is often a list of supplies by category that you can review. This is the grocery list for the menu provided and also what you can expect to be delivered to your boat in boxes and bags prior to departing on your chartered boat. When you are in the planning stages of your trip, have each person who will be on the charter review the supply list and check off items they will *not* eat. You may be able to make some changes before the food is delivered to your boat, otherwise you will need to cart unwanted items back to the provisioning post and exchange them for ones you prefer.

Translating a Charter Company Menu

A charter company menu reads like a restaurant menu, which can be deceiving, because you are still doing all the food preparation, cooking, serving and cleanup. It doesn't take long to figure out the hidden meaning behind a sumptuous-sounding menu. Here's wording taken from an actual menu.

Suggested Menu for Split Provisions

Day 1- boat pickup begins at noon

Lunch:	Toasted ham and cheese sandwiches, stuffed with slices of lean ham and Swiss or American cheese melted to perfection, accompanied by pineapple wedges and chips
Hors d'oeuvres:	Veggies and zesty curry dip
Dinner:	Barbecued chicken basted in sauce accompanied by oven-baked potatoes with your favorite topping, old-fashioned coleslaw, fresh steamed vegetables
Dessert:	Fresh tropical fruit compote and cookies

Remember that your first day is busy. You will be attending a briefing on the use of the boat and its systems, and hauling and unpacking your belongings. Boats are normally turned over to charterers at noon, unless there is a holdup, such as a mechanical problem. We had a blowfish caught in our exhaust pipe one year, and it was late afternoon before we could leave the dock. We've found the better the reputation of the charter company, the fewer the delays.

Tasks Involved

If you do your own cooking, it is likely you will simplify this menu. The only way your sandwiches will be "melted to perfection" is if you leave them in the sun too long. What sane boater will want to be belowdecks toasting sandwiches and coring pineapple when it's time to set sail? You'll serve cold ham and cheese sandwiches, pass around a bag of chips and save the pineapple for another time. Trying to do this menu underway, or even at the dock, will be a sweaty, messy task that will take your time and attention away from the day. The veggies needed for the hors d'oeuvres and for dinner need to be cleaned and prepared. You'll be slicing, dicing and shredding the cabbage and carrots for the old fashioned slaw. Ditto the fruit compote for dessert. Also, the chicken will be frozen, so it will need to be defrosted, rinsed off and prepared for the fire.

Supplies Provided

Another thing the menu tells you is what foods will be supplied on your boat. Some charter companies provide an organized provision list to accompany the menu. If not, you can create your own from the suggested menu. Based on this suggested first-day menu, you should find:

Ham
Cheese
Sandwich bread
Potato chips
Fresh pineapple and other tropical fruits
Packaged zesty curry dip
Barbecue sauce
Chicken, enough to feed your group
Baking potatoes
Cabbage
An assortment of fresh vegetable, such as carrots, onions, peppers and
    squash
Cookies

Note: If you check the supply list, you will probably find mustard, mayonnaise and butter or margarine (to fry the sandwiches in).

Custom Provisioning

Some provisioning companies will deliver a custom order to the boat, so you may be able to preorder what you will need to fill out a menu you have planned. Ask to have a list of available food supplies faxed or sent. The Ample Hamper in Tortola has a Web site, which allows you to place an order on-line. Before making your selection, review the list carefully to see what is (and is not) available. Keep a calculator handy to determine how much you will need for the number of people on board, and take into consideration the package size of each item. A bottle of juice, for example, may be sold by individual 12-ounce sizes or in 48-ounce cans. This is good to know when you are ordering multiple cases.

I have used both split and custom, or a la carte, provisioning and find the custom provision plan offers more control. We recently used split provisioning and, having only one hour to inventory supplies and make exchanges, were left with a number of items we wouldn't or didn't use.

Pack Your Treats

Regardless of which method of provisioning you choose, it's always nice to bring along special foods you enjoy that may not be available in your cruising area. It's our tradition to keep a big box of chocolates cooling in the fridge on a charter trip. I have a special kind of coffee I love, so I always pack a pound or two for our charter. My captain is lactose-intolerant and can't have milk in his coffee, so if the provisioning company doesn't have nondairy coffee creamer on their list, I bring a large jar from home.

SETTLING IN

If you thought finding spots to unpack your clothes was difficult, wait until you try to stow a mountain's worth of provisioning in an unfamiliar galley. When you arrive, the galley will look very neat. In the cabinets, you'll take inventory of the number of pans with covers, dishes, cups, forks, spoons, cooking utensils and match boxes. This is the easy part. Take a last look at those neat cupboards, because that's where you'll be stowing the gargantuan load of supplies that will be heaped unceremoniously aboard your boat in cartons, bags or boxes. These will litter your countertops and the saloon table, and as soon as you think you've got it all, another load will have arrived and be sitting in the cockpit, screaming to be stowed. It's apt to be the frozen goods, so pay attention.

Before you set sail, all these supplies will need to be counted and stowed. You'll need to take inventory to see what is missing or has been substituted, and you'll need to do it quickly for the cold foods will defrost rapidly in the hot tropical temperatures. This is a sweaty job and often left to the would-be cooks, because the others are off learning how to operate the boat, certainly a more critical task.

Remain calm and in control. One of the problems is that in an effort to get the job done, supplies are often stowed helter-skelter, which ultimately makes a scavenger hunt out of locating a particular item. Take a minute to search out likely stowage areas, and point any assistants toward them. Take a systematic approach by grouping like items—snack foods, canned fruits and vegetables, paper goods and so on. If you can conveniently do so, mark down locations on the inventory list. If you are self-provisioning and have your own menu, create an inventory control worksheet prior to your trip and use this. There is never any air in a slip, so by the time you're through, your special crew T-shirts will be sweat-soaked, and you will be badly in need of a cold soda, which hasn't yet had time to chill. That's when you realize you need to buy more ice. Ice is critical. Get enough!

Heed the Briefing

No matter how involved you are with stowing provisions, at the very least make sure to listen to the instructions on lighting the oven, operating the refrigerator, changing over the water tanks, running the generator or inverter, turning on the engine, and turning on and hooking up the CD player. Knowing how to operate these basics can be invaluable, even critical, at times.

Get Off the Dock

All this comes on top of trying to leave the dock and dealing with growling stomachs, because it is now, of course, well past lunchtime. Despite all the provisioning ado, departure always brings instant relief. The feel of fresh cool wind and the movement of the boat through turquoise waters calm the confusion. It's time to don bathing suits, consume quarts of water, stuff yourself with the quickest sandwiches you can make and instantly swing into vacation mode. If you plan to anchor at a spot without a restaurant, it's soon back in the galley trying to remember how far down in that pit of a freezer the steaks are stored, while the others are lathering their bodies with sun screen, flexing their muscles and tipping beer cans.

Leftovers

At the end of the trip, everyone is always dismayed at the thought of leaving un-used food on board. The first time we chartered, we trucked home jars and cans of this and that only to realize that the dollar value of what we had brought was minimal. Now, we limit ourselves to specialty items—local spices and sauces—that we cannot buy at home. Unused food, if it is still fresh and unopened, will never go to waste if left behind as a tip for the cleanup crew.

SHARE THE COSTS, SHARE THE WORK

On a charter, when costs are equally divided among several couples or individuals, we have learned to select a boat with a layout that allows equal accommodations: a double or single berth, head and a door to close for privacy. It is assumed we will all share the cooking, and it will be fun. Right? I'm not saying it can't be. We've had some of our best trips with couples who understand that everyone must do his or her part. But when the crew starts calling me *Mama Joy*, I know I'm in trouble, because I have just been dubbed the galley slave. Wait a minute. What happened to *my* vacation? And what about all the rest of the female species who got roped into the deal thinking they might enjoy a respite from dealing with the food. We want to eat it, not necessarily fiddle with it.

The food-handling issue starts out as a hassle and sometimes doesn't get much better, depending on the people in your group. If you've got some love-to-cook crew aboard, they may be happy to take over. On the other hand, if they don't, it could mean that the host or hostess is stuck with the meal preparation. Resent-ments build when the same people are doing the bulk of the work, and this isn't worth it. Vacation is for everyone.

I've gotten smart over the years and learned to judge my group. If people we've invited are the cooking kind (you'll know this because they will bring some of their favorite seasonings and recipes along, or make the first move to turn on the coffee pot and start making breakfast) then you are home free. But they have to *want* to do it or their lack of enthusiasm will spoil the trip for everyone. If you have an inkling that your group may let you down in the cooking area, here's a solution that has worked for us.

Hire a Cook!

Most charter companies offer captain-cook teams. We've had no need for a cap-tain, but a cook? YES! In the scheme of things, putting an official cook in the galley settles the whose-turn-is-it-now issue and allows *everyone* to relax and enjoy the trip. When the cost is divided among several couples, it really is minimal. Depend-ing on the area and charter company, a hired cook may cost as little as $60 to $100 a day. Divided by three couples, this may only add $20 to $35 dollars a day to the total trip cost—a pittance to pay for a major relief. If you decide it's worthwhile to hire a cook, you will also need to buy provisions for an extra person and allot to the cook a private sleeping and grooming area on your charter boat. This could mean renting a slightly larger boat, which will cost more. Just think "vacation" and shell out the extra bucks.

What we love about having a cook is that when we arrive, all the food has been stored. Your hired cook will interview you to determine your food preferences—whether you like salads, what you usually eat for breakfast, the kind of meats and vegetables you will want, and your customary dining times. She or he will also work with you to arrange for trade-ins at the charter company supply store. One other perk we've enjoyed is arriving to find that our cook has made up our berths with fresh linens and put towels in the heads. *Now* we're talking vacation!

Just not having to hassle with the freezer is reason enough to take on a cook. If you need a drink from the refrigerator or want to retrieve a candy bar from the freezer, all you need do is ask, and the cook will get it for you. We usually make our own drinks, but hors d'oeuvres magically appear at the predinner cocktail hour. We'll go for a swim and return at lunchtime to find our cook stationed at the stern barbecuing burgers for lunch. It's like when you were a child and your mom took care of everything for you. Wonderful! No dishes to wash, no food worries except when and what you want to eat. You can get so spoiled you'll want to take your cook home with you when the trip is over.

The cook gets a break when you go out to eat, which on a split provisioning plan is sometimes every other night depending on your itinerary. You need only tell the cook your plans and she or he will adapt the menu accordingly. In addition to curing your culinary worries, a cook has local knowledge and, if encouraged, will steer you toward the prettiest harbors and may even invite you to participate in some very special island experiences. When we chartered in the Tahitian islands, our cook, a 22-year-old man, arranged a personal tour of his uncle's vanilla plantation. On that same trip, we were invited to watch fishermen spearing the same fish that we would later enjoy for dinner at a local restaurant. Show appreciation for your cook by treating him or her to a restaurant meal near the end of a trip and by leaving a hefty tip.

This should do it. Now go have a blast—and don't forget to pack some good sun screen to protect your winter-white skin.

Chapter 29
Serious Sailing

You're going offshore? What now? As an offshore passagemaker, I'm sorry to say, you'll have to shuck that vacation attitude because this is work. This type of cruising requires around-the-clock alertness, watch taking, and preparing and providing food for a crew in a constantly moving boat in all manner of weather and sea conditions. The food supplies you have aboard are those you'll dine on—unless someone aboard is a pro at catching fish.

If you are anxious to try offshore sailing, start by taking a simple overnight sail to get the feel of watches and to help guide your provisioning instincts for longer trips. The whole category of serious sailing encompasses both short and long passages and is defined by the nonstop nature of the voyage. A more casual trip may

involve a night or two on the water and be within 25 miles of land, while a more involved trip may carry you so deep into the ocean that the closest point of land is beneath your boat. Our trip to Bermuda from Tortola took us over 200 miles off-shore.

FIRST-TIME JITTERS

Your first offshore trip is a rite of passage. Once you've passed the test and set aside your largely unfounded fears, future trips will be less traumatic and much more enjoyable. The hardest part of my first passage, a seven-day stint between the British Virgin Islands and Bermuda, was making the commitment to go. Many folks feign bravado, but feeling nervous about embarking on such a gutsy venture is quite normal. The longer the passage, the stronger the resolve needs to be, because there is no turning back.

When you and your crew first depart, everything feels rather routine, except for the undercurrent of excitement and challenge that electrifies the air. You back out of the slip, stow the dock lines and fenders, and snap your harnesses to the jack lines. As home become distant, however, it's common for panic to strike like a sledgehammer, spinning waves of regret and nausea. It's the calm assurances of your more seasoned fellow crewmembers that will help you through those first-day jitters. Tomorrow is another day, and often a better one as you adjust to the routine of a passage. On these trips, it's hard to anticipate whether the crew will be ravenous or seasick. People's bodies react differently on a nonstop trip, than when we anticipate traveling only a few hours. A good pre-departure plan is to ensure that each crewmember is armed in his or her own way against seasickness.

THOUGHTS FOR FOOD

There are varying ideas on handling provisioning for passages, not all of them good. When I provisioned for my first trip, I sought suggestions from a woman sailor who had made many passages and I was told to get a few boxes of pizza, shove them in the freezer and let each person take out a slice and add fixings whenever they got hungry. "They can just warm it up in the microwave," she said. One delivery captain confided to me that he nearly ran out of food and drink on one trip and survived on sauerkraut and anchovies. This same person expected to lose weight on our trip. It's no wonder! These folks don't eat! If you read and digested (no pun intended) the earlier section on nutrition, you know how essential healthy eating is to a crew's well being.

For any offshore passage, particularly one lasting more than a day or two, food preservation, storage capabilities, nutrition and meal balancing are more important than ever to sustain energy, alertness and speedy reaction time. Why *shouldn't* the provisions be carefully considered and planned to support the effort? People who are dealing with erratic sleep patterns and enduring winds, rain and sun need good food to fight back, to retain stamina.

Expect that wives and girlfriends will offer send-off foods. Enjoy the bounty. We once had on board homemade pickles and brownies from Lorraine, frozen stuffed clams from Kathy, frozen chocolate chip cookies from my neighbor Julie, and a large pan of lasagna and two sour cream coffeecakes from Diane. In addition, you'll find that each crewmember will arrive with a personal stash of treats.

All meals will be taken aboard, and even though crewmembers may claim they aren't hungry on some occasions, in my experience, they will wolf down whatever is offered. Your menu plan needs to be flexible, yet exact, regarding the quantities and types of foods you intend to serve. With no stores along the way, the key is to leave with a fully stocked boat. When it comes to nonperishables, it seems you can never have too much. The leftovers will remain as part of your staples, which you will continue to draw from while at your destination or while continuing on at sea. Here, storage will be a greater concern, since large quantities of beverages and supplies are space hogs that need to be carefully stowed.

Knowing the dietary needs of each crewmember is paramount on an offshore passage, because they've nowhere else to eat. Lactose intolerance is so common today—50 percent of my friends and family seem to have it— that for long trips I always stock soy-based veggie cheese and nondairy creamer. The refrigerated Coffeemate, which we prefer, is impossible to find in many places, but travels well.

On Watches
Any cruise extending beyond 24 hours requires that some sort of watch schedule be in place. The exact arrangement will be contingent on the number of people aboard and their levels of experience. On my first passage, we had a crew of four and set a schedule of three hours on, six hours off. I got the 6-to-9 p.m. stint, which meant I needed to prepare dinner and serve it around the time my watch began, leaving someone else to do the dishes. After dinner, one by one, the others slipped below to rest up, while I spent the darkest hours of 7 to 9 p.m. in the company of the glow of our running lights and the glitter of stars. I wasn't up again until dawn, but I know there was some nibbling going on throughout the night.

If you will be on watch while others are asleep, you'll be unable to leave the helm, so just before taking on the task, pack yourself a goodie bag of snacks and drinks. A typical cache might include a large bottle of water, yogurt, a power bar and raisins.

When on watch, you are on a 24-hour clock, which puts you in a jet lag mode. Until you become acclimated, it may seem as if you are always tired and never quite know when it's time to eat. To help combat this, rest as often as possible. End each watch with a meal or snack and a nap. To keep your body clock in sync, try to eat meals in sequence, breakfast, lunch and dinner. Expect that you will need some sort of protein-based snack or mini-meal to keep your energy up throughout the wee-hours watches between midnight and 6 a.m. My captain and I shared this watch on our last passage, a $2^1/_2$ day trip between Block Island, Rhode Island, and Annapolis, Maryland, and found we needed a lift every couple of hours. We ate fruit, hot chocolate, peanut butter sandwiches and cookies before our watch was up. If nothing else, munching food helps pass the time. Books on tape also are beneficial to alertness, as long as you don't get so engrossed that you forget to watch for ships crossing in the night.

On Snacking

Some articles and books recommend that snacks be pre-portioned and meted out over the course of the trip, so there will be enough for everyone. With plenty on board, I wasn't worried about all the goodies being gobbled down the first day, so I employed a laissez faire policy by operating on a help-yourself basis. I had individual snacks ready to distribute and kept a thermos of hot water available to make it easy for a crewmember to grab a hot cup of something—soup, tea, instant coffee—if they ever got a 3 a.m. chill. For safety's sake, store it in the sink.

In the treat category, I've read suggestions that the cook squirrel away a few surprises like chocolate bars to present as gifts to lift tired or weather worn spirits. But I find this only works if the cook is allergic to chocolate. Regarding treats, the trick is to sense when one is needed and then act. One of our crewmembers, Ron, traditionally offers a cup of coffee and a few cookies as a reward to the person taking over his watch. It's the element of unexpectedness that makes something ordinary feel special, like handing up a plate of brownies at breakfast time or a hot cinnamon bun at the midnight watch.

Prepare Your Galley for Others

The reality of a passage is that, although there is a main cook, there are times when others will take over. It's important to understand that even though you plan provisioning and have in place a menu, it may not necessarily be followed. Whoever cooks, gets to create his or her own specialties. They will use items you have aboard or may bring along additional supplies that will allow them to prepare a favorite dish.

If the provisioning is interactive, your crew will take an interest in meal making and pitch in when necessary. When you are preparing your galley for a trip, set it up so that others can easily navigate your domain. Be specific about the whereabouts of items in your galley. For our first passage I organized everything into a booklet that was stashed in a galley cupboard. It included a typed copy of the planned menu, a provision inventory with item locations and status, and a layout of the boat lockers and what they contained. On the inside of each cupboard and locker door, I taped a small piece of paper listing its contents.

FISHING

What more obvious way to enjoy deep-sea sailing than to cast a line overboard and troll along the way. Luckily, we had one crewmember on our southbound trip who knew something about fishing. He put aboard a laminated chart of the types of fish that could be found in our cruising area, so we would be able to recognize anything we'd caught. (Some fish aren't good eating.) Wild Bill, the owner of the Noank Bait Shop, set us up with some surefire lures and a special reel we could affix to the stern. And while we weren't fortunate enough to land any edible fish in the super-deep waters between Bermuda and Tortola, they were jumping in the Gulf Stream.

Be careful what you troll for because you might catch it. Be prepared to cut the line when a monster fish takes the bait. It may be good sport to land such a beauty, but unless you are an expert and your boat is equipped for the task, you are liable to jeopardize your safety when, in a survival frenzy, the fish takes you all for a ride. We once quickly cut the line when we realized that the blue marlin leaping in the distance was ours, and did the same thing whenever we drew up a snapping barracuda. However, on several occasions, some tasty tuna—fine dinner fare—was hauled aboard and laid out on the filleting table to be cleaned.

Oh, by the way, make sure you have at least one crewmember aboard who is willing, able and expert enough to perform this unsavory task. Be certain the designated slicer is harnessed or supported in some way, so as to maintain balance while wielding a sharp knife. The goal is to cut up the fish, not the carver. Wearing a rubber or waterproof apron will save sailing attire from needing to be tossed overboard afterwards, as this is a bloody task. If you and your crew are total novices, I suggest either packing a few how-to books on deep-sea fishing or buying your fish from the market.

SAMPLE MENU PLANNING AND IMPLEMENTATION

Clearly, the provisioning for any trip lasting more than a couple of days needs to be meticulously planned. I can't claim to have *all* the answers, but I can share with you the menus I planned, as well as what worked and what didn't.

Short Passage

You may find that cruising through a night or two will allow you to travel much farther in a short amount of time. One year we took the offshore route to Maine, so we could take our time exploring all its wonderful little inlets as we harbor-hopped our way home. Planning for this type of trip doesn't need to be very intense. We expected our cruise to Maine to take a little over two days of nonstop travel. Armed with some extra crew—five of us in all—we followed familiar coastal waters to the Cape Cod Canal and then set a direct compass heading for Mount Desert, which is better than halfway up the Maine Coast.

Complying with the captain's request to keep it simple, I planned breakfast foods, sandwich fixings and prepared a hearty dinner stew. Even though it was August, it would be cool as we neared Maine. I cooked my usual batch of hard-boiled eggs the day before we left. We had aboard some bakery muffins as well as some sweets and the makings for bacon and eggs. Our boat was well-stocked with enough staples to carry us through our lazy return trip, as well. As it happened, I was the only one suffering from mal de mer. Lisa, who took over lunch, was in one of her culinary moods, so she booted the sandwich idea and created a wonderful pasta dish that everyone but I enthusiastically devoured.

SHORT OFFSHORE TRIP: INFORMAL MENU

    Day 1: Departed after dinner, no meals, 1 night snack
    Day 2: 3 meals, 3 or 4 snacks
    Day 3: 1 meal, arrive before noon

Actual Menus

Here's an example of how a flexible menu can and should work! Don't forget that a good provisioning plan should allow for creativity and change. There's not much to do when things are calm and you are offshore. Surprises that entice the palate are always welcome.

Noank, Connecticut to Mount Desert, Maine

Day 1: Depart Noank – 8 p.m.

We left in squallish rain and wallowing seas. With a batch of homemade brownies tucked away, but accessible, and a hot pot of coffee brewed, I didn't worry about the night crew going hungry. In addition to sweets, I had cheese and lunch meat in the fridge, and cereal bars and assorted crackers in the snack cupboard. Water is always an essential. Ours is tasty enough to be taken from the tap at the galley sink. We labeled several individual bottles with names, then kept a supply washed, refilled and chilled.

Day 2: The seas have calmed, and it promises to be a decent day.

Breakfast

Hard-boiled eggs (The crew had hot cereal, instead)

English muffins with peanut butter, jam

Fruit juice and coffee

Mid-morning Snack

Fruit or baby carrots

Beverage

Lunch

Choice of turkey, ham or roast beef sandwiches on rolls with lettuce and tomato (Lisa made pasta sauce using the ham, frozen peas and canned tomato sauce, and served it over linguini with rolls to sop the sauce.)

Beverage

Cookies

Late Afternoon Snack:

Deviled eggs (the rejected hard-boiled eggs in disguise)

Beverage

Dinner

Chicken stew, dumplings (premixed and stored in plastic zippered bag—only needed to add water)

Green salad (1 bag of prepared salad, complete with dressing packet)

Beverage, including 1 alcoholic drink per person

Brownies

Day 3: We are now in sight of the Maine coastline and expect to arrive at our destination late morning.

Snack- 6 a.m. watch

Brownies, coffee and binoculars

Breakfast

Bacon and eggs

Toast and jam

Juice, coffee

Arrival Snack

V-8 Juice with gin and celery stalks

Lunch Ashore

Lobster rolls and more cocktails at Southwest Harbor's Head of the Harbor Restaurant

Passagemaker's Two-week Menu Plan

When I provisioned our boat for its first southward voyage to the British Virgin Islands, I set up the galley for another cook, as I would not be going along. I made up a detailed menu plan, right down to the desserts, and shopped and cooked like a maniac. To simplify the process, I planned a five- to seven-day menu, and then repeated it for the second leg. This same menu also worked well for the return trip in the spring. By adhering to a stock menu, I was able to make double recipes of each dish, and then package them and place them in the freezer according to when they might be needed.

By the time I was through, every spare crevice in our boat was stuffed with bottled beverages and dry and canned foods, and we had enough staples to last through much of the boat's winter stay. Our freezer overflowed with heat-and-eat meals. I am fortunate in that our boat is equipped with a stove, microwave oven and a reliable refrigerator and freezer. I had the foresight to stock the food locker with individual portion sizes of stews and soups. This proved to be a godsend for the rest of the crew on the leg of the trip I was in charge of the galley, as I was spending the rough days nursing a heaving stomach. Am I the first to disprove the theory that after two days one gets accustomed to the motion and seasickness goes away for the duration? I started the trip feeling ill, and ended it that way; however, during the calm seas in between, I felt just dandy. Here's how my menu worked out on this trip.

TORTOLA TO CONNECTICUT MENU

When I first got onboard, I had two crewmen tell me they didn't need formal meals, but preferred to just nosh. Well they managed to nosh their way through all of the food in the menu below without much trouble. Breakfast was often a casual affair, with each person helping themselves, although we tried to eat lunch and dinner together. The leg I was on was very calm, making it easy to prepare more complicated meals at dinnertime, which is why we could adhere to my planned menu. In the event of rough weather, I had plenty of individual canned stews available in the dry locker. Although we nixed alcoholic beverages for most of the trip, we permitted ourselves one drink with dinner each night.

The second leg, between Bermuda and Connecticut, crossed the Gulf Stream so the seas were livelier and so were the fish, which made fine dinners and caused a few frozen casseroles to be left uneaten in the freezer. With a crew of five on this leg, one person acted as a floater on watches and helped with the cooking. The first night the crew ate plain pasta, most of which ended up over the side. There were several cases of seasickness. The crew arrived in Noank late afternoon on the fifth day out.

LEG 1: TORTOLA TO BERMUDA: 7 DAYS AT SEA

Day 1: Leave Tortola, BVI. Boat rocked like a cradle all day; rain at night.

Breakfast
Hard-boiled eggs (prepare one day in advance and chill)
Muffins (purchased)
Juice (individual assorted juice boxes left from trip down), coffee

Lunch
Roast beef sandwiches on French bread with mango chutney, lettuce, and cheese
Pickles
Beverage

Dinner
Chicken and rice casserole (frozen in ready-to-heat oven bag; heat in micro-wave)
French bread (use it fast since it will go stale)
Celery and carrot sticks (I cleaned and cut up a quantity of these for use throughout the trip)
Beverage
Dessert (see choices at end of menu)

Day 2: Partly cloudy, no wind, calm seas.

Breakfast
See choices at end of menu
Fruit or juice, coffee

Lunch
Roast beef sandwiches (eat it or it will spoil)
Olives
Beverage

Dinner
Ground beef zucchini bake (with potatoes)
Green salad
Fresh orange wedges

Day 3: No wind, calm seas.

Breakfast
See choices at end of menu
Choice of juice, coffee

Lunch
Ham sandwiches
Pickles
Beverage

Dinner
Shrimp and rice with green beans (shrimp is cooked, frozen)
Cucumber salad
Beverage
Pound cake

Day 4: No wind again, calm seas.

Breakfast
Bacon and cooked-to-order eggs
Toast and jam
Juice, coffee

Lunch
Tuna salad on pita bread
Carrot and celery sticks
Beverage

Dinner
Roasted turkey with gravy (cooked in Tortola and frozen in ready-to-heat oven bag)
Mashed potatoes (instant)
Peas (boil-in-bag from freezer)
Cranberry sauce
Dessert, beverage

Day 5: Still no wind, calm seas; motoring full sail at 4 knots to save fuel!

Breakfast
French toast with grilled ham
Juice, coffee

Lunch
Turkey sandwiches with
    cranberry sauce and
    lettuce
Pretzels
Carrot sticks

Dinner
Spaghetti with Joy's ground beef
    sauce (sauce in ovenproof bag
    for microwave or stovetop
    heating)
Garlic bread (in freezer)
(Need a salad, but the lettuce
    died. Bag lettuce won't last
    past a few days!)
Beverage

Day 6: No wind!! Used last can of spare fuel. Calm seas.

Breakfast
See choices at end of menu
Juice, coffee

Lunch
Hotdogs and rolls
Pickles, carrot sticks
Beverage

Dinner
Charcoal-grilled steak
Mount Gay sautéed onions
Baked potato
Broccoli (boil-in-bag from freezer)
Beverage
Coconut cake

Day 7: Finally, 15–25 knot winds, 6- to 8-foot seas; cook is seasick.

Breakfast
See choices at end of menu
Juice, coffee

Lunch
Grilled-cheese sandwiches or
    deli meats
Beverage

Dinner
Hamburgers (crew ate left-
    over spaghetti, instead)
Baked beans
Macaroni salad

Here's the flexible part of the menu that anyone on board could feel free to make, heat or eat.

Breakfast choices:
Yogurt (fridge)
Hard-boiled eggs (fridge)
Cereal, oatmeal (dry storage)
Bagels (freezer) with peanut
    butter or cream cheese
English muffins (freezer) with
    peanut butter or cream cheese
Toast with butter and jam
Honey buns (freezer)
Cinnamon rolls (Pillsbury, in
    fridge)

Lunch choices:
Tuna salad, crabmeat salad
Grilled-cheese sandwiches
Deli meats (fridge)
Hotdogs (freezer)
Hamburgers (freezer)
Cooked turkey (freezer-refrigerator)
BLTs (microwave bacon
    between paper towels)
Leftovers from previous
    evening's dinner

Appetizer/snack choices:
Conch fritters (freezer)
Deviled eggs
Shrimp cocktail (frozen
    shrimp in freezer)
Nuts
Pretzels
Crackers and cheese-pep-
    peroni
Smoked oysters (canned)
Vienna sausages (canned)
Spreads (savory mint pesto,
    mango chutney, sun-dried
    tomato tapenade)

Desserts/sweets:
Cookies (cupboard)
Coconut cake (freezer)
Pound cake (freezer)
Chocolate candy (fridge)
Fresh fruit
Granola bars
Individual gelatins, puddings,
    applesauce, fruit cups
    (cupboard)

We arrived at St. George's Harbour, Bermuda, at midnight with light rain and cool weather. The seas were up during our layover, and the weather predictions were for more of the same, delaying departure for half a day. I flew home leaving the galley chores in Lisa's capable hands.

A WORD ABOUT LIVING-ABOARD CRUISING

For liveaboards, boats are their homes; their galleys are stocked in an ongoing manner, much the same as we do our kitchens at home. While recreational boaters look to time on their boats as a release from a pressure-cooker life, liveaboards are free to roam the wild blue ocean (living every male boater's dream). Certainly liveaboard life isn't as idyllic as it may seem to us outsiders. They have budget concerns and maintenance problems, and they constantly have to reckon with Mother Nature.

Section Ten:
Food, Glorious Food ~~~~~~~~~~

You should be expert enough at this cooking thing to have earned the title of chef by now. Now it's time to have some fun in the galley and to reap the rewards. This final section will help you make the most out of your galley supplies and dinner leftovers and to enjoy meals out.

Chapter 30
Creative Cookery

Welcome to the experimental galley. Here you can revel in the true glories of your kitchen afloat. When cooking on the fly becomes creating on the spur, consulting a recipe isn't always convenient; but ingredients on-hand are. Whip up your own miracles from staples, leftovers, herbs and condiments. Put together a last-minute hors d'oeuvre or salad for a party, or make dinner for unexpected company. Some of my best recipes and cooking ideas have come under the guise of desperation. Although a few unsavory ones have nearly gotten me keelhauled. Creativity in the galley is a game of odds, but once you start to play, you may surprise even yourself. As you create, follow my habit of writing down ingredients and amounts, and before long you'll have developed your own cookbook of favorites.

THE ART OF ILLUSION

Use the element of surprise to elevate store-bought foods or leftovers to fancy status.

Shop and Decorate

There is a wealth of ready-made foods available from the deli. Let your imagination fly. Unmold a packed bowl of store-bought potato salad upside down onto a platter, and then decorate it with bits of vegetables and herbs on hand. Go simple by topping it with a wreath of tomato rings, or get exotic by fashioning a palm tree from a standing celery stalk, leaves left on and strings curled down. Give deviled eggs a nautical twist by turning them into hulls of sailboats and letting them "cast off" on a blue platter.

Dress up cheeses for a party. Find appealing chutneys, tapenades, relishes and salsas in gourmet food departments and keep a few aboard. Slice Brie in half, fill with topping and then spread more over the top. Serve heated gently or cold, along with crackers. I've tried this with both an olive tapenade and dried tomato pesto, and both got rave reviews. A block of cream cheese works equally well. Try cranberry pepper relish or a fruited salsa. Instead of plopping a block of cream cheese

210

onto a platter, shape it into a fish and trim it with your chosen topping. Poke the edges of wheat thins into the cream cheese to make fins.

Use, and Reuse

Store-made bruschetta, which is a diced tomato salad seasoned with olive oil, garlic and basil, can be made into a sandwich dressing, or a topping for fish, chicken or pork. For a welcome change, simply pour salsa in a nicer bowl and set it on a platter surrounded by thin slices of a French baguette. Coleslaw and potato salads are also good on sandwiches, and by using them you can eliminate the mayonnaise and lettuce. Cucumber slices and other vegetables make colorful, healthy stand-ins for crackers.

Be inventive with dinner leftovers. I once made a delicious chicken soup by plunking the leftovers from a chicken, broccoli and rice dinner in a pot with some canned chicken broth. The leavings of a fish and asparagus dinner make a delicious rollup when layered on a tortilla with a slice of cheese. Add a tiny bit of salad dressing for some zing and heat in a skillet, secured with a toothpick. One of our favorite lunches is a barbecued beef sandwich made with leftover steak. You could easily use pork or chicken.

NO RECIPE!

Cookbooks are great, but they can get wet and be in the way in a small galley. Once you get the hang of creative cooking, you'll want to toss written recipes to the wind and let your ingenuity soar. As you gain confidence, putting on the proverbial apron and wielding shakers of this and that will be as familiar as hauling up the mainsail. Start your trek toward freedom by breaking the measuring cup habit and understanding the basics of combining and substituting ingredients; then go for the golden brown.

No Measuring Devices, Either!

The majority of dishes—casserole, entrees, dips and marinades—are forgiving, so train yourself to judge how much to add using these simple methods. Bear in mind that certain dishes, like soufflés (which I doubt you'll make aboard), cakes, breads and other mixes that depend on exact measurements *do* require liquid and dry measuring cups and official measuring spoons.

- If you don't already use the cupped-palm method of estimating dry ingredients, teach yourself to do it at home. Take a set of measuring spoons and fill the various sizes with a dry ingredient, such as oregano or basil flakes. Dump each one, as filled, into the curved palm of your hand and note the fill level. Do this a few times, and before long you'll be able to tell the difference between teaspoons, tablespoons and portions thereof. An eighth of a teaspoon is one or two finger pinches.
- Ordinary dinner teaspoons and tablespoons can be used instead of measuring spoons, although wavering between heaping versus level spoon measures will affect the consistency of a dish.
- Once you know which cups and glasses in your galley hold eight ounces (one-cup), it will be easy to figure out how much of the cup

represents one-half, one-quarter, and one-third of a cup. One-eighth cup is the same as two tablespoons.

Play by the Rules

The difference between a "Wow!" and an "Ick!" is understanding the basics of recipe development and alteration.

- Substitute like for like.
- Maintain the balance of liquid and dry ingredients.
- Season with caution.
- Be prepared with a plan B should your creation bomb.

Substitute Like for Like

So often we scour our shelves for just the right ingredient to complete a recipe and come up empty. See the Recipe Appendix for alternatives to commonly used items that can be used without sacrificing the flavor of a good dish. Use like for like. Vegetable oil will give different results than melted butter. Egg whites can replace whole eggs. Milk can usually replace water without a problem, or vice versa, but keep the weight the same. If the recipe calls for heavy cream, using water or regular milk will affect the texture, and the result is apt to be runny. When you need to add a liquid, look around the galley for a viable alternative. Some fruit juice, an open bottle of wine or some liquor might easily stand in for chicken or beef broth or water in the right recipe.

Balance Ingredients

Maintain the balance between liquid and dry ingredients, always keeping these in the same proportion as the original recipe. Suppose the recipe calls for one cup of water, half a cup of milk, two tablespoons vegetable oil and one egg (the equivalent of an eighth cup). Pretend you are in math class and convert everything to cups and add them up. In this instance, the recipe contains a total of $1^3/_4$ cups of liquids, which means you should add no more than this amount of another liquid. The Measurement Conversion Chart in the Recipe Appendix will help simplify these types of calculations.

Be sensible about making substitutions. Avoid drastic changes and consider the end result. For example, in biscuits, breads and cakes, omitting the egg could mean a flop, while the egg will hardly be missed if omitted from a Caesar dressing. Oil carries flavor, so reduce the quantity called for, if you must, but avoid eliminating it entirely.

Oops, Too Much!

Somewhere in the back of your mind you've got a sense of what works and what doesn't. For example, a tablespoon of black pepper will be too much for most recipes, six cloves of garlic will fight off werewolves, and a quarter cup of chili powder will send anyone hopping up and down in agony. To avoid overdoing when doubling or tripling a recipe, adjust the seasonings in lesser amounts.

2 times the recipe: use $1^1/_2$ times the amount called for

3 times the recipe: use 2 times the amount called for

4 times the recipe: use $2^1/_2$ times the amount called for

Sometimes we go crazy sprinkling a bit of this and a bit of that until we either over season a dish or manage to have such a laundry list of ingredients that we don't care to make it ever again. The trick is to figure out the ratio of one seasoning to another in order to obtain the best flavor, without being overpowering—salt to pepper and oregano to parsley, as an example.

Save Your Soup (or whatever)
Once you've added too much of a good thing, launch a rescue mission by trying some of these ideas.

- Strain out bits of herbs and spices, or scoop off any that have not yet dissolved.
- Simmer a raw, peeled, quartered potato in the mixture for 10 to 15 minutes to absorb some of the excess flavor. Remove and discard the potato afterward.
- Reduce the amount of salt, if it has not already been added in, and stir in a little sugar.
- If a mixture is overly sweet, sharpen the flavor with a teaspoon (small squeeze) of lemon juice, lime juice or vinegar.
- Cold numbs the palate, so if possible, serve the dish well-chilled.
- Prepare a second batch, omitting the seasoning, and combine it with the first.

Good Seasonings
Dry herbs and spices take little attention and storage space, so keep a supply of your favorites on hand to add character to a dish. Certain combinations of herbs and spices work together to give dishes their distinct flavor. Some blends are so common we don't think of them as combinations, but as seasonings in themselves. You can make yours from scratch as you go, premix them for the boat, or buy them ready made. Experiment to find those you like to cook with most.

Keep this list of ethnic combinations in mind.

Italian: parsley, basil and oregano
French: rosemary, tarragon and thyme
Mexican: chili powder, cumin and cilantro
Indian: coriander, curry
Chinese: ginger and soy

The quickest way to enhance the flavor of a dish is to add a dash of a pre-blended sauce or herb mixture. This saves storage in the galley and gives a gourmet appeal to plain foods. Popular manufacturers like McCormick and Bell-Carter Foods have developed lines of regional sauces and spices, and on the international front, standard Chinese and Mexican fare are being overrun by the more exotic Indian, Thai and African seasonings. Find a favorite that you can sprinkle like magic dust to transform bland foods.[38]

Practice with Dressings and Dips

One of the easiest things to concoct is a salad dressing, yet we buy bottles and bottles of it. With vinegar, oil and a few herbs you can make a dressing that folks will talk about wildly. My "wing it" vinaigrette involves boldly pouring the oil and vinegar directly on the salad, then sprinkling on the seasoning. Toss the salad and do a taste test, adding a little more of this and that. Add mustard for mustard vinaigrette, or take a different tack and make your own Thousand Island dressing by mixing catsup and mayonnaise until a shrimp pink color emerges; then add a smattering of pickle relish.

You'll find that common condiments like mayonnaise, catsup, soy sauce, hot sauce and barbecue sauce (which you can also easily make from scratch) can be the basis, either alone or in combination, for many interesting marinades and sauces. Add an unexpected ingredient—fresh herbs, a tangy pepper sauce or a squeeze of lime juice—and you'll have a winner.

Use Ingredients on Hand

If you have an opened bottle of a favorite dressing or sauce, use it until it's done. If it's creamy, spread it on sandwiches or use it as a base for a dip. Spread chunky blue cheese dressing on a roast beef sandwich; use it as a dip for celery or spicy chicken wings, or stir it into mashed potatoes.[39] I put an open jar of mango chutney to work by adding it to guacamole and including in an entree with chicken and fruit over rice.

Have a Happy Accident

Many of my often-used recipes are the results of either happy accidents or pure laziness. I was looking for an easy way to combine garden tomatoes and squash with ground beef and arrived at my ever-popular Ground Beef Zucchini Bake, which I prepare often, both at home and aboard. I did a similar one-pot dish using chicken, broccoli and a few simple seasonings. Being short an ingredient or out of it entirely is reason enough to scour the galley in pursuit of a substitute—and who knows, the stand-in item may be just the thing you needed to turn a good recipe into a fabulous one.

GET IDEAS FROM RECIPES

If you're not quite ready to let go of written recipes, use them as a springboard for ideas for combining textures and flavors, and for presenting foods. I find the newspaper food section and cooking magazines are great sources. Zero in on recipes that look appealing and easy to make. I keep my collection, which as you might imagine is pretty hefty, in a file box sorted by food type—entrees, side dishes, sauces and marinades, appetizers, beverages, breakfast foods and desserts. I go looking in my box whenever I need an idea. Suppose I have chicken breasts on hand. I pull the file of entrees, select all the chicken recipes, scan the ingredient lists and, if I have most of the items, give one of the recipes a whirl. Seldom do I ever follow a recipe exactly. I substitute whenever I need to, keeping in mind the end result.

To apply your own twists to recipes you've collected or use routinely at home, start with a comfortable base recipe and each time you make it, vary an ingredient or amount, or make a substitution. Limit the number of changes you make to avoid overdoing or throwing the original recipe off balance. Use pork instead of chicken in a stew; try ground turkey instead of ground beef. Add extra vegetables, beans or pasta. When altering a printed recipe in any way, always mark down the changes so you can either find your error when it flops or re-create the alteration when it doesn't. Once you have developed a recipe that has gotten rave reviews, fine-tune it so it will be simple to prepare.

The most rewarding part of cooking without a recipe is the pride felt when the crew asks for more. But wherever there are winners, there will always be losers; some, in fact, you'll never live down. My family still laughs about the hot broccoli and the "yellow" chicken incidents. On days when your best intentions meet the trashcan, suggest an alternative. Dinner out!

Kitchen Afloat proverb
  Nothing could be finer, than to be a diner.

Chapter 31
Oh Heck, Let's Eat Out

Boating puts us in a vacation mode, and there are many of us who find this synonymous with *not* cooking. There are few things finer than to discover that you have
the night off. It's not that you mind the work; but there are times when you'd like to
relax, to be a Lazy Lucy or Clueless Karl, and pretend that the galley doesn't exist.
Did you know it takes more water to cook and clean up after a dinner aboard than
it does to shower? The amount of potential water saved alone makes dining out a
worthy cause. Although there are many ways to dine out, the ultimate means is
going to a restaurant and being served.

CHOOSING A RESTAURANT

If being served is your goal, choose a destination *on* the beaten path. Think about the type of restaurant you want. The differences between dining out and eating out are price and atmosphere. If you're seeking a romantic evening with the captain, you won't find it at Burger King or Pizza City. However, if you are harboring a gang of kids aboard, fast, cheap food may be your best option.

Let your trusty waterway guide, as well as other coastal publications, direct you to harbors with amenities. Those with grocery stores typically have some sort of dining establishment as well. A comprehensive travel guide will provide you with important information about a harbor, so this is an ideal place to begin your quest for dining facilities. Save old guides at home so you will have telephone numbers available during the week for information gathering and reservation making.

Read All About Them

Pick up independently published area guides to restaurants and activities, such as *The Captain's Seaside and Restaurant Guide,* available in coastal towns throughout the Northeast. Browse through magazines and clip restaurant reviews. Read boating newspapers, note the advertisements, and save articles on potential cruising destinations. The author may give you the *real* scoop on that well-publicized restaurant or direct you to some gem you might otherwise have missed.

The Chamber of Commerce will also offer a wide selection of free information about the area you are visiting. In addition to a descriptive listing of restaurants, you'll often find a calendar of events that lists times and places for lobster fests, clambakes and other food-oriented happenings common to the summer season. Download data from their Web pages or call to have an information packet mailed to you.

At new destinations, collect local flyers and newspapers geared toward the tourist trade. In your daily trip journal, make notations about the places where you ate and refer to them whenever you revisit a particular harbor.

Ask Around

Before you head out, talk to friends who share your tastes in food and are familiar with your destination. Write down the names of the places they suggest—you won't remember them—and note their comments. Once you arrive, ask around, although remember that the information is only as good as the source. Find out where the locals dine, since these usually have the best food. If time permits, stroll over and check the place out before committing to it. Scan the menu and the prices, and note the type of attire required. You may find a fabulous rib place, or a dinner-and-show combo.

Never assume a restaurant is open. Some, especially those in quaint villages, are seasonal or have specific serving hours. One summer we brought our flotilla to Marion, Massachusetts, with the intention of dining at a restaurant my husband and I had discovered the previous year, only to find it was closed; and it was the only one in the area! Had we called ahead for reservations, we might have rescheduled our Marion stop to a different night and averted the hotdog and bean dinner that ensued.

Getting to the Restaurant

First you have to get on shore. Then you need to decide whether to travel to your restaurant choice by foot or by car. Getting ashore may be a problem if you are not on a slip or don't have a reliable dinghy, or if your marina doesn't offer a launch service. For weekend or holiday stays at popular harbors, check on berth availability before you commit to dinner reservations. A full-service marina will often have a restaurant either on the premises or within close walking distance of the dock. Some oceanfront restaurants even monitor marine radio channels. (This information will often be listed in the waterway guide.) If your chosen restaurant is farther away than you can comfortably walk, ask at the marina about cab service, courtesy transportation or shuttle services offered by the restaurants themselves. In popular tourist towns like Hyannis, Plymouth, Falmouth, Massachusetts, and Boothbay, Maine, you'll find trolley, bus and even ferry service.

Make a Reservation

A cell phone and a marine radio will save you searching the marina for a pay phone. Don't wait until you arrive to make a dinner reservation at a top-notch restaurant. Some places are booked several weeks ahead. It is common to call around for reservations for the same day and find there is either nothing at all or that they can't take your party until late into the evening.

Going along with a late reservation is seldom a good move. As the evening wears on, a restaurant gets backed up on serving, meaning you'll be seated well past your reservation time. Worse, they'll start to run out of their specialty dishes. In one such instance, we were served steak over pasta, instead of the expected side dish of garlic-mashed potatoes—at 11 p.m. To avert this type of situation, it's common to make the late reservation, and then proceed to call around to other restaurants to get a better time slot. If you do this, be sure to have the courtesy to cancel the other reservations.

It's always smart to inquire about a restaurant's reservation policy. Some will only reserve for large parties of six or more. If you are one short of the quota, perhaps you might fib a bit, and then plead a no-show for the missing person. Many will not accept reservations at all, which could leave you and your growling stomachs standing in a queue on the sidewalk or over-imbibing at the bar. In heavily visited areas like Newport, Rhode Island, the standard wait is two hours on weekends. Many folks put in their names at several places, and then make the rounds to check back until they can be seated. We've found that by sticking around and making sure the host knows we are waiting—we smile and periodically ask how we are doing—we are often seated well before the quoted time. So curb that urge to roam and stay put. It works.

Go Ashore Incognito

If your group tends to be rowdy, it may be wise to put in your reservation under an alias to avoid being denied a reservation on your next visit. Be aware that you are advertising the fact that your boat will be unattended by making a reservation under your boat's name, a practice prevalent in harborside restaurants. Once when chartering in the Grenadines, our boat was robbed while we dined ashore. One solution might have been to give a bogus boat name or to have used my captain's first name. A dinghy named after your primary boat bobbing at the dinghy dock is also a tip-off that the captain and crew are not aboard the main ship. Our dinghy carries registration numbers, but otherwise remains nameless.

Paying the Bill

Just as you've savored the last mouthful, and are considering ordering another drink, the tab arrives. If you have joined with other couples and need to split the bill, have the soberest person check it over to be certain it is correct. We find it saves haggling to divide the bill evenly among us. Most waiters don't mind if you hand them three or four credit cards. It is customary to tip 15 or 20 percent, depending on the quality of the service. Maybe we boat cooks should form a union so we can get a nice tip too!

Notes

1 Seagull IV X-FP drinking water enhancement system from General Ecology, Inc. 151 Sheree Blvd. Exton, PA 19341 (800 441-8166)

2 Collapsible rolling cooler, item # 6433ID, $79.95. Available from Hammacher Schlemmer (800 543-3366 or www.hammacher.com)

3 Max Grip makes a high impact fastening kit that will support up to 1200 pounds selling for about $20. Sold by Fastening Solutions, Inc. 15230 Burbank Blvd, Suite 106, Van Nuys, CA 91411 (800 232-7836 or email dj-fsi@pacbell.net)

4 I use bags by Horizons, LTD, Converse, GA (800 969-4583). Marine cooler bags are now manufactured by other companies, as well.

5 Suggestion from Tom and Jane Petipas of the catamaran Jane-O (*Latitudes and Attitudes* Magazine)

6 "Super Q" ice saver blanket standard 18 x 24 inch costs $23. Order from Standout Yacht Fittings, 6826 Cliff Ave. KPS, Longbranch, WA 98351 (800 622-1877)

7 Tips for Cruisers by Dave Schaefer, *The ENSIGN* magazine, October 2001

8 *The Meatless Galley Cookbook* by Anne Carlson, Seaworthy Publications: Brookfield, WI, 1995

9 See the earlier section on portable refrigeration for more detail on thermoelectric operation.

10 Seacook gimbaled stove by Force 10 or Forespar Mini-galley 2000 marine stove; costs range between $10 to $150.

11 Portable I.R. mini gas stove, #MAT122, $29.95 (800 669-0987 or www.shoplifestyle.com)

12 Mini kitchen by Avanti; 13 x 23 x 15 1/4 inches self-contained unit with two burners and oven with broiler. Costs about $275.

13 HeaterMeals (www.heatermeals.com or 800 503-4483)

14 For under counter dispensers, shelf organizers, and more, Get Organized Catalog (800 803-9400 or www.getorginc.com)

15 Chrome Cabinet Organizers #27-4016499C-can dispenser, $14.00, Hold Everything Catalog, P.O. Box 379906, Las Vegas, NV 89137 (800 421-2264)

16 Trash Trapper $12.95, plus shipping (to order: 877 487-2773)

17 Kimberly Amaral, "Plastics in Our Ocean," (from web)

18 Ibid

19 CHEF'S catalog offers professional cooking gear at discount prices (800 338-3232 or www.chefscatalog.com)

20 Antibacterial cutting board, $20 in Williams Sonoma Catalog #57-3863586 (to order: 800 541-2233 or www.william-sonoma.com)

[21] Chef's caddy, a 3-piece knife set, stores in a waterproof nylon sheath that can convert to a stand. Montane, Inc, in Portland, OR specializes in portable food gear (www. Montane.com or 877-MONTANE)

[22] FoodTool #KFT231, $29.99 (less with other purchases) Life Style (www.shoplifestyle.com or 800 669-0987)

[23] 800 543-3366; www.hammacher.com item #60934D

[24] Little Nemo's hideaway, sells for about $200; Contact Eagle Engineering, 735 W. Knox Rd., Tempe, AZ 85285 (877 278-6366)

[25] Ross Marine Ideas, 2756 North Dixie Hwy, Ft. Lauderdale, FL 33334 (www.rossmarineideas.com or 800 327-8929 or 954 561-4200; fax 954 561-0537)

[26] One company that advertises such supports is Galleyware Company, 330 Water St. #108 in Newport, DE. (Order their catalog on www.galleyware.com or by calling 302 996-9480)

[27] Doctors Foster & Smith Catalog

[28] Roberta Larson Duyff, MS, RD, CFCS, The American Dietetic Association, Complete Food and Nutrition Guide, Chronimed Publishing, 1996, p. 299

[29] Ibid, p. 157

[30] USDA pamphlet, Use a Food Thermometer. For more information call Meat and Poultry Hotline 800 535-4555 or on line, www.fsis.usda.gov/themy

[31] Most custard based recipes or puddings will tolerate these substitutions without sacrificing flavor or appearance. Use coffee creamer instead of light cream in mashed potatoes or custard cream pies, and lactose free or soymilk to make puddings. The soymilk will change the flavor somewhat.

[32] Recommended by Garrett and Georgeann Goheen, Entre Nous, Royal Passport 47

[33] Many safety hints used in this chapter and in Chapter 1 have been adapted from Cooking on the Move, Common Sense Cruising, by Beth Leonard, SAIL magazine, Living Aboard, March 1999)

[34] Motion Eaze, Alta Labs, POB 251, Alta, WY 83422 (www.motionease.com or 888 212-5503)

[35] VitaMotion-S from Sky Sailing. (Check www.skysailing.com or call 760 782-0404)

[36] ReliefBand, Class II battery-operated medical device for relief of nausea and vomiting. Sold OTC at pharmacies for upwards of $50, depending on model. (For more information www.aeromedix.com)

[37] J.E. Stantomenna, Cruising is a Breeze, Windspirit Publisher, 1994

[38] Otwell's Foods in Hartford, CT (860 523-7647) makes a Venetian seasoning salt I use constantly, and I can't live without Sunny Caribbe's Jerk Sauce from Tortola, BVI (www.sunnycaribbee.com)

[39] This idea came from The Back Eddy Restaurant in Westport, MA. We loved their blue cheese mashed potatoes—they use, of course, real blue cheese.

Recipes

MEASUREMENTS, CONVERSIONS AND SUBSTITUTIONS

Teaspoons

10 drops = dash
$1/8$ teaspoon = a few grains
3 teaspoons = 1 tablespoon
8 teaspoons = 1 ounce

Tablespoons

1 tablespoon = $1/2$ fluid ounce
2 tablespoons = 1 fluid ounce or $1/8$ cup
4 tablespoons = $1/4$ cup or 2 ounces
16 tablespoons = 1 cup or 8 ounces

Cups

$1/8$ cup = 1 oz or 2 tablespoons
$1/3$ cup = 5 tablespoons + 1 teaspoon
$1/2$ cup = 8 tablespoons or 4 ounces
2 cups = $1/2$ pint or 8 ounces
2 cups = 16 ounces or 1 pound
4 cups = 1 quart

Dry Volumes

2 cups = 1 pint
2 pints = 1 quart
4 quarts = 1 gallon

1 Pound Equivalents

2 cups butter
$3^1/2$ cups all-purpose flour
$3^1/2$ cups powdered sugar
$2^1/3$ cups brown sugar
2 cups milk
$3^1/2$ cups nuts

Liquid Measures

$1^1/2$ oz = 1 jigger
1 quart = 2 pounds
2 tablespoons = 1 fluid ounce
1 cup = 8 ounces
1 quart = 32 ounces

Butter
1 pound = 2 cups
$1/4$ pound = 1 stick
1 stick = 4 ounces or $1/2$ cup

Cheese
$1/2$ pound cream cheese = 1 cup or 8 ounces
1 pound cottage cheese = 2 cups
1 pound = 4 cups grated

Eggs
1 whole = 2 whites
2 large or 3 medium = $1/2$ cup
6 medium = 1 cup

Fruits
1 lemon = 2 to 3 teaspoons juice
1 lemon = 2 teaspoons zest or peel
1 lime = $1^1/2$ to 2 teaspoons juice
1 orange = 6 to 8 teaspoons juice
1 orange = 2 to 3 teaspoons zest or peel
1 banana = $1/2$ cup
1 pound bananas = 3 to 4 medium bananas
1 pound apples = 3 cups sliced

Starches
1 cup uncooked macaroni = 2 to $2^1/2$ cups cooked
1 cup uncooked noodles = $1^1/2$ cups cooked
1 pound uncooked rice = $2^1/2$ cups cooked
1 pound potatoes = 2 cup mashed

Temperature Conversions
0 degrees Celsius (centigrade) = 32 degrees Fahrenheit, which is the freezing point of water.

100 degrees Celsius = 212 degrees Fahrenheit, which is the boiling point of water.

To convert centigrade Celsius to Fahrenheit: multiply the centigrade degrees by 9, divide by 5 and add 32.

To convert Fahrenheit to centigrade: Subtract 32 from Fahrenheit degrees, multiply by 5, then divide by 9.

Oven Temperatures
Below 300°F – very slow, low heat
300°F – slow

325°F – moderate
350°F – moderately hot
400-425°F – hot
450-475°F – very hot
500°F or higher – extremely hot

Substitutions

Dairy
1 cup buttermilk = 1 cup milk, with 1 tablespoon milk substituted with 1 table-spoon vinegar. Let stand 5 minutes.
1 cup milk = $1/2$ cup evaporated milk and $1/2$ cup water, or 5 tablespoons dry milk and 1 cup water
1 cup light cream = 1 cup evaporated milk, 1 cup half and half, or 1 cup non-dairy creamer
1 cup sour cream = 1 cup plain yogurt and $1/3$ cup butter
1 oz. chocolate = 3 tablespoons cocoa and 1 tablespoon butter
6 oz semisweet chocolate chips or squares = 6 tablespoons unsweetened cocoa powder and 7 tablespoons granulated sugar and $1/4$ cup shortening.

Flours
1 tablespoon flour = $1/2$ teaspoon cornstarch
1 tablespoon flour = 2 teaspoons quick-cooking tapioca
1 cup sifted cake flour = $7/8$ cup sifted all-purpose flour
1 cup all-purpose flour = 1 cup, 2 tablespoons cake flour

Other
1 small onion = $3/4$ teaspoon onion powder
1 small clove garlic = $1/4$ teaspoon garlic powder
1 pound fresh mushrooms = 6 ounces canned
1 tablespoon fresh ginger = $1/4$ teaspoon ground ginger
$1 1/2$ tablespoons balsamic vinegar = $1/4$ cup wine vinegar

Equal Alternatives for Herbs and Spices
Basil = oregano
Caraway = anise
Celery seeds = minced celery
Chervil = parsley, tarragon
Fennel = anise, tarragon
Oregano = marjoram
Sage = thyme
Allspice = equal parts cinnamon, cloves, and nutmeg
Chili peppers = cayenne
Nutmeg = mace

FAVORITE RECIPES

I couldn't write a book on the galley without including some recipes I've developed. I hope you enjoy these.

Appetizers

When preparing and serving any type of appetizer, keep in mind that its appearance and presentation are what will make it appealing. Take a few extra minutes to give some thought and attention to whatever you are serving. You'll find it's easy to turn ordinary foods, even leftovers, into tempting hors d'oeuvres.

Make-do Shrimp Cocktail

Here's a simple version of shrimp cocktail I came up with when hard pressed for a sauce.

1 pound fresh, cooked shrimp (frozen also works)
$1/2$ teaspoon Paul Prudhomme's Seafood Magic or other Cajun seasoning

Make-do Cocktail Dip

2 tablespoons catsup
1 teaspoon jerk sauce (Sunny Caribbe Jerk Sauce is a stock item in my seasoning bin. If you don't have it, try 1 teaspoon Worcestershire sauce and a drop or two of hot sauce.)
1 teaspoon lemon or lime juice

    Place cooked shrimp in a plastic bag along with the seasoning and shake until coated. Chill until ready to serve. Mix together the dip ingredients. To serve, place the shrimp on a platter, atop some lettuce if desired, and offer the dip on the side. Note: For peel and eat shrimp, simply leave on the shell.

Louie Lobster

2 cups fresh lobster meat, cut into bite-sized chunks (crabmeat will work also)

Louie Dip

$3/4$ teaspoon fresh chopped oregano leaves or $1/4$ teaspoon dried
$11/4$ teaspoon lime juice
$1/4$ cup (4 tablespoons) mayonnaise
2 tablespoons ketchup
$3/4$ teaspoon pickle relish
1 teaspoon jerk

    Mix together dip ingredients. To serve: Line a serving platter with lettuce leaves. Pour dip into center and spread toward sides. Distribute lobster meat evenly over the top leaving a ring of dip showing. Serve with spreader and wheat or plain crackers.

Lobster Spread

$1/2$ cup cooked lobster (or crabmeat), chopped
1 tablespoon minced onion
$1/2$ teaspoon minced jalapeño pepper
1 teaspoon fresh lime juice
2 tablespoons mayonnaise
$1/2$ teaspoon dried cilantro

Place lobster meat in a small bowl. Add remaining ingredients and stir in well. Chill for at least $1/2$ hour before serving to allow flavors to meld. Serve as a spread with wheat crackers.

Salmon Spread

$1/2$ cup cooked salmon
4 teaspoons mayonnaise
1 tablespoon minced onion
$1/8$ teaspoon liquid smoke
$1/4$ teaspoon jerk sauce
1 teaspoon fresh lime juice

Mash salmon with fork in a small bowl. Add remaining ingredients and mix well. Serve with pumpernickel cocktail bread sliced in triangles.

Quick Dip

2 tablespoons mayonnaise
1 teaspoon Dijon mustard
$1/4$ teaspoon red pepper flakes or dash of hot sauce
1 squeeze or a lemon or lime wedge

Mix and chill for about one half hour before serving. Good with veggies or seafood.

Island Guacamole

1 California avocado, peeled and mashed
1 clove garlic, minced
Juice of $1/2$ fresh lime
$1/4$ teaspoon salt
Dash black pepper
$1/8$ teaspoon hot sauce, or to taste
2 tablespoons mango chutney

Add the remaining ingredients to the mashed avocado and mix well. Serve with pita chips.

Steamers

3 to 5 pounds fresh steamer clams
1 large clove garlic, chopped
1 onion, chopped
2 tablespoons butter
2 12 oz cans beer

Place clams in a large covered pot with the beer. Add remaining ingredients and stir to mix. Bring to a boil. Cover pot, and then reduce heat to medium and cook until clams open. Serve with dipping cups of clam broth and of melted butter. (Courtesy Lorraine Morecraft, SCARAMOUCHE, Tartan 42)

Sailboat Deviled Eggs (makes 12 boats)

6 hard-boiled eggs
3 tablespoons mayonnaise

$^1/_2$ teaspoon Paul Prudhomme's Seafood Magic, or to taste
1 sheet plain white paper
12 toothpicks

Peel eggs then slice in half lengthwise. Slip out yolks into a small mixing bowl. Add the mayonnaise and the Seafood Magic seasoning and mash together until blended. Fill each scooped-out white portion with a spoonful of yolk mixture and place in a platter. If you are doing this underway, be sure serving platter is secure and somewhat level or these little devils will set sail on their own. To complete sailboats, cut 12 triangles from a sheet of plain white paper. White napkins or paper towels will do in a pinch. Label sails with names of crewmembers and their boats. For each boat, thread a toothpick in and out of one side of the triangle, and then set one end of the toothpick into the bow of the egg boat. (Courtesy Lorraine Morecraft)

Fish-shaped Appetizer
1 16 oz package cream cheese
1 8 oz container Otwell's Nip N' Tang brand fruited horseradish sauce or red pepper jelly
1 black olive and scallion or celery tops for garnishes
1 box Wheat Thins

Spread softened cream cheese on a platter, using your fingers to form it into an elliptical oval. Cover the cream cheese "fish" by pouring Nip N' Tang sauce over all. To make fins, stand crackers on end. Make several rows. Use the olive to make a fish eye, and the scallion greens to form a tail. (Courtesy Lisa Musumeci, GABRIELLA, Macourdy and Rhodes 48. Note: Lisa is also the owner of Otwell Specialty Foods 860 523-7647.)

Rosemary Pecans (makes 3 cups)
This combination of seasonings is amazingly complementary. Whenever I serve these nuts, I find my guests virtually licking the crumbs from the bottom of the bowl.
4 tablespoons ($^1/_2$ stick) butter or margarine
1 tablespoon dried rosemary leaves
$^1/_4$ teaspoon dried basil
2 teaspoons seasoned salt
3 drops hot sauce
3 cups pecan halves

Preheat oven to 325°F. Melt butter, then stir in the rosemary, basil, salt and hot sauce. Add the pecans and mix until coated. Spread pecan mixture on a large baking sheet in a single layer. Bake in oven for about 10 minutes, until pecans are aromatic and slightly dried, but not burnt. Let cool and serve at once, or store in a tightly covered container.

Beverages

Sun Tea (makes 48 oz)
Fill a clean, empty plastic juice jug with water. Add 2 teaspoons of sugar. Stuff 4 tea bags into the mixture, leaving the tab ends of the strings hanging outside the jug. Screw the cap onto the bottle and set it in a snug spot in your cockpit for several hours until the tea turns amber. Serve over ice with a squeeze of lime.

Block Island Mudslides (makes 2–3 drinks)

This recipe originated aboard our boat on a rainy Fourth of July weekend, when we tried to re-create those we had enjoyed at sundry frozen drink bars. If you've never tasted a mudslide, here's your chance. They are pure alcohol, except for the ice, but taste like a chocolate ice cream soda, so go easy.

$^1/_3$ cup Baileys Irish Creme
$^1/_3$ cup Kaluha
$^1/_4$ cup vodka
2 cups crushed Ice

Working in a blender, pour in the Bailey's, Kaluha, and vodka. Add the crushed ice and blend on high speed for $1^1/_2$ to 2 minutes until ice becomes slush. Add more ice if needed. Serve in a large, stemmed glass. For strawberry mudslides, blend in about 1 cup hulled fresh strawberries in your final whirl of the blender. For Nantucket-style mudslides, dribble some chocolate syrup down the side of each glass before filling it with mudslide. (Developed in the JOY FOR ALL SEASONS galley by Mike Poole, my wonderful son-in-law.)

Joy Juice

Here's a simple version of rum punch.

By the Jug

8 oz Mount Gay rum
48 oz Ocean Spray Mauna Loa Island guava juice
4 oz lime juice
Crushed ice to fill remainder of container

Mix all ingredients in a 64-oz. plastic jug and shake well. Serve over additional ice with a dash of nutmeg if desired.

By the Glassful

Fill a 12 oz cup or glass with ice and add 1 part rum to 3 parts guava juice. Squeeze in a wedge of fresh lime.

Lunch Fare

Oregano Tuna Salad (serves 2)

1 6.5 oz can solid tuna in water
2 - 3 tablespoons mayonnaise
1 small tomato, chopped (about $^1/_4$ cup)
1 teaspoon fresh chopped oregano leaves, or $^1/_4$ teaspoon dried

Mix tuna, mayonnaise and oregano until blended. Fold in tomato. Serve as a salad on a bed of lettuce, or scoop into two or three soft rolls to make sandwiches.

Barbecued Beef Sandwiches (serves 2)

1 cup sliced cooked steak, pork or chicken
$^1/_4$ cup barbecue sauce
2 sandwich rolls or hamburger buns

I use leftover meat from the previous evening's dinner or deli roast beef. This is good on a cool day when the last thing you want for lunch is a cold sandwich. Place barbecue sauce and beef in a skillet over medium-high heat. Sauté until sauce bubbles and beef is warmed. Serve on split rolls.

One-pot Meals and Main Dishes

Provincial Chicken Stew (makes 2^1/$_2$ quarts, serves 8)
Bon Appetit magazine liked my recipe well enough to publish it, so maybe your crowd will enjoy it. This chicken stew makes a good meal onshore as well as offshore. Leftovers freeze well.

2 pounds chicken breasts, skinned (boneless, or bone-in)	2 teaspoons salt
3 cups chicken broth	1 tablespoon dried oregano
1 14^1/$_2$ oz can stewed tomatoes	2 tablespoons dried parsley
1 large yellow onion, chopped	1 tablespoon dried basil
1 clove garlic, minced	1 15 oz can cannelloni beans
1 10 oz package frozen green beans	^{1}/$_2$ cup red wine

Place all ingredients except the cannelloni beans in a large stockpot or Dutch oven. Bring to a boil over medium heat. Drain and rinse the cannelloni beans and set them aside to add to the stock later. Reduce heat to low, then cover and simmer for about 40 minutes or until chicken is cooked and falls away from the bone. Remove chicken breast from broth and break meat up into large chunks, de-boning breasts if necessary, then return chicken to the broth and add the cannelloni beans and the wine. Continue cooking another 10 minutes. Serve hot.

To make dumplings:
Mix together 1^2/$_3$ cups Bisquick reduced fat baking mix and ^{2}/$_3$ cup skim milk (or use your own dumpling recipe.) Drop by spoonfuls onto the boiling chicken stew. Cook uncovered for 10 minutes, then cover and continue cooking another 10 minutes. Makes 8 dumplings.

Mango Chutney Chicken and Rice (serves 2)

1 tablespoon butter	^{1}/$_4$ cup mango chutney
1 pound chicken tenders	^{1}/$_4$ teaspoon nutmeg or ginger
1 fresh peach, peeled, pitted and cut into bite-sized chunks	Salt and pepper to taste
^{1}/$_4$ cup water	1 package boil-in-the-bag rice, cooked
1 cube chicken bouillon (or 1 teaspoon granules)	

In a large skillet, melt the butter. Sprinkle chicken pieces liberally with salt and pepper, then sauté them along with the peaches on medium heat until chicken is cooked. Remove from pan and set aside. Pour the water in the same pan, then stir in the bouillon cube, chutney and nutmeg. Bring to a boil stirring constantly. Return the chicken mixture to the pan and stir. Continue to cook until mixture is syrupy. To serve, pour mango chicken over cooked rice.

Shrimp and Rice (serves 4)

1 tablespoon butter
1/2 onion, sliced
1 cup frozen French-cut green beans, defrosted
1/2 pound frozen shrimp, pre-cooked, shelled and deveined
1 141/2 oz can stewed tomatoes
2 2-cup serving packets boil-in-bag rice, cooked
1/2 cup white wine
1/2 teaspoon dried basil
Salt and pepper to taste

Melt butter in a 10- or 12-inch skillet on medium-high heat. Add the onions and sauté until they begin to soften. Stir in the green beans, then the shrimp. Add the stewed tomatoes, cooked rice, wine, basil, salt and pepper. Mix well. Reduce heat to low. Cover and cook another 5 minutes.

Ground Beef Zucchini Bake (serves 4)

I usually make this dish without the potatoes and serve it with either rice or rolls and a salad for a complete meal.

1 pound ground beef
1 tablespoon butter
1 sliced onion
1 large, sliced Idaho potato
1 or 2 zucchinis, sliced
2 tomatoes sliced
1/2 teaspoon oregano
1 teaspoon dried parsley
Salt and pepper to taste
4 slices deli cheese

Sprinkle pan with salt and pepper and crumble the ground beef into a large 12-inch skillet on medium high heat. Sauté until cooked. Drain excess fat from pan. Melt the butter in the same pan, then add the onion and potatoes and sauté until they begin to brown. Reduce heat to low, then evenly distribute the cooked ground beef on top of the potatoes. Top with a single layer of the zucchini rounds. Follow with a layer of tomato rounds. Sprinkle additional salt and pepper between layers. Sprinkle the oregano over the zucchini layer and the parsley over the tomatoes. Place the cheese slices over the top and cover pan tightly. Simmer for about 20 minutes until zucchini is cooked.

Chicken Breast Sauté (serves 2)

1 pound boneless, skinless chicken breasts
1 egg
2 tablespoons milk
1/2 cup seasoned breadcrumbs (or flour)
3 tablespoons cooking oil
1/2 cup white wine
1 tablespoon lemon juice
1 tablespoon dried parsley
1 fresh tomato, sliced into wedges
1/2 head broccoli, cut into spears
Salt and pepper to taste

Season chicken breasts on both sides with salt and pepper. In a shallow bowl, beat the egg and milk together with a fork. Pour the breadcrumbs onto a piece of waxed paper. Heat the oil in a 10-inch skillet on high or medium high. Dredge the chicken pieces first in the egg mixture, then in the breadcrumbs and place in hot oil. Brown on one side for a minute, then turn and brown for another minute. Reduce heat to medium-low. Add the wine and lemon juice to the pan. Sprinkle with the parsley. Add the tomatoes. Then lay the broccoli spears over the top of the chicken. Sprinkle again with salt and pepper. Cover pan tightly and continue to cook another 15 minutes or until chicken is cooked through. If pan becomes dry add a bit more wine. Serve with rice or orzo.

Barbecued Chicken Strips (serves 4)

Strips cook more quickly than chicken breast halves, and they are more versatile. Leftovers make good snacks or sandwiches. Children love these.

2 pounds skinless, boneless chicken breasts
1 cup of your favorite barbecue sauce

Rinse chicken and pat dry. Cut lengthwise into 1-inch strips, leaving chicken strips connected at one end for easy handling, then place them in a resealable plastic bag with the barbecue sauce. Squish the chicken around in the bag with your fingers to thoroughly coat it with the sauce, then chill or freeze it until you are ready to grill or sear it in a skillet. Serve with potato salad and some chilled baby carrots on a warm night, or offer with canned baked beans and buttered noodles if there's a chill in the air.

Magic Scallops (serves 2-3)

Any grilled fish can be prepared this way. If your barbecue is rained out, sauté the scallops belowdeck.

1 tablespoon olive or vegetable oil
2 tablespoons dried parsley (optional)
1 $^1/_2$ tablespoons Paul Prudhomme's
 Seafood Magic

1 pound bay scallops, rinsed and patted dry
3 wedges of fresh lime for garnish

Place oil and seasonings in a plastic bag along with the scallops. Close bag and mush scallops around in the oil mixture to coat. Remove scallops with a slotted spoon. Place them on a hot grill on a piece of foil punched with holes to allow the heat through, or on a special grilltop for fish. Turn them frequently with a spatula. Scallops will be done in five minutes or less. Do not overcook them, or they will be tough. To serve, remove to a platter and offer with lime wedges. A packaged rice mixture makes a nice accompaniment.

Pork Cutlets with Oranges, Green Onions and Coriander (serves 4)

My recipe won honorable mention in the 1994 National Pork Council's "Lick Your Chops" contest. Try it also with turkey, veal or chicken cutlets.

1 pound pork cutlets
2 to 3 tablespoons margarine
$^1/_4$ cup green onions or scallions, sliced
2 navel oranges, peeled and sliced in
 circles

$^1/_4$ cup orange juice
$^1/_4$ cup chicken broth or water
$^1/_4$ teaspoon ground coriander
$^1/_4$ teaspoon salt or to taste
Pinch black pepper

Rinse cutlets, pat dry and season with the salt and pepper. Melt 1 tablespoon of the margarine on medium high heat in a 12-inch skillet. Add the green onions and sauté lightly. Add the pork cutlets in a single layer in pan and cook for 1-2 minutes on each side. Add the second tablespoon of the margarine as needed to keep cutlets from sticking to pan. Remove to a serving platter and cover to keep warm. Melt the third tablespoon of the margarine, if needed. Add orange slices and sauté lightly. Remove the orange slices. Arrange over the cutlets on the serving platter. In a small cup, stir together the water, orange juice and coriander. Pour the juice mixture into the skillet to deglaze pan, scraping browned bits from bottom to form a sauce. Simmer a few minutes until liquid reduces slightly. Pour sauce over cutlets. Serve on a bed of white rice with a green vegetable or salad.

Chicken Chardonnay (serves 2-3)

1 pound package chicken cutlets
Salt and pepper to taste
$1/4$ cup flour
3 tablespoons butter
1 pound Portobello or other mushrooms,
    sliced

$1/2$ cup chicken broth
$1/2$ cup Chardonnay or dry white wine
1 tablespoon fresh chopped parsley, or 1
    teaspoon dried

Sprinkle cutlets on both sides with salt and pepper. Dip cutlets in flour to thinly coat on each side. Heat the butter on medium in a 10- or 12-inch skillet. Add the mushrooms and sauté for one minute. Pushing mushrooms aside, add the veal cutlets and brown for 1 to 2 minutes on each side. Remove cutlets to a warm platter and continue cooking mushrooms until browned. Remove mushrooms to the platter. Add the wine and chicken broth and parsley to the pan and stir to deglaze pan. Return veal and mushrooms to pan and simmer uncovered for an additional 10 to 15 minutes until sauce is reduced and slightly thickened. Serve over white rice.

Not So Hot Chili (makes about 6 cups)

2 tablespoons olive oil
1 pound lean ground beef or turkey
1 medium onion, chopped
1 clove garlic, minced
1 14 $1/2$ oz can stewed tomatoes with
    juice
1 12 oz can beer

1 tablespoon chili powder
1 teaspoon ground cumin
$1/2$ teaspoon molasses (optional)
Salt and pepper to taste
1 15 oz can black beans, drained and
    rinsed
1 tablespoon cornmeal (optional)

In a 10-inch skillet, heat 1 tablespoon of the oil on medium high heat. Add the garlic and onion and sauté briefly. Cover and cook for 3 to 5 minutes until onions are softened. If pan is dry, add the remaining oil then add the ground beef or turkey. Sauté the meat until browned and cooked. Drain off excess fat and add the remaining ingredients, except for the cornmeal. Cook uncovered on medium low heat for about 45 minutes. About 5 minutes before cooking is complete, stir in cornmeal to thicken chili. Serve with cornbread. Freezes well.

Classic Beef Stew (serves 4)

$1/4$ cup flour
$1/2$ teaspoon salt
$1/4$ teaspoon black pepper
$1 1/2$ pounds cubed stew meat
3 tablespoons olive oil
1 clove garlic, crushed and minced
1 large onion, sliced into wedges
$1/2$ pound mushrooms, sliced
$1 3/4$ cups beef broth (or bouillon
    cubes or granules and water)

4 medium potatoes, scrubbed and
    sliced into 1-inch chunks
4 carrots, scrubbed and sliced into 1-
    inch chunks or use $1/2$ bag baby carrots
$1/4$ cup chopped fresh Italian parsley, or 3
    tablespoons dried
1 teaspoon basil, dried
1 teaspoon thyme
$1/2$ cup red wine, or water

Place flour, salt and pepper in a large plastic bag or mixing bowl. Add the beef cubes and shake until thoroughly coated with the flour mixture. Set aside. Heat 2 tablespoons of the olive oil on medium high in a 12-inch skillet or Dutch oven. Add the garlic and onions and sauté for a few minutes, then stir in the mushrooms and cook until all vegetables soften. Remove vegetables to a small bowl and set aside. Add the remaining oil to the pan, then add the beef, including any excess flour mix, and brown meat on all sides. Stir in the beef broth to deglaze pan, scraping browned bits from bottom of pan. Add the cooked mushroom and onion mixture, potatoes, carrots, parsley, basil, thyme and wine. Bring to a simmer and cook covered, stirring occasionally, until beef is tender and potatoes and carrots are cooked (about an hour). Add additional salt and pepper to taste, and more wine or water if sauce is too thick. Serve at once with crusty bread and a green salad.

Mussel Stew (serves 4)

2 slices bacon, cut into 1-inch pieces
1 clove garlic, minced
1 medium onion, sliced
1 bell pepper, sliced
3 pounds mussels, shells on and
    scrubbed
1 cup dry white wine

2 teaspoons dried thyme
1 14.5 oz can stewed tomatoes
$1/2$ cup water
$1/2$ teaspoon salt
$1/8$ teaspoon black pepper
1 large potato, chopped and cooked in
    salted water (optional)

Sauté the bacon in a Dutch oven or stockpot over medium high heat until it begins to cook. Add the garlic, onion and bell pepper and continue to sauté until bacon is cooked. Add the mussels to the pan, then pour in the white wine. Sauté for a minute. Add the tomatoes, thyme, salt and pepper. Bring to a boil and then reduce heat to low and cook covered until the mussels open, about 5 or 10 minutes. Stir in the cooked potato, if desired. Ladle into bowls and serve with crusty bread.

Ground Beef Pasta Sauce (makes $1^{1}/_2$ quarts)

Why use bottled pasta sauce when you can make your own from scratch in under an hour? Try adding different meats or vegetables to this basic recipe.

1 pound lean ground beef
1 small onion, sliced
1 large clove garlic, crushed
8 oz mushrooms, sliced
1 tablespoon olive oil
2 28 oz cans crushed tomatoes in
    tomato puree (or 1 can chopped
    tomatoes, 1 can puree)
$1/4$ cup red wine

$1/8$ cup fresh, chopped Italian parsley, or
    3 to 4 tablespoons dried parsley
2 tablespoons oregano, dried
3 tablespoons sweet basil, dried
$1/8$ cup water or red wine
$1/8$ teaspoon salt or to taste
$1/4$ teaspoon black pepper
$1/8$ teaspoon crushed red pepper, dried
    (optional)

Heat olive oil in a 12-inch skillet or heavy saucepan. Add garlic and sauté briefly. Add onion and mushrooms and sauté until softened. Remove vegetables from pan and set aside. Sprinkle the skillet with salt and pepper. Put the ground meat in the saucepan, breaking it up, and sauté until cooked. Remove cooked meat from pan and pour off excess fat. Return meat and reserved vegetables to pan. Add remaining ingredients and simmer for 30 to 45 minutes or until ready to serve over any type of cooked pasta.

Fresh Herb Turkey Sauce (makes about $1^1/_8$ quarts, serves 4-6)

Cook long enough to let the herbs permeate this delicate sauce, and use only fresh herbs. My recipe was not only published in *Bon Appetit* magazine, but was selected to be in its "Light Cooking" booklet.

2 cloves garlic, sliced
2 tablespoons olive oil
1 pound ground turkey
2 28 oz cans crushed tomatoes in
   tomato puree
$^3/_4$ cup chopped fresh parsley

$^1/_2$ cup chopped fresh basil
$^1/_4$ cup chopped fresh oregano
$^3/_4$ cup dry white wine
$2^1/_8$ teaspoons salt
$^3/_4$ teaspoon black pepper

    Heat the olive oil in a large 12-inch skillet or Dutch oven on medium high heat. Sauté the garlic until browned. Sauté the turkey until it turns white. Drain excess juices from skillet, then add the tomatoes, parsley, basil, oregano, salt, pepper and $^1/_2$ cup of the wine. Reduce heat and simmer about 30 minutes, adding additional wine if sauce is too thick. Serve immediately over linguini or penne. Sauce may be made ahead. Store chilled, or freeze until ready to use again.

Salads and Sides

Parsleyed Potatoes (serves 5-6)

These taste like mashed potatoes, but don't require as much work or forethought. New potatoes are nice, but I use whatever I have on hand.

10 red or white new potatoes,
   scrubbed and cut into 1 inch (bite-
   sized) chunks
1 teaspoon salt

$^1/_4$ teaspoon black pepper
4 tablespoons butter
$^1/_3$ cup fresh chopped parsley, or 3
   tablespoons dried

    Boil potatoes, salt and pepper in a large pot until tender when pierced with a fork. Drain excess water from pan. Add the butter and parsley and stir for a minute with a wooden spoon until butter is melted and potatoes are coated. Do not over mix or potatoes will be too mushy. Serve at once.

Minted Peas (serves 2-3)

1 package frozen peas
$^1/_2$ teaspoon dried mint, or 1 teaspoon
   fresh chopped mint

Salt and pepper to taste

    Steam all ingredients in a covered saucepan with about $^1/_2$-inch of water, or use the microwave oven. To microwave, place all ingredients in a 1-quart microwave safe casserole dish. Cover and microwave on high for a few minutes until peas are defrosted and tender. Serve.

Grilled Vegetable Packets (serves 3)

No pots to clean! Be creative and create your own combinations of vegetables. I usually place my prepared vegetable packets on the grill while it is preheating. By the time the meat or fish is cooked, they are ready, too.

Heavy-duty aluminum foil
3 medium potatoes, sliced in $1/8$-inch
    circles
$1/2$ yellow pepper, julienne cut
$1/2$ small zucchini, julienne cut
$1/2$ Vidalia or other mild onion, quartered,
    then cut into $1/8$-inch slices

$1/4$ cup chopped fresh basil leaves, or 1
    tablespoon dried basil
1 tablespoon butter
Salt and pepper to taste

Make individual portion packets or one large one. Cut 2 squares of foil per person, one square for the base, and the other for the lid. Place the vegetables and seasonings on the foil in the order listed, dividing them evenly among the packets. Dot each with $1/3$ tablespoon of the butter. Cover with the top layer of foil and fold over each edge two times to seal. Do not pierce with fork. Cook on the grill for 10 to 15 minutes, turning once with a large metal spatula, being careful not to tear foil. Pierce to ventilate the steam once packet is turned to its second side.

Mount Gay Onions (serves 4)
I serve these with grilled steak. Sliced Portobello mushrooms are also good cooked this way. Often I mix them with the onions.

2 tablespoons butter
2 Vidalia or other mild onions, sliced
1 teaspoon dried parsley

$1/4$ cup Mount Gay or other dark rum
Salt and pepper to taste

Heat butter in 10-inch skillet on medium-high. Add onions and sauté. Sprinkle with parsley, salt and pepper. Cook until they begin to soften. Stir in the rum. Continue to cook until onions are browned and begin to caramelize. Serve as a side dish with steak.

Twister Pasta Salad (serves 6-8)
6 cups spiral pasta, cooked, drained
    and rinsed (1 pound uncooked)
$1/2$ cup chopped scallions
$1/2$ cup canned corn, drained
$1/2$ cup black beans, drained and rinsed
$1/2$ teaspoon ground cumin
$1 1/2$ teaspoons dried cilantro

$1 1/2$ tablespoons chopped fresh oregano
    leaves, or 1 teaspoon dried
Pinch black pepper
3 teaspoons salt
2 teaspoons lime juice
$1/4$ cup olive oil
$1 1/2$ tablespoons wine vinegar

Place the pasta in a large mixing or serving bowl. Mix in the scallions, corn and beans. Add the remaining ingredients and stir gently until well mixed. Cover and chill at least one hour before serving.

Perfect Potato Salad (serves 4 to 5)
As simple as potato salad is to make, I've always had a problem getting the dressing just right. Why else would Hellmann's bottle a special potato salad dressing? When I finally got the balance of seasoning correct, I wrote it down for posterity.

5 medium baking potatoes, scrubbed
    and cut into bite-sized chunks
1 egg
2 tablespoons chopped fresh parsley,
    or 1 teaspoon dried

1 teaspoon chopped fresh jalapeño
    pepper (optional)
$1/2$ cup chopped Vidalia or other mild
    onion
1 cup chopped celery, 3 to 4 stalks

Perfect Dressing

1 tablespoon Dijon mustard
1 teaspoon wine vinegar
1 tablespoon olive oil
6 tablespoons mayonnaise

$^1/_2$ to 1 teaspoon salt or to taste
$^1/_8$ teaspoon black pepper or to taste
$^1/_4$ teaspoon paprika

Place potatoes and the egg in a medium saucepan filled with a few inches of water. Bring to a boil. Cover pan and reduce to medium heat and continue to cook for 20 to 30 minutes until potatoes are soft, but not mushy. Drain and rinse in cold water. Peel and chop egg. Place cooked potatoes and egg in a large mixing bowl and chill to room temperature, then mix in the onion, green pepper, celery and dressing ingredients. Return to the cooler for at least an hour before serving.

Broccoli Orange Salad (serves 4-6)

1 head broccoli, cut into florets
$^1/_2$ Vidalia or other mild onion, sliced
2 large navel oranges, peeled and sliced

Orange Mint Dressing
$^1/_2$ cup olive oil
$^1/_4$ cup wine vinegar

$^1/_4$ cup orange juice
1 tablespoon minced onion (optional)
1 teaspoon dried mint, or 2 tablespoons chopped fresh
$^1/_2$ teaspoon salt or to taste
$^1/_8$ teaspoon black pepper

Combine the broccoli, onion and oranges in a salad bowl. Add the mint, orange juice, oil, vinegar, salt and pepper. Toss well and chill for at least 30 minutes before serving.

Pineapple Tossed Salad (serves 3-4)

4 cups mixed greens, torn into bite sized pieces
2 scallions, sliced
$^1/_8$ cup pitted black olives
$^1/_8$ cup canned pineapple chunks, drained with juice reserved

Pineapple-Balsamic Dressing
2 tablespoons pineapple juice
2 tablespoons balsamic vinegar
$^1/_4$ cup olive oil
$^1/_4$ teaspoon fresh, minced ginger or one pinch ground ginger
$^1/_4$ teaspoon salt
Pinch black pepper

Mix pineapple juice, vinegar, oil, ginger, salt and pepper together to make dressing. Place the pineapple chunks, olives, scallions and greens in a salad bowl. Toss with dressing and serve at once.

Garlic Bread (serves 6-8)

Make good use of stale bread. It reheats well, as long as it is kept in foil. For an extra hearty snack, top toasted bread with any soft cheese and return it to the broiler for a couple of minutes until cheese melts.

1 loaf Italian or French bread
4 tablespoons butter or margarine

2 cloves garlic, crushed
$^1/_8$ teaspoon dried oregano

Slice the bread lengthwise to make two long pieces. Combine the butter, garlic, and oregano in a small saucepan or microwave safe bowl and heat until butter is melted. Lay bread halves on a large piece of aluminum foil, crust side down. Using a pastry brush spread the butter mixture evenly over the cut bread halves. If bread is fresh and at room temperature, broil the topsides until it sizzles and begins to brown. If you are using chilled or not-so-fresh-bread, put halves together to reassemble loaf and wrap tightly in the foil. Bake at 350°F for about 15 minutes, or until bread is heated through. Remove the bread from the oven and turn on the broiler. Open the halves and top brown. Serve hot.

Marinades, Seasoning Mixes

Italian Seasoning
2 tablespoons dried parsley
1 tablespoon dried basil
1 teaspoon oregano

Salt Blend
Make up a batch and use instead of salt and pepper in everything.

$^1/_4$ cup salt
1 teaspoon ground black pepper
$^1/_8$ teaspoon dried, minced garlic
   (or $^1/_4$ teaspoon garlic powder)
1 tablespoon dried minced onion
   (or $1^1/_8$ teaspoons onion powder)

2 teaspoons parsley flakes
1 teaspoon dried basil
$^1/_8$ teaspoon thyme
$^1/_4$ teaspoon celery seed

Measure the parsley, basil, thyme, celery seed, and minced garlic and onion into a blender or coffee or spice grinder and whirl until fine. Pour mixture into a small jar, brushing the excess from the blender or grinder with a pastry brush. Add the salt and pepper. Put the lid on the jar and shake well. Pour salt blend into a shaker and store the rest. Keeps indefinitely. Add a few grains of rice to the mixture to absorb moisture and keep it dry.

Mustard Vinaigrette (makes $^1/_4$ cup)
3 tablespoons olive oil
$1^1/_8$ tablespoons wine vinegar
1 teaspoon Dijon mustard

1 teaspoon minced onion
Salt and pepper to taste

Balsamic Vinaigrette (makes $^1/_4$ cup)
1 teaspoon salt
$^1/_8$ teaspoon pepper
1 small clove garlic, minced
1 tablespoon chopped fresh parsley, or
   1 teaspoon dried

$1^1/_2$ tablespoons balsamic vinegar
3 tablespoons olive oil
1 tablespoon Parmesan cheese (optional)

Low-cal Balsamic Vinaigrette (makes $^1/_4$ cup)
1 teaspoon olive oil
2 tablespoons balsamic vinegar
1 tablespoon, plus 1 teaspoon orange
   juice

1 tablespoon water
$^1/_2$ teaspoon salt and pepper mix
$^1/_4$ teaspoon basil

Tequila Marinade (makes about $1/2$ cup)
Use for fish. Marinate for about 20 minutes, then grill or broil fish for about 10 minutes per inch of thickness per side.

1 whole, fresh lime
$1/4$ cup tequila gold
2 tablespoons catsup
1 tablespoon olive oil
1 teaspoon chili powder

1 teaspoon sugar
2 stalks scallions, trimmed and thinly
    sliced
$1/2$ teaspoon dried cilantro

Grate the zest from the lime and place in a small bowl. Cut the remaining lime into quarters and squeeze out all juice into bowl. Add the tequila, catsup, oil, chili powder, sugar, scallions, and dried cilantro. Mix well.

Mount Gay Marinade
Use for steak or pork. Will marinate up to six pounds of meat.

1 tablespoon olive oil
$1/4$ cup soy sauce
1 teaspoon jerk sauce

1 clove minced garlic
$1/4$ cup Mount Gay rum
1 teaspoon dried parsley (optional)

Place all ingredients in a zippered plastic bag. Add meat and allow to marinate at least one half hour before grilling or broiling.

Bibliography

Reference Books

- Brown, Larry *Frugal Yachting*, International Marine, 1994
- Carlson, Anne *The Meatless Galley Cookbook*, Seaworthy Publications, 1995
- Duyff, Roberta Larson, MS, RD, CFCS *The American Dietetic Association Complete Food and Nutrition Guide*, Chronimed Publishing, 1996
- Gershoff, Stanley, Ph.D *The Tufts University Guide to Total Nutrition*, Harper Perennial, 1990
- Gibb, Jane *The Reluctant Cook*, Adlard Coles Nautical, 1991
- Greenwald, Michael *The Cruising Chef Cookbook* 2nd edition, Paradise Cay Publications, 1996
- Groene, Janet *Cooking on the Go*, Hearst Marine Books, 1987
- Groene, Janet *How to Live Aboard a Boat,* Hearst Marine Books
- Jorgensen, Eric *Sailboat Maintenance*, CLYMER Publications, 1975
- Mallory, Elbert S. *Chapman Piloting, Seamanship and Small Boat Handling*, Hearst Marine Books, 1996
- Pardey, Lyn with Larry Pardey *The Care and Feeding of Sailing Crew*, 2nd edition, W.W. Norton Co., 1995
- Payne, John C. *The Great Cruising Cookbook,* Sheridan House, 1996
- Robinson, Jan *Slim to Shore*, Ship to Shore Inc., 1993
- Rombauer, *The Joy of Cooking,* Scribner, 1997
- Santomenna, J.E. *Cruising is a Breeze*, Windspirit, 1994
- Sharp Electronics Corp. *Carousel Convection Microwave Cookbook*, 1983
- Somers, Elizabeth MA, RD *Food & Mood,* Henry Holt & Co., 1995

Miscellaneous Sources

Practical Sailor
Motorboating & Sailing
Sail
Cruising World
Boating World
Latitudes and Attitudes
The ENSIGN

Assorted Gadget Catalogs

West Marine Master Catalog 1999-2001
Boat/US Catalog
Defender Catalog

Web site Sources

www.fda.gov US Food & Drug Administration
www.fsis.usda.gov
www.mealsforyou.com
www.mymeals.com
www.fightbac.org/fbi
www.SailNet.com
How things work/Univ. of VA site
www.oceanconservacy.org

Index